BIG BLUE BOOK
OF BICYCLE REPAIR

A Do-It-Yourself Bicycle Repair Guide From Park Tool

2nd Edition

Big Blue Book of Bicycle Repair— *2nd Edition*
A Do-it-Yourself Bicycle Repair Guide from Park Tool

Park Tool Company

Copyright © 2008 Park Tool Company

® The color BLUE is a registered trademark and trade dress of Park Tool Co.

The Big Blue Book of Bicycle Repair is published by Park Tool Company.
For more information or to contact us:

Park Tool Company
6 Long Lake Road
Saint Paul, MN 55115
(651) 777-6868
Fax: (651) 777-5559
http://www.parktool.com

To report errors, please send a note to info@parktool.com

For the latest on all our products and services please go to
http://www.parktool.com

Written by: C. Calvin Jones
Editor: Rick Fuentes
Contributing Editor: Dan Garceau
Art Director: Ken Wangler

ISBN 978-0-976553-02-1

Printed and bound in the United States of America

CHAPTER 9 - *Derailleur System*

CHAPTER 10 - *Internal Gear Systems*

CHAPTER 11 - *Caliper Disc Brake System*

Introduction

The bicycle, possibly the perfect combination of simplicity and complexity, is more than just a vehicle that transforms your muscular energy into motion. The bicycle provides transportation, exercise, a way to escape, and a way to be together with your friends. The bicycle itself consists of numerous levers, bearings, pivots, and parts that require proper care and maintenance. Without a basic understanding of these parts and how they all work together, fixing your bike can be intimidating, but gaining that understanding is easier than you think. Knowledge of the mechanics of the bicycle will change the way you ride. It gives you the confidence to ride longer and farther; the skills to do trail or roadside repair; and the ability to maintain your bike to get it ready for the next ride.

Whether you own a single, high-end bike or a fleet of bikes for the family, the second edition of the Big Blue Book of Bicycle Repair is designed to help you, the home mechanic, keep your equipment in top-notch condition. This book is a natural for Park Tool Company. We've been designing and manufacturing bicycle tools for professional and home mechanics since 1963. With Big Blue 2, we pull together more than four decades of knowledge about bicycle repair into one comprehensive, easy-to-use manual.

With the Big Blue Book of Bicycle Repair-2 and practice, you should be able to make most adjustments to your bike and install or upgrade many components, but Big Blue is not a substitute for a good bike shop. Bicycle shocks, for example, vary greatly in design and service procedures. Therefore, shock repair is best left to the professional mechanic. Wheel building also involves complex procedures and component selection, such as choosing proper spoke length, and other procedures require tools that are too expensive to justify purchasing for one time or occasional use. Your favorite bike shop is the most reliable source for information about upgrades, new products, compatibility of components, and the tools you will need to do the repairs in this book.

The service procedures outlined in this book include a list of tools and supplies needed to do the repair. Look for the Tools & Supplies icon. These items may be general-purpose tools, such as hammers and screwdrivers, or special purpose tools such as crank removers or cone wrenches. Most bike shops carry the bicycle specific tools mentioned in the tool list.

Read through any procedure first before taking apart the bike. Also look for the CAUTION icon. This indicates an issue of safety, such as with wheel installation or seat post installation. Pay special attention to the text and discussion on these topics. Lastly, you will find TECH NOTE icons that call out points of technical interest.

Bicycle design has not changed from the basics of two wheels, a place to sit, and a handlebar. That said, however, modern bikes are becoming more proprietary in their details. There are components that may fit only one bike and one model. It is very difficult for a book to include all possibilities of component service. There will be situations where it is necessary to contact the manufacturer for additional information. Bicycle and component design can change rapidly and without notice, and portions of this book may be obsolete the moment it hits the store shelves. Still, this book looks ahead to new products coming to market, and we try to make this edition a tool you will turn to for years to come.

The Big Blue Book of Bicycle Repair has several features that you will find useful. There are eighteen chapters in the book and four appendices. The appendices include a glossary of terms and a table of recommended torque values. You will also see references to Park Tool's website www.parktool.com. Whenever Big Blue does not cover the service of a particular item, or we feel that more discussion of a topic will be valuable, you'll see a reference to Park Tool's website. When visiting www.parktool.com, click the "Repair Help" button on the navigation panel. You will find comprehensive coverage of many topics that are too complex to deal with in this book.

Creating a bicycle repair book is like creating a new bicycle tool. It takes time and effort and the process is never as straightforward as one would hope. I want to thank Eric Hawkins, the owner of Park Tool Company, for his continued support and patience as we worked through this new edition of Big Blue. I also want to thank Dan Garceau, National Sales Manager, for his help with organizing the chapters, evaluating the repair procedures, and double-checking the references to Park Tool products. My editor, Rick Fuentes, and the Park Tool Art Director, Ken Wangler, were indispensable in this project. I have also received invaluable help and advice from manufacturer's technical people about the proper procedures to use when preparing or maintaining their products.

Finally, I would like to dedicate the BBB-2 to all the people who have written or called Park Tool with questions on your bike repairs, comments on my articles, or critiques of what I have written. Your feedback is valuable and irreplaceable.

Thanks for purchasing the Big Blue Book of Bicycle Repair-2. I think you will find it the most comprehensive and easy-to-use bicycle repair manual ever published.

– Calvin Jones
Park Tool Company

Foreword

The year was 1956. My father Howard and his partner Art Engstrom had just bought a small fix-it shop on the east side of St. Paul, Minnesota, named Hazel Park Radio and Bicycle. Both loved to get their hands dirty. So the shop seemed to be a good fit with their skills. Along with the lawn mowers and ice skates, the shop sold bicycles, and I admit neither knew much about bikes. As they dug in to their new venture and bicycles evolved to include hand brakes and shifting systems, Howard and Art soon tired of working on bikes turned upside down while squatting on the floor. With the help of a longtime friend, Jim Johnson, they designed their first bicycle repair stand. Soon, they realized there was a need for other tools that could make their lives easier, and a tool business was born. At first Howard and Art produced tools under the Schwinn label, then shortened Hazel Park Cycle Center Repair Stand Company into Park Tool Company. So begins our history.

Today, Park Tool produces and supplies over 300 different bicycle specialty tools to more than 60 countries worldwide. Go into any bike shop in America or just about any shop around the globe, and you'll find our famous Park Tool Blue tools in use in the back room and for sale on the showroom floor. Our goal is simple: Build the best bicycle tools. We are constantly improving and expanding our line to meet the expectations of team and professional mechanics as well as those doing their own work at home or on the trail.

This manual, the second edition of The Big Blue Book of Bicycle Repair, represents one more tool in our constantly expanding lineup. While we love to sell tools, we feel strongly that information and knowledge are the most valuable tools of all. Once you gain some of this knowledge and the confidence to use it, a whole new side of bicycling opens up to you. With a basic understanding of the bicycle and how it works, you'll be free to ride longer and farther. You'll understand what makes one bike or one component better than another. You may even take apart your bike and put it back together just for fun. This manual is designed to give you a complete, well-rounded look at the mechanics of a bicycle. We've designed the BBB-2 to help guide you through a wide variety of repairs from flat tires to bearing replacement; from repairing a chain to lacing spokes; and from truing a wheel to dropping in a headset. Road or mountain, recumbent or kids bike, tandem or city bike, whatever you ride, we've included information that can help you maintain or repair your bike. This 2nd edition is packed full of new subjects and updated information to help you keep pace with the ever-changing bicycle industry.

When we decided to produce a guide for home mechanics, we knew it had to be great, full of photos and tables, up to date information featuring the latest components and tools, and an easy to use format. Our author, Calvin Jones, is truly one of the world's most qualified mechanics and instructors. With over 30 years in the industry: Calvin lives, eats, and breathes bicycles. Here is a short list of his qualifications.

- US Olympic Team Mechanic, Los Angeles 1984

- 10-time National Team Mechanic and Manager of National Team Mechanics at MTB World Championships

- Instructor at USA Cycling Mechanics Licensing Clinics at the U.S. Olympic Training Center in Colorado Springs, Colorado since 1985

- Eight years instructor at Barnett's Bicycle Institute for Bicycle Mechanics

- Author, Park Tool School Manual. Park Tool's in-store clinic presented by your local bike shop

- Park Tool Director of Education since 1997

- Mechanical advisor for countless bicycle industry manufacturers, professional racing teams, and retailers

We're sure you'll agree that Calvin has done his homework and created a complete and concise manual. It's sure to be a reference for nearly any mechanical procedure you choose to tackle. This is the book Howard and Art could only dream would ever be written. With a special thanks to Calvin for all his hard work, we're proud to present the 2nd Edition of The Big Blue Book of Bicycle Repair.

– Eric Hawkins
Owner
Park Tool Company

CHAPTER 1

Basic Mechanical Skills

Equipment and machinery all share many commonalities. Leverage, friction, tension, material strength, and bonding are all part of automobiles, coffee makers, satellites, and bicycles. Understanding some basic concepts of engineering will help you understand and service any equipment.

Threaded Fastener Tension & Torque

Manufacturers use threaded fasteners to hold many components to the bike, and the bike itself can act as a nut for certain threaded parts. Understanding threaded fasteners, i.e. bolts and screws, is an important part of bicycle maintenance. These fasteners are made of two parts. One is the external thread, which is the bolt or screw. The other is the internal thread, which is the nut. Threaded bike parts, such as bottom brackets or cups, operate the same way.

It is important to align threads correctly when you first begin to engage the inner and outer threads. The critical threads are the first ones, and damaging these threads from misalignment can make the component very difficult to install. Take note of the axis of both inner and outer threads and make sure you are rotating the parts square to this axis. An old technique for beginning a thread is to actually turn the threaded backwards to feel first thread engagement. You will feel a click or give in the part, which tells you to then rotate the correct direction.

Threads are made in many different sizes. Bolts that appear visually similar may actually made for different nuts or fittings. The size of the thread is designated and named by the external thread diameter and pitch of the thread. The pitch is the distance from the crest of one thread to another measured along the length of the thread. Thread diameter can be measured with a caliper, and pitch is best measured with a thread pitch gauge.

The so-called "English" or SAE (Society of Automotive Engineers) threads are designated by the frequency of how many threads are counted along one inch. This is called "threads per inch" and is abbreviated as "tpi." An example of an SAE thread is 9/16" x 20 tpi (for pedal threads). Metric threading uses the direct pitch measurement in millimeters from thread crest to the adjacent thread crest measured along the thread axis. An example of metric thread would be 10mm x 1mm (common rear derailleur bolt).

Threads are made to advance and then tighten as they rotate. Many threaded fasteners, but not all, tighten when turned clockwise. These are called "right hand threads." Some threads on the bicycle are made to tighten when turned counter-clockwise and are called "left hand threads." All threads are made at a slight angle. If the threaded bolt or screw is held vertically, it will appear to slope upward toward its tightening direction. Right hand threads slope upward to the right, and left hand threads slope upward to the left (figure 1.1).

FIGURE: 1.1

Left hand threads are seen on the left pedal, and right hand threads are seen on right pedal. Threads slope upward toward the direction of tightening.

As a fastener is tightened, the fastener and threads actually flex and stretch, much like a rubber band. This stretching is not permanent. It gives force to the joint, holding it together (figure 1.2). The stretching force is called "preload," or tension. Each fastener is designed for a certain range of tension. Too much tightening will deform the threads or damage the parts. A thread with too little preload will loosen with use, which in some cases can also damage the part. For example, riding with a loose crank bolt will eventually damage the crank. Loose bolts and nuts are also a common source of creaking noises on the bike as the component parts move and rub one another.

FIGURE: 1.2

A crank bolt under tension keeps the arm pressed to the spindle

Typically it is necessary to lubricate threads. Without being lubricated, bolts or nuts cause threads to rub and scrape rather than tighten fully. Lubrication also aids in preventing corrosion. As a rule of thumb, if the threads are relatively small with a fine thread pitch, a liquid lubricant is adequate. If the thread size is relatively large, grease is preferred. For example, a small bolt holding derailleur cables can be oiled, but the large threads of pedals should be greased.

There are exceptions to always lubricating a thread. Either the internal or external thread may have nylon fittings, commonly called "Nylock." The nylon in the thread prevents the screw or bolt from turning. Nylock systems are used for adjustments when there is low torque or even no torque on the fastener. For example, derailleur limit screws use plastic fittings to prevent the screws from turning and changing the derailleur adjustment. Do not lubricate the limit screws.

Generally, bolts and nuts should be tightened as tight as the weakest member of the bolt-nut component system can withstand. For example, crank bolts are large and can take a very high torque. Cranks, however, are typically made from aluminum and cannot withstand as much pressure as the bolt could potentially generate. The crank is the weak link in that system.

To prevent over-tightening and under-tightening, many manufacturers provide specific torque values, best achieved by using a torque wrench (figure 1.3). Torque wrenches are like a tape measure or a ruler and are simply a type of measuring tool. Torque wrenches measure the amount of turning effort applied to the bolt or nut. A torque wrench should be part of the bicycle tool kit, but it is possible to work without one at some risk.

Measured torque may be given as Newton-meters or as inch-pound or foot-pound units. This refers to the force at the end of a lever. For example, 60 inch-pounds are equal to sixty pounds of force at the end of a one-inch wrench. If the wrench were two inches long, thirty pounds of force would be required to achieve the same torque on the bolt. If force were applied at twelve inches from the bolt, only 5 pounds of effort would be required.

To convert inch-pound units into foot-pound units, divide the inch-pound number by 12. For example, 60 inch-pounds of torque is equal to 5 foot-pounds. To convert foot-pound units into inch-pounds, multiply foot-pounds by 12. Three foot-pounds are equal to 36 inch-pounds. To convert Newton-meters to inch-pounds, multiply Newton-meters by 8.85. There is a list of recommended torque specifications in Appendix C. Use the component manufacturer's recommended torque when available.

With experience, a person may learn the amount of force to apply to a wrench when tightening a fastener. It may require both over-tightening and then under- tightening fasteners in order to learn acceptable torques. Tightening by feel relies on "perceived effort." Perceived effort is subjective and will change with the length of the tool used and where the hand holds the tool. Think about lifting a six-pack of 12-ounce beverage cans. The six-pack weighs approximately 4.7 pounds. This effort applied to a wrench held six inches from the bolt is about 30 inch-pounds of torque, just about what is required to tighten a derailleur cable pinch bolt. Now consider hefting, with one hand, a case of twenty-four 12-ounce beverage cans. Typically, that effort will be close to 20 pounds. That much effort on a wrench held six inches from the bolt is 120 inch-pounds or approximately the amount of torque required for hub cone locknuts and for many stem bolts. Cranks typically require about 300-400 inch-pounds, which is one of the highest torque values on a bicycle. That is at least 50 pounds of effort holding a wrench six inches from the crank bolt.

FIGURE: 1.3

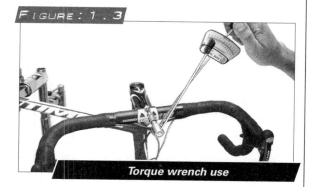

Torque wrench use

If you are not using a torque wrench, it is still useful to use torque values as a guideline for perceived effort. To determine the effort, divide the inch-pound torque by the number of inches from the middle of your hand to the bolt or nut. For example, in the image below, a 300 inch-pound torque is desired to hold the wheel to the frame. The hand is holding a wrench 6 inches from the nut. Apply an effort of 50 pounds force (figure 1.4).

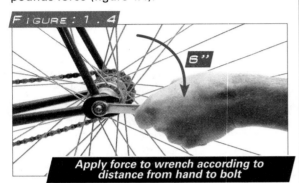

FIGURE: 1.4

Apply force to wrench according to distance from hand to bolt

It is very useful to understand the concept of "mechanical advantage" especially when working on tight bolts and nuts. The wrench acts as a lever that pivots on the bolt or nut. In situations where two wrenches are used, position the wrenches to form a "V," with the bolt or nut at the point of the "V." This position allows more force to be applied effectively to the bolt head. Avoid positioning the wrench so the levers form an angle greater than 90 degrees. When using one wrench, look for the second lever. This will sometimes be in the form of the opposite crank when working on pedals or the frame tubing while working on the bottom bracket (figure 1.5 and 1.6).

FIGURE: 1.5

Poor mechanical advantage

FIGURE: 1.6

Good mechanical advantage

Lubrication, Thread Lockers & Cleaners

Bicycles require various types of lubricants depending upon the part and how it is used. Lubricants vary in how well they work, what they are composed of, and how they are sold.

Lubrication prevents friction, corrosion, and rust. Engines use motor oil under pressure to ensure that pistons and bearings run smoothly. The car engine has pumps to maintain oil pressure to keep friction between parts low. That's a luxury the self-propelled cyclist cannot afford. Lubrication on bicycles is based on a much simpler system called "boundary lubrication," which refers to a very thin film of lubricant that separates moving bearing surfaces. This boundary of just a few molecules of lubrication is all we have to prevent metal from being ripped off a hub bearing or chain rivet.

A good lubricant should stick to the part requiring lubrication. Unfortunately, that may mean dirt and grit will want to stick to the part as well. Water tends to wash off lubricants. Liquids such as chain lubricants vary in their resistance to being washed off. It is useful to have available several lubrication choices. A light liquid lubricant will penetrate easier into smaller areas, such as derailleur cable housing. Examples of a light lubricant are Park Tool CL-1 Synthetic Blend Chain Lube and Triflow®. Heavy lubricants stick better in very wet conditions and are good for lubrication where grease is not useful. A chain used in the rain, or the internals of a freehub, would be good areas for a heavier lubricant. An example of a heavy lubricant would be Phil Wood® Tenacious Oil, or Finish Line® Cross-country.

Grease is simply oil suspended in a mixture of surfactant soap or other compounds. The grease keeps the lubricating oil in place on the component part, but it is the oil in the grease that provides the lubrication. When grease gets pushed out of the way of the bearings, there will be little or no lubrication left. Grease should be changed when it becomes contaminated with grit and dirt or when the oil in the grease becomes old and dry, which reduces its lubricating properties. Water may also wash out grease, and the bottom bracket is especially vulnerable.

It can be difficult to know when the grease used in the component parts is contaminated. It will be necessary to simply disassemble a hub or part and inspect. By the time a bearing is making noise, the damage from poor lubrication is already done. As a rule of thumb, the grease should be replaced once a year. If the bike is used for racing or ridden daily, replace the grease 2-3 times per year.

Grease is commonly sold in tubes or in tubs. Use care to always replace the lid when using the tub so the grease does not become contaminated. Liquid lubricants come in spray aerosol and non-aerosol bottles. The non-aerosol bottles use a tube for dripping the lubricant, which allows the user to place it where it does the most good. Aerosols can easily over-lubricate parts by spraying too much lubrication, but they can be helpful when flushing away dirt. If the bike is ridden in heavy rain, taken through stream crossings, or is washed with soap and water, liquid lubricants should be applied to the pivot points. Do not drip or spray oil into greased bearings such as hubs, headsets, and bottom brackets.

Another option for thread preparation and some press fits is anti-seize compound. This provides a thick and durable coating for surfaces. Anti-seize solutions are typically made of ground metals such as aluminum or copper and are combined with lubricants. These compounds are not appropriate for moving bearing surfaces such as hubs or headset bearings. Anti-seize compounds tend to outlast grease when exposed to water, which makes a long lasting preparation for uses such as bottom brackets.

Thread-lockers and retaining-compounds are special liquid adhesives for metal fasteners and fittings. These liquids are available at home improvement centers, hardware, or automotive parts stores. Thread-lockers are made by the Loctite® Corporation, the Wurth® Company, ND® Industries, and the Devcon® Company. Retailers commonly sell a type of thread-locker called "anaerobic." These liquids cure independently of air and will harden and expand when sealed in the threads of the part. This process is what gives the thread-lockers and compounds their special features. It should be stressed, however, that these products should not be used to replace proper torque and pre-load when the clamping load is important. Most thread-lockers are designed for use with metals. They may harden and weaken plastic and generally are not intended for that purpose.

Lighter duty thread-lockers are considered "service removable." This means the part can be unthreaded and removed with normal service procedures. An example of a service removable thread-locker is Loctite® #242. Stronger compounds require extra procedures to disassemble the part, such as treating with a heat gun. In a pinch, even hot water poured on the part can be enough heat to soften the compound.

Retaining-compounds are intended for press fit applications. On a bicycle, they may be used for poor cartridge bearing press fits and poor headset cups fits. The retaining-compounds tend to have a higher viscosity than the thread-locking compounds. Many retaining-compounds require special techniques for removal, such as excess force or mild heat or both. An example of a retaining-compound is Loctite® #RC-690.

Servicing bicycle components, such as the chain, will require cleaners and solvents. Never use highly flammable liquids, such as gasoline, kerosene, or diesel as a cleaning solvent. There are safer solvent choices on the market, including Park Tool CB-2 Chain and Parts Cleaning Fluid. Dispose of used and spent solvent by contacting your local hazardous waste disposal site, which is typically with a state or county agency.

For cleaning the paint on the frame use mild cleaners such as window cleaners or simply soap and water. Isopropyl rubbing alcohol is usually adequate for cleaning rim-braking surfaces. It is important that cleaners for braking surfaces not leave an oily film.

Diagnosing and Solving Mechanical Problems

As you develop mechanical skills and become more experienced with the technical side of the bicycle, diagnosing particular problems will become easier. To learn this skill, begin by paying attention to your bike while you ride and become accustomed to how it sounds and feels when things are operating properly.

A basic component of diagnosing and discussing technical or mechanical issues is knowing the names of the component parts. Being familiar with what shop mechanics call an item will enable you to converse and provide useful information. Appendix D is a Bike Map, showing the common names of the various component parts of the bike. Additionally, a glossary of bicycle specific terms can be found in Appendix B.

Diagnosing from the saddle while riding can be quite useful when repairing the problem later. For example, note if an unusual noise is repetitive or occurs with every pedal revolution. This would place the problem in the crankset area, like the pedal, bottom bracket, or chainring. A noise every second or third revolution might be in the chain, such as a stiff link as it passes by the derailleur pulley wheels. Ask yourself if the noise occurs when pedaling only or also when coasting. Make a mental note if the noise or problem occurs under load, such as on a hill, or when you hit a small bump.

It can be very helpful to use another mechanically-minded friend when diagnosing problems. For example, a friend can stress the suspect part of the bike, such as the crank, while you listen and feel for creaking. Creaking can often be felt through the frame and parts as a resonance. It can also be useful to ride with a friend, first describing what you think you are hearing and experiencing before you both ride. Use extra care during these diagnosing/riding sessions so you don't run into each other or parked cars.

Tools and Tool Selection

Having the correct tool for the job makes the work easier. Bicycles require both general maintenance tools common to any toolbox and specialty tools unique to the bicycle industry. There are a wide variety of sources for tools, such as bicycle retailers, department stores, automotive stores, and general tool retailers. In some cities, there are also public workshops that rent special tools and workbench space by the hour.

It is possible to purchase tools only as they are required. This is economical in one sense but not timely in another. When a part fails, the tools to repair the problem must be sought out, which can create a long delay in fixing the bike. Anticipating the use of tools and purchasing them ahead of time means initially spending money, but the tools are there when you need them. The priority in purchasing tools depends upon the bike components, the type of maintenance, the frequency of the work, and the mechanic's growing skill level.

Look for the "Tool Box" icon throughout the book, which lists tools and supplies typically required for the described procedure. Some tools are common, such as screwdrivers. Other tools, such as crank pullers, are more specific to the bicycle industry. Bikes are not all equipped the same and don't require every tool listed in the Tool Box. Keep in mind that older bikes may need special tools as well. Consult your local bicycle professional for recommendations on specific tools.

Tools differ between manufacturers in many ways including tool finish, fit in the hand, type of material, and tool fit to the part. The finish affects both the look of the tool and how it will resist corrosion. A hand tool should fit the hand comfortably and not be awkward to use. The type of material may affect the durability of the tool. Good quality steel will last longer than softer grades. Tools are typically made to a certain size. The size should fit the part correctly without being too large or too small. Bicycle component manufacturers sometimes limit what tool companies can do for tool design. For example, if a component part was poorly thought out and service only considered after the design was completed, a "correct" fitting tool may not be possible.

Box-end wrenches and open-end wrenches fit over the outside of a bolt head or nut. When choosing a wrench for a particular bolt, pick the smallest size that will fit over the head/nut. This also applies to spoke wrenches. Two different wrenches can appear to fit, but the smaller one will grab the part better.

Hex wrenches and screwdrivers (Phillips®, cross-tip, and straight blade) fit inside a screw head. The proper size here is the largest one that will fit inside. Although two different screwdriver

tips may fit inside a screw head, always choose the larger one for more engagement to the head.

A complete tool table for a very complete home shop is listed in Appendix A. However, the table does not include some tools professionals might use, such as frame machining equipment.

It is important for all mechanics, whether casual home mechanics or professional mechanics, to always use tools correctly. Wrenches should be placed fully on the nut or bolt head before turning. Hex wrenches should be fully inserted into the socket fitting before turning. Hold wrenches for comfort and good mechanical advantage. When using a file or hacksaw, apply pressure on the forward cutting stroke, not on the backstroke. These basic habits may seem obvious and pedestrian, but they are what make good mechanics.

Repair Stands

The repair stand (work stand) is the basic and most crucial piece of equipment for any shop or home. Getting the bike off the ground makes the repair quicker, easier, and more fun. A work stand brings the work up to the mechanic, rather than force the mechanic to bend over to get to the work. Work stands also allow the mechanic to pedal the bicycle and quickly diagnose problems. Many stands come with a rotational feature that allows the bike to rotate up to the mechanic. Repair stands often have a height adjustment feature, which allows for raising and lowering the bicycle.

Some bike frames have oval, square, or other non-round shaped tubing, making it difficult to clamp onto the frame tubing. For certain frames, the bicycle manufacturer may recommend clamping only on the seat post, rather than the frame tubing. Most bikes can be clamped on the seat post. When in doubt, check with the manufacturer for acceptable areas to clamp.

There are several clamp and stand designs available. Models vary in adjustability, range of working height, and how they hold the bike (figure 1.7 to figure 1.10). There are also repair stands available that do not clamp the bike on any tube (figure 1.11).

FIGURE: 1.7

Screw-type clamp with an opening cam

FIGURE: 1.8

The adjustable linkage of an over-the-center clamp offers adjustable pressure at any diameter setting

FIGURE: 1.9

This screw-type clamp fits a wide range of tube sizes

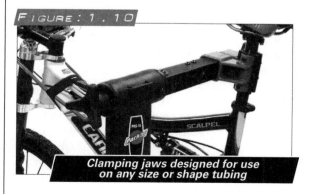

FIGURE: 1.10

Clamping jaws designed for use on any size or shape tubing

FIGURE: 1.11

Popular with race teams, the PRS-21 stand holds the bike without clamping the frame tubes

Home Shop Set Up

Home mechanics may enjoy setting up a dedicated repair area, or, basically, their own "bike shop." The primary requirement for a shop is space for a workbench, a repair stand, the bike, and enough room to maneuver. A common size for commercial workbenches is 72 inches by 30 inches (182cm by 75cm). This is deep enough to hold a wheel. It is possible to use a bench shorter than the 72 inches, but avoid benches narrower than 30 inches deep. If you are building a custom workbench, it can be set for the height of the user. This may range from 32 inches to 40 inches high. For general technical work, the top of the workbench should be approximately 4 inches to 6 inches (100-150mm) below the height of the user's elbow. The bench top can be made of many different materials, but expect the top to take some punishment during work. It is very useful to bolt the bench to the floor and to a wall. This is especially important if you plan to mount a vise to the bench.

Tools may be mounted to a board on the wall. This allows the mechanic to quickly find the right tool. A pegboard provides a versatile system to hang and arrange tools. The higher quality pegboard measures 1/4-inch thick. The pegboard should be at least as wide as the workbench. Hardware stores and home supply stores stock pegboard hooks. A mix of short and long hooks will be needed. However, the short hooks are better, as this avoids stacking too many tools on one hook. A tool magnet is also a very useful item for the work area. It can hold odd shaped steel tools, and even bolts that you don't want to lose during a repair.

If possible, select an area with good light. You may need to supplement the work area with extra lighting. Painting the pegboard surface white or off-white will reflect more light onto your work area.

A good repair stand is the most critical part of the repair shop. The repair stand should be positioned next to the work area. Keep the stand close to the workbench to avoid taking even one step to the bike, but not so close you are crowded. Be sure to use the rotation and height adjustment features of the stand to move the work area of the bike closer to you, rather then bending over. Save your back for riding.

If possible, get a bench-mounted vise. A four-inch vise is typically adequate for bicycle repair. Mount the vise on a corner of the bench so the non-moving jaw is even with the bench edge.

When arranging tools on the wall, place the tools likely to be used in conjunction with the vise close to the vise. For example, place the axle vise, cone wrenches, hammer, and freewheel tools closer to the vise.

Another very useful piece of equipment is an air compressor. A floor pump can, of course, provide enough air pressure for tires. A small air compressor, however, is useful for drying parts after washing them with a solvent. A compressor is also very useful when inflating tubeless tires.

Tool arrangement preferences will vary from mechanic to mechanic but try to group specialty tools together. Brake tools should be with other brake tools. Non-specialty tools should be together with hex wrenches grouped together and combination wrenches lined up in order (figure 1.12). With time you will develop the system that is best for you.

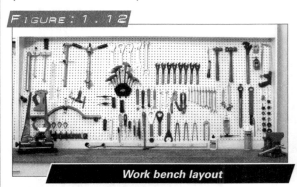

FIGURE: 1.12

Work bench layout

Maintenance Schedule

The idea of a schedule of maintenance is that it will encourage you to check certain items on a regular basis. No two bikes are used in identical conditions, and your bike may benefit from more checking than a list suggests. If you ride in conditions of rain, mud, sand, dust, salt water, pot-holed roads, or aggressive trails, these will take their toll on the bike. Table 1.1 should be viewed only a general reference. Add your own items to the list that you feel are needed.

TABLE: 1.1   Maintenance Schedule

EVERY RIDE

1. Check pressure in tires. Use tire gauge when available. Squeeze sidewalls at a minimum.
2. Check tires for tread cuts
3. Grab brake levers with force, note any differences between rides
4. Bounce bike, listening for rattles and odd noises, such as loose headset
5. Spin pedals backwards, note any squeaky or dry chain
6. Clean/wash if very gritty and dirty

EVERY 100 MILES (160 KILOMETERS)

1. Check chain stretch
2. Inspect cable for cuts
3. Clean chain if necessary or dirty
4. Inspect brake pads for wear
5. Inspect tires for tread wear, replace as needed
6. Check hand pump for ability to create pressure
7. Check for bearing play in wheel hubs
8. _____
9. _____

EVERY 500 MILES (800 KILOMETERS)

1. Grab cranks and pull side-to-side checking for play.
2. Lubricate pivot points
3. Lubricate brake and shifter cables
4. Check crank bolts
5. Full suspension bikes, check swing arm pivot bolts
6. Inspect frame for cracks or other anomalies
7. _____
8. _____

EVERY 1000 (1,600 KILOMETERS)

1. Inspect rims for wear if using rim calipers
2. If ridden in muddy and hard conditions, overhaul bearings
3. Inspect shoe cleats and replace as needed
4. Remove seat post and clean. Re-grease as appropriate.
5. _____
6. _____

EVERY 3000 (4,800 KILOMETERS)

1. Grease bearings if non-cartridge
2. Remove tires and inspect rim strip
3. Install new cables and housing, especially shifting systems
4. Replace cartridge bearings if worn or play is present
5. _____
6. _____

ParkTool

CHAPTER 2

Tires and Tubes

The smooth ride of the bicycle is due in large part to the air in the tires. The common bicycle wheel uses pneumatic tires referred to as "wired on" tires or "clinchers." The wheel's rim is shaped to hold the tire beads or edges of the tires. Inside conventional tires is an inner tube to hold the air. The tire's body and casing around the inner tube take the pressure, bumps, and bruises of riding. There are also "tubeless" systems available, which are similar to car tires. Many professional-level road racers also use sew-up or tubular tire systems.

Servicing tires and tubes is a basic skill required for any cyclist. Anything from sharp thorns, glass, or nails can puncture tires and inner tubes, and the tire itself will wear out with use and time.

TOOLS & SUPPLIES:

Wrench of correct size for wheels with axle nuts (15mm is common)

Removing Wheels

The wheel must be removed to replace the tube and tire. If possible, begin by mounting the bike in a repair stand. If no stand is available, the bike should be laid on the non-drive side to avoid damage to the rear derailleur when the rear wheel is removed. Do not stand the bike upright without the rear wheel in place, as this will damage the rear derailleur. The bicycle may be turned upside down on the ground if there is no chance of lever or accessory damage. Bikes with quick-release wheels do not require tools for removal. Bikes with axle nuts will require the correct size combination wrench or adjustable wrench.

Quick-release wheels use a hollow-hub axle fitted with a shaft, a lever that operates a cam mechanism, and an adjusting nut. Tightening the lever puts tension on the shaft and pulls both the cam and the adjusting nut tight against the dropouts. This tension holds the wheel securely to the frame. The adjusting nut determines the amount of tension on the quick-release lever and cam.

Non-quick-release hubs use a solid axle with nuts outside the dropouts. The axle nut may also have a built-in washer, or there may be a separate washer under the nut. If the washer has teeth or a knurled surface, these face the dropout to help secure the wheel. Lubricate the axle threads with the wheel off the bike. For wheel removal with axle nuts, loosen both nuts outside of dropouts.

The procedure for wheel removal:
  a. REAR WHEEL: Shift derailleur to outermost rear cog and innermost front chainring.
  b. Release rim brake caliper quick-release, if any (figure 2.1, figure 2.2, figure 2.3, figure 2.4).
  c. Release wheel quick-release by pulling quick-release lever outward. If necessary, loosen quick-release adjusting nut to clear any tabs at end of fork (figure 2.5). If the quick-release is used on a through-axle fork and hub, it is necessary to remove axle completely from hub. For non-quick-release wheels, loosen both axle nuts.
  d. FRONT: Guide the wheel through the brake pads and out the fork ends.
  e. REAR: Pull back on rear derailleur to allow cogs to clear chain (figure 2.6). Lower wheel, guiding the wheel down through caliper brake pads and forward to clear chain and derailleur. (Note: some bike dropouts are rear facing. Pull wheel back to remove it from the dropouts. Unhook chain from cog to removal.)

FIGURE: 2.1

Side pull or dual pivot rim brake caliper may have quick-release lever at caliper arm

FIGURE: 2.2

The quick-release engagement is located at the brake lever on some models

For linear pull calipers, squeeze lever arms together and disconnect cable from linkage

For cantilever calipers squeeze lever arms together and disconnect straddle wire cable

Pull lever from closed to open position

Pivot derailleur back to clear wheel and cogs

Removing Tire & Tube from Rim

To fully inspect the tube and tire, it is best to remove the tire completely from the rim. The mounted tire has a bead that is fitted to the inner wall of the rim. Use tire levers to pry tire bead up and over rim sidewall. Tire levers come in different shapes and materials. A plastic lever (Park Tool TL-1 or TL-4) is typically adequate and will not leave blemishes on the rim. However, some tire and rim combinations are extremely tight and may require a steel lever, such as the Park Tool TL-5. Some cosmetic marring may occur with any metal lever.

CAUTION!

Do not use a screwdriver, knife, or other sharp lever object, which might damage tire or tube.

The procedure for tire and tube removal:

a. Remove valve cap. Fully threaded valve shafts may also have a locking nut next to the rim. Loosen and remove locking nut before deflating.

b. Deflate tube completely. Even a small amount of air left in the tube can make it more difficult to get the tire off the rim. For best results, press downward on wheel while depressing the valve.

c. The tire bead will be pressed tight against rim sidewall. Push both sides of tire toward the center of the rim to loosen the bead (figure 2.7).

d. Engage one tire lever under bead of tire. Engage second lever 1-2" (2-5 cm) from first lever then push both levers down towards the spokes to lift the bead up and off the rim (figure 2.8).

e. Disengage one of the levers. Move it approximately two inches (5 cm) along the rim and engage this lever under the bead. Push lever to lift the next section of bead off rim.

f. Repeat engaging the lever until the bead loosens. Then slide the lever along the rim under the bead until the bead is completely removed from the rim.

g. Starting opposite the valve, pull inner tube out from inside of the tire. Lift valve from valve hole and remove tube from wheel.

ParkTool

h. Remove second bead from rim, which removes the tire completely from the rim. To fully inspect the tube and tire, it is best to remove the tire completely.

FIGURE: 2.7

Push bead toward middle of rim

FIGURE: 2.8

Engage levers under bead

Inspecting the Inner Tube

When servicing a flat tire, always inspect the tire and tube carefully to locate the cause of failure. This will help prevent future flats. It can be useful to mark the tire at the valve to help in referencing any holes in the tube to the location in the tire. It is always best, however, to inspect the full surfaces of both tire and tube.

The procedure for inspecting the inner tube:

a. Re-inflate inner tube, if possible, to twice its normal width. This extra tension makes small leaks easier to locate (figure 2.9 and figure 2.10).

b. Inspect for air leaks. Move the tube closely past the sensitive skin such as the lips or cheeks. Small leaks can also sometimes be heard. Check around the entire tube. If this does not work, then submerge the tube in water and watch for bubbles at the hole.

c. If you plan to repair the inner tube, use a marking pen to make four marks, one on each side of hole (figure 2.11). Do not mark directly on the hole, as the marks may be sanded off, making the hole's location difficult to find.

d. Inspect the remainder of inner tube for more holes.

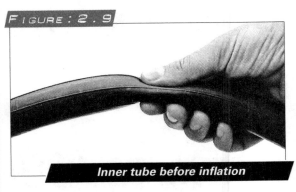

FIGURE: 2.9

Inner tube before inflation

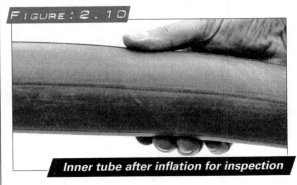

FIGURE: 2.10

Inner tube after inflation for inspection

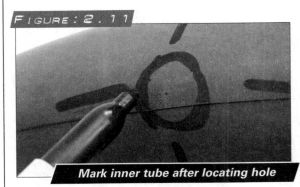

FIGURE: 2.11

Mark inner tube after locating hole

It is important to inspect the flatted inner tube even if it is to be replaced with a new one. The type of cut or hole in the tube will help determine the cause of the flat. Knowing this can help prevent flats in the future. Common cuts and their causes include:

• Cut at valve

Misalignment of tube in rim, a crooked valve, or riding with low pressure. Be sure the tube is mounted straight inside the rim and check tire pressure before every ride.

• Leaky valve core

Loose core inside stem. Test mounted tube and the tire at full pressure with soapy water or saliva sealing the core. Inspect for bubbles appearing at the core (figure 2.12). Tighten with a valve core tool.

FIGURE: 2.12

Test valve for core leak

• Large shredded hole

Blowout. Usually not repairable. Check tire and rim for seating problems. Also check for hole in the tire casing (figure 2.13).

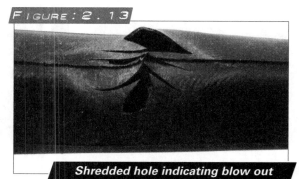

FIGURE: 2.13

Shredded hole indicating blow out

• Hole on the rim strip side of tube

Rim strip failure. Inspect inside of rim for protruding spokes, sharp points, or lack of strip coverage of inner rim holes.

• Long cut or rip

Tire blow out. Tube is usually not repairable. Check tire and rim for seating problems. Use care when seating tire during installation.

• Single puncture or small hole

Thorn, wire, glass. These holes may be repairable. Check tire as well. The cause of the puncture may still be embedded in the tire. Hole typically located against top of tire casing.

• Double slits

Rim pinch. Tube was pinched between the rim and an object on the road or trail. Increase air pressure or use wider tires (figure 2.14).

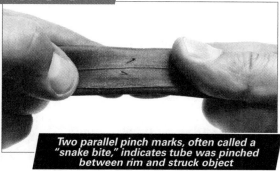

FIGURE: 2.14

Two parallel pinch marks, often called a "snake bite," indicates tube was pinched between rim and struck object

Inspecting the Tire

It is important to always inspect the tire as well as the inner tube. The cause of the flat, such as a nail or piece of glass, may still be embedded in the tire or tread. Inspect both the outside of the rubber tread and the inside of the casing.

Inspect for protruding nails, pieces of glass, thorns, or other objects. Squeeze any cut to look inside for objects such as slivers of glass. Visually inspect the inside of tire casing for nails, glass, or debris. Wipe inside of casing with a rag and then carefully feel inside with fingers. Proceed slowly as there may be sharp objects still in the casing (figure 2.15).

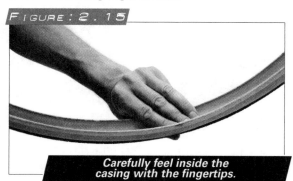

FIGURE: 2.15

Carefully feel inside the casing with the fingertips.

Inspect tire bead for damage. A broken or cut bead will not permit the tire to hold to rim. Any exposed bead will require tire replacement (figure 2.16).

ParkTool

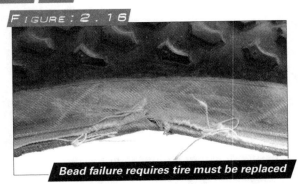

Bead failure requires tire must be replaced

Check for "tire rot," or a deterioration of the tire casing. Old and rotted tires are more susceptible to punctures and blow outs from sidewall failure (figure 2.17).

Rotted tire casing will not resist thorns or glass, and will eventually fail by blowout

Inspect sidewall for rips, abrasions, holes or damage to casing (figure 2.18). Damage to the cords may only be seen when the tire is fully inflated. Failed cords will show as bulges and anomalies to tire shape.

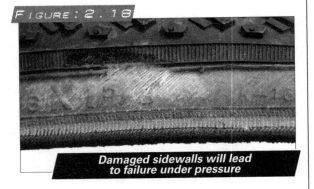

Damaged sidewalls will lead to failure under pressure

The tire tread will eventually wear out. For tires used on pavement, look for a flattening of the tire crown in the middle. For off-road tires, the top knobs will become worn and rounded compared to knobs on the side. If the cord is showing or the casing appears deformed, it should be replaced (figure 2.19).

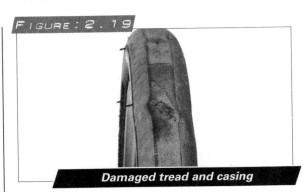

Damaged tread and casing

Rim Strip

The wheel rim may have holes between the rim sidewalls for spoke nipples. The rim strip covers the holes or nipples. It protects the inner tube from nipples and sharp edges in the base of the rim. The rim strip can be made of cloth, rubber, or polyurethane plastic. It should be wide enough to cover the bottom of the rim, but not so wide that it interferes with the seating of the tire bead. Inspect the rim strip whenever changing a tire or inner tube. Look for tears and rips. Make sure the rim strip is centered over the nipple holes and completely covers each hole (figure 2.20).

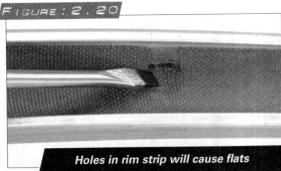

Holes in rim strip will cause flats

High-pressure tires require a strong rim strip. Without a sturdy support, the inner tube will push down into the nipple holes, resulting in a blow out. Do not use soft and flexible rubber rim strips in rims with eyelet holes.

Repairing Inner Tubes

Inner tubes are commonly made of butyl rubber and are black in color. Latex inner tubes are lightweight and tend to be a cream color. The latex material is more porous than butyl rubber and will require air before every ride. Both types can be patched.

Replacing the punctured inner tube with a new tube is always the safest and most reliable procedure. In some cases, it's safe to repair a small hole in an inner tube. If the hole is large, however, it may not be possible to repair. When in doubt, replace the tube.

Pre-Glued Patch Repair

The Park Tool GP-2 Super Patch Kit uses pre-glued patches. The patch relies on the tube pressing against the tire for the hole to be sealed. If the inner tube is too small relative to the tire casing, the patch may become too stretched to hold effectively. Double check if the inner tube is an appropriate size for the tire when using a pre-glued patch.

The procedure for repairing inner tubes with Park Tool GP-2 pre-glued super patch:

 a. Locate the hole marked during inspection. (See Page 14, Inspecting the Inner Tube.) Using a fine emery cloth or sandpaper, clean the tube by lightly abrading the area around hole. Excessive sanding or heavy pressure can cause grooves in the rubber leading to patch failure.
 b. If possible, clean the area with a rag and alcohol. Allow it to dry completely.
 c. Peel patch from patch backing. Handle patch as little as possible and by edges only (figure 2.21).
 d. Center patch to hole and lay patch on tube.
 e. Apply pressure for patch to seal. Roll patch and tube between thumb and forefingers.
 f. Tube is ready to install. DO NOT test patch by inflating tube while outside of mounted tire. This may stretch the tube body and weaken the patch bond.

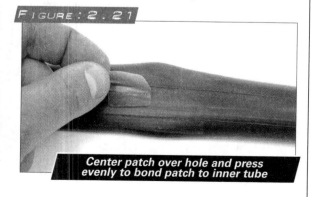

FIGURE: 2.21

Center patch over hole and press evenly to bond patch to inner tube

Repairing Inner Tubes with Self-Vulcanizing Patches

Self-vulcanizing patches require the application of a thin layer of self-vulcanizing fluid on the tube before the patch is applied. The patch reacts with the fluid to bond with the inner tube, but inner tubes differ in their component chemical compounds. Patching may result in mixed success.

The procedure for repairing tube with self-vulcanizing patch:

 a. Locate hole marked during inspection. (See page 14, Inspecting the Inner Tube.)
 b. Using a fine emery cloth or sandpaper, lightly abrade area around hole. Abrade an area larger than patch size.
 c. When possible, clean area with alcohol and allow it to dry completely.
 d. Open self-vulcanizing fluid tube and puncture seal. Apply thin coat of self-vulcanizing fluid and spread evenly around hole area (figure 2.22). Use a clean finger or the back of patch to spread the self-vulcanizing fluid evenly over an area that is larger than the size of the patch. Do not apply too much fluid. The layer should not appear "glopped" on.
 e. Allow self-vulcanizing fluid to dry. This may take several minutes. Test by touching the perimeter area of self-vulcanizing fluid only. Do not touch self-vulcanizing fluid where the patch will contact.
 f. Peel patch from backing. Leave clear plastic cover on patch. Handle patch by its edges.
 g. Center patch to hole and lay on the tube.
 h. Apply pressure to patch, especially at the edges, to seal. If possible, maintain pressure for several minutes.
 i. Inspect edges of patch. Edges should lay flat and appear bonded to tube (figure 2.23 and figure 2.24).
 j. Tube is ready to install. Do not remove plastic cover from patch. It could pull on the freshly-bonded patch.

ParkTool

Spread a thin, wide layer
of self-vulcanizing fluid

FIGURE: 2.22

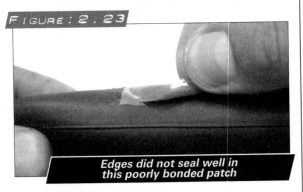

Edges did not seal well in
this poorly bonded patch

FIGURE: 2.23

Edges lay flat in a successful patch

FIGURE: 2.24

Inner Tube Sealants

Liquid sealants can be added to the inner tube. These products are available from various manufacturers and are only intended to seal small holes in the tube. To add sealant to the inner tube, install the inner tube into wheel as normal. For Schrader valves, remove the core using a valve core remover. Only some Presta model tubes use a valve with a removable core. Place the valve at the three o'clock or nine o'clock position, making the valve horizontal. Inject the sealant according to the manufacturer's directions. Replace the valve and inflate tire, keeping the valve horizontally. Spin the wheel to spread the sealant. When inflating or deflating the tire, the valve should be placed horizontally.

The sealant will make patching the inner tube difficult or impossible. The sealant tends to prevent good patch bonding. The valve core can also become plugged and sealed with time. Sealants can even plug a tire pump head used to pump this tube. Always keep the valve at horizontal position while inflating.

Tire Liners

Tire liners are specially made strips of a tough, flexible material placed inside the tire body. Liners are installed between the tire and inner tube and may help prevent thorns, glass, and other sharp objects from reaching the inner tube (figures 2.25). Liners should be installed centered to tire. Liners will not prevent pinch flats and do not protect from sharp object penetrating the side of tire.

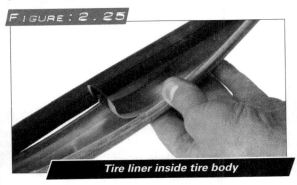

Tire liner inside tire body

FIGURE: 2.25

Temporary Repair of Tire with Tire Boot

If the tire has been ripped and the casing damaged, it may not hold an inner tube. It is possible, in some cases, to make a temporary repair with a Park Tool TB-2 Emergency Tire Boot. A booted tire should not be considered a permanent repair. The tire should be replaced as soon as possible.

Begin repair by locating rip in tire. Compare rip to size of tire boot. Tire boot must completely overlap the rip to be effective. Clean inside the tire adjacent to the rip. Cut patch to size. Align the patch making sure the edges do not extend beyond the tire bed. Center the patch to the rip and press it inside of the tire casing (figure 2.26). It is possible to affect a temporary boot using other material. If possible use a strong material that is resistant to tearing. Notebook paper or paper currency should not be considered acceptable boot material.

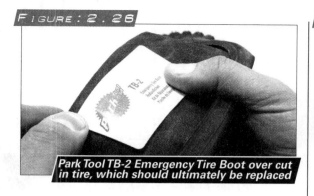

FIGURE: 2.26

Park Tool TB-2 Emergency Tire Boot over cut in tire, which should ultimately be replaced

FIGURE: 2.28

Valve core remover checks security of Schrader valves

Inner Tube Valves

There are two common types of valve stems on bicycles, Schrader and Presta ("French" type) (figure 2.27). The Schrader or American-type valve is common on cars and motorcycles. It is also found on many bicycles. The valve stem is approximately 8mm (5⁄16") diameter and has an internal spring plunger (core) to assist in shutting the valve.

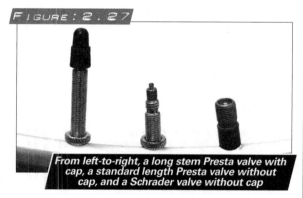

FIGURE: 2.27

From left-to-right, a long stem Presta valve with cap, a standard length Presta valve without cap, and a Schrader valve without cap

To deflate the Schrader valve tube, it is necessary to stick a small hex wrench or other object into the valve in order to press on the stem and release the air. Upon release of the stem, the valve spring shuts. Schrader-compatible pump fittings press on the internal stem with a plunger, which allows the tube to be filled.

The Schrader valve core can be removed from the tube if necessary. This is rarely necessary, but a valve can become stuck and cause a slow leak. A loose core can also be the source of a slow leak. A valve core remover allows removal or tightening of the core (figure 2.28).

The rim's valve hole should match the valve of the tube. If a rim has been made with the smaller valve hole for Presta, it can be drilled and enlarged to the 8mm size by using an 11⁄32-inch (8.5mm) hand drill. After drilling, use a small round file to remove any sharp edges. Rims that are less then 15mm outside width should not be drilled. It is also possible to use the smaller Presta valve in a rim intended for the larger Schrader by using an adapter sleeve.

The Presta or French-type valve is common on mid- and higher-priced road bikes and on higher-priced mountain bikes. Presta stems are 6mm diameter (nominally ¼") and thinner than Schrader valves. Stem length will vary. Deep section rims require longer valve stems (approx. 60mm). At the top of the stem is a small valve locknut, which must be unthreaded before air can enter the tube (figure 2.29). To deflate the inner tube, unthread the locknut and depress the valve stem. To inflate the tube, unthread the locknut and inflate using a Presta-compatible pump.

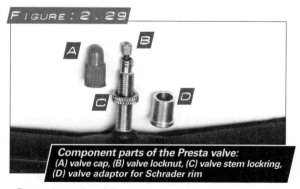

FIGURE: 2.29

Component parts of the Presta valve: (A) valve cap, (B) valve locknut, (C) valve stem lockring, (D) valve adaptor for Schrader rim

Some brands of Presta tubes use a valve shaft that is fully threaded. These come with an extra locking nut or ring. Loosen the ring by hand and remove it before installing the tube. Install and fully inflate the tube. Then install the lockring and snug by hand. When deflating the tube,

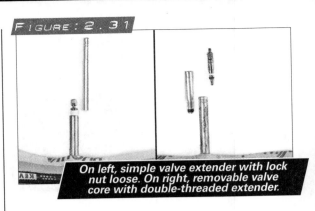

On left, simple valve extender with lock nut loose. On right, removable valve core with double-threaded extender.

loosen and remove the nut first. When a tire is fully inflated and then deflated, the valve moves back into the tire casing. If the valve is locked to the rim by the nut, the valve may be ripped from the inner tube.

Presta-compatible pump heads have no plunger. The seal of a Presta pump head is smaller than the pump head of a Schrader pump. To inflate a Presta tube, unthread the valve stem locknut and tap lightly to release the seal. The seal tends to stick over time and tapping the stem breaks it free, which makes it easier to inflate. Press the Presta-compatible pump head onto the stem and inflate the tube. Some pump heads may have a lever to help seal the valve.

There is no performance difference between the two kinds of valves. The Schrader valve, however, is wider and requires a larger rubber base to bond it to the tube. Consequently, very narrow tubes use the Presta valve. A Presta-to-Schrader adapter is available, which allows Schrader pump heads to be used on Presta valves (figure 2.30).

Tire & Tube Sizing

Tires are made with a steel wire or fabric cord, called the "bead", which is molded into each edge of the tire. The bead forms a circle. The diameter of this circle determines the tire fit to the rim. The tire bead is made to fit into the rim bead seat, which is the area below the outer rim edge (figure 2.32).

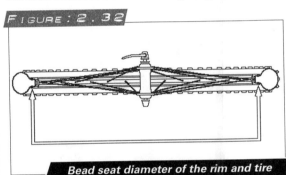

Bead seat diameter of the rim and tire

A Presta to Schrader valve adapter in place

Some models of Presta valves use removable cores. If the valve has two wrench flats, use a small adjustable wrench to secure or remove the core.

Aerodynamic rims with a very tall cross section require longer valve stems built into the inner tubes. There are also valve extenders available that screw onto the Presta valve and allow the tube to be inflated (figure 2.31). However, it is the design of the Presta valve that the locking nut be shut to fully secure the valve. If the nut cannot be closed, there may be some leaking from the valve. Some extenders do not allow the valve nut to be tightened, which may result in a slow leak.

Do not attempt to mix tires and wheels with different bead seat diameters. Although the bead seat diameter determines the tire and wheel fit, there is little consistency between manufacturers in how tires are labeled or identified. Different countries at times have used different nomenclature marking systems. This can cause confusion when selecting a tire for a wheel and frustration when installing a tire.

An antiquated, but still common method, uses "inch" designations, such as 27-inch or 26-inch. The inch size does not directly refer to the bead seat measurement. It is simply a code, and it refers to the approximate outside diameter of an inflated tire. For example, there are several 26-inch tires that use different bead seat diameters. A 26" x 1⅜" tire, for example, will not interchange with the modern MTB 26" x 1.5" tire. There are three even more obscure tire standards also referred to as 26-inch diameter, but none are interchangeable.

Another common system is the older French system of sizing. The sizing numbers are reference numbers only, but they're not actual measurements of anything. Road bicycles commonly use a 700c tire that has a bead diameter of 622mm. The "700c" does not refer to bead diameter. The "c" is part of the code system. There are also 700a and 700b tires and wheels, but none interchange with the more common 700c.

The ETRTO (European Tire and Rim Technical Organization) system, which is the same as the ISO system (International Standards Organization) is now becoming more common. The ISO or ETRTO system uses two number designations for the tire and rim sizing. The larger number is always the bead seat diameter. Rims and tires with the same number are made to fit one another. For example, tires marked 622 will fit rims marked 622, because the bead seat diameter is 622 millimeters for both. Look for this sizing system on the tire. Rims may also have ISO sizing on the label (figure 2.33).

FIGURE: 2.33

25-622 (700X25C)
WARNING MOUNT ONLY ON HOOKED TYPE RIMS
WARNUNG: NUR AUF HAKENFELGEN MONTIEREN

ISO (ETRTO) sizing on tire label along with French sizing system

The rim marking may also have a smaller number. This is the width in millimeters between rim sidewalls. Generally, a wider rim will accept a wider tire. A narrow tire on a relatively wide rim will mean the tire profile shape will be less rounded. A wide tire on a narrow rim will result in less support for the tire in cornering, which can cause the tire to laterally roll or twist. Additionally, rim caliper brakes will have very little room to clear the tire with this combination. As a loose rule, the ISO tire width should be between 1.5 to 2 times ISO rim widths. A rim width 25mm between the sidewalls should use an ISO tire width of about 37 to 50.

The inner tube should match the tire size diameter closely. Tires that are close in bead diameter may use the same inner tube. For example, an inner tube for an ISO 630 tire

(27-inch) will also fit an ISO 622 (700c) tire. The inner tube must also match the tire width, but, because inner tubes are flexible, one inner tube may fit a range of tire widths. If the inner tube is too narrow for the tire width, it will become very thin when inflated inside the tire body. This will cause it to be more susceptible to punctures and failures. If the tube is too wide for the tire, it will be difficult or impossible to fit inside the tire casing. Part of the tube may stick out of the tire and blow out when the tire is fully inflated. Refer to Table 2.1 for common sizes for the tire and wheel bead-seating systems.

TABLE: 2.1 — Tire Sizing

COMMON SIZING NAME	ETRTO OR ISO BEAD SEAT DIAMETER	COMMON USES
29"	622	MTB using the 29" tires. Rim is same diameter as 622 below
27"	630	Older road bikes, and less expensive road bikes
700C	622	Road bikes, hybrid bikes
26" x 1 ⅜"	597	Older Schwinn
26" x 1 ⅜"	590	Department store three speeds, English 3-speeds
26" x 1" to 26" x 3.7"	559	MTB bikes
26" x 1 ½" or 650c	571	Smaller road bikes or special tri-athlete bikes
24" x 1" to 1.75"	507	Juvenile MTB bikes
20" x 1" to 2.2"	406	Juvenile bikes, BMX, freestyle bikes, recumbents
16" x 1" to 2.2	305	Some recumbents and juvenile bikes

Fraction
Decimal } can't inner-change

ParkTool

Installing Tire & Tube on Wheel

Tires are sized to match the rim. However, even within the same rim and tire sizing standard, certain tire/rim manufacturer combinations can be easily mounted by hand. Other combinations will be tight and may be difficult to mount by hand. These combinations require tire levers for installation. Never use a screwdriver, knife, or other sharp tool to mount the tire.

The procedure for tire installation:

a. Note any directional arrows of the tire manufacturer. Directional arrows printed on the sidewalls indicate rotation of wheel. Not all tires have direction orientation.

b. Inflate tube enough for tube to hold its shape.

c. Install tube inside tire. Install with tube valve adjacent to air pressure recommendations written on tire sidewall (figure 2.34).

d. Lean rim vertically against your legs with the valve hole facing up.

e. Lower tire and valve into rim valve hole and align valve so it is pointing straight toward hub. A crooked valve can lead to a flat tire later (figure 2.35).

f. Install one bead at a time. Begin with the bead adjacent to your legs.

g. Work tire bead onto rim with hands. If tire bead will not seat using hands, use a tire lever as a last resort. Use caution when using tire levers to avoid pinching inner tube. Use tire lever in same orientation as removal method.

h. Work tube over rim sidewall and into rim cavity.

i. Install second bead onto rim (figure 2.36). Use care if using a tire lever. Do not lift lever beyond 90-degrees from the wheel plane (figure 2.37).

j. Inspect both sides of tire for bead seating and for any sign of the inner tube sticking out. If the tube is visible under the tire bead, remove the tire and re-install.

k. Inflate to low pressure and inspect bead again on both sides. Look for a small molding line above the bead. This line should run consistently above rim (figure 2.38).

l. Inflate to full pressure and check with a pressure gauge. It may be necessary to press downward above the valve in order to engage the pump head. For fully threaded valve shafts, re-install any locking nut. Turn the nut finger tight only. Do not use a wrench or pliers.

FIGURE: 2.34

Place tube into tire before mounting tire to rim

FIGURE: 2.35

This valve will eventually be cut by the rim valve hole

FIGURE: 2.36

Push bead onto rim

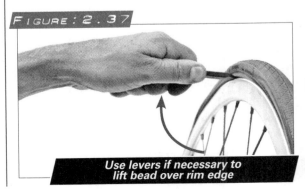

FIGURE: 2.37

Use levers if necessary to lift bead over rim edge

FIGURE: 2.38

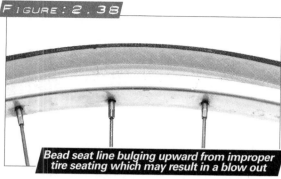

Bead seat line bulging upward from improper tire seating which may result in a blow out

Installing Wheels on Bike

The wheels must be properly mounted to the bicycle frame. Misalignment can result in problems with shifting, brake pad alignment, and bike handling. If the wheel is not securely mounted in the dropouts, it may come out and possibly injure the rider. Wheels may be held to the bike with a quick-release system, axle nuts, or a "through-axle" system.

The quick-release is fitted with two conical shaped springs. The small end of the spring faces the axle, and the large end faces outward. These springs make the wheel easier to install. If one or both springs become twisted or damaged they can be removed. The springs serve no purpose once the wheel is tight on the bike (figure 2.39).

FIGURE: 2.39

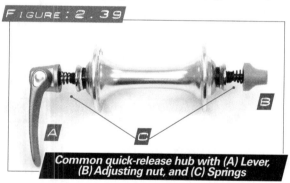

Common quick-release hub with (A) Lever, (B) Adjusting nut, and (C) Springs

The quick-release skewer uses a cam device to hold the wheel securely to the frame dropouts. It is important that the skewer be fully and consistently tightened before each ride. This is also important for the pressure applied to the hub bearings. For most brands of skewers, hold lever parallel to the hub axle, which is half way through its swing from fully open to fully closed (figure 2.40, figure 2.41, figure 2.42). Tighten adjusting nut snug against the dropout. Check results by moving the lever. Lever should meet resistance to closing halfway through the swing. Lubricate the cam mechanism if it appears sticky or dry.

FIGURE: 2.40

Lever in fully open position

FIGURE: 2.41

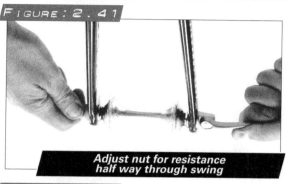

Adjust nut for resistance half way through swing

FIGURE: 2.42

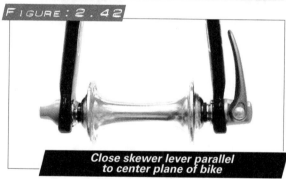

Close skewer lever parallel to center plane of bike

The cam mechanism is designed to lock when the lever is parallel to the center plane of the bike. Inspect section of lever adjacent to the cam. If the lever arm is not fully closed, the wheel is not properly secured (figure 2.43). Double-check the skewer adjusting nut and the pressure on the lever.

FIGURE: 2.43

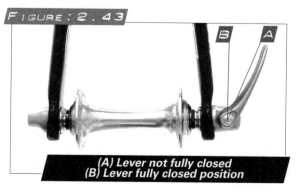

(A) Lever not fully closed
(B) Lever fully closed position

Park Tool

A common skewer design is called the "open cam" (figure 2.44). The cam mechanism and press points are visible and exposed to dirt and grime. Setting lever resistance at halfway through swing may be too tight for some models. However, these skewers should still close with force. The open cam especially needs lubrication to work effectively. Consult specific manufacturer for recommended pressure of closing.

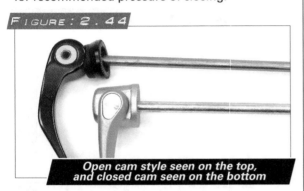

FIGURE: 2.44

Open cam style seen on the top, and closed cam seen on the bottom

The procedure for installing wheels:

a. Open brake quick-release mechanism.
b. Move wheel quick-release skewer to open position.
c. FRONT WHEEL: Install between dropouts with skewer on non-drive side.
d. REAR WHEEL: Check that rear derailleur is in most outboard position. Pull rear derailleur back to open chain (figure 2.45). Place cogs between upper and lower sections of chain and guide wheel between brake pads and engage smallest cog on chain.
e. Guide rim or disc rotor between brake pads. Guide axle up and into dropouts. Pulling up and/or back depending upon dropout style. It may be necessary to flex dropouts open to get wheel in. Pull wheel fully up into dropouts.
f. Adjust closing tension of quick-release skewer and close skewer. FRONT: Wheel should be centered between fork blades. If necessary, open skewer, move wheel either left or right until wheel appears centered, then close skewer. The quick-release skewer must be fully engaged on the dropout surfaces
g. Close brake quick-release mechanism.
h. Determine final closing position of quick-release lever.
   FRONT: Move lever and adjusting nut so lever is just in front of fork (figure 2.46

and figure 2.47). However, with some dropout designs or suspension forks, it will be necessary to use an alternate position if lever will not fully close. REAR: Orient skewer so lever will end up between the seat stay and chain stay, unless this prevents lever from fully closing (figure 2.48).

i. Adjust closing tension of quick-release skewer and close skewer. Wheel should be centered between fork blades. If necessary, open skewer, move wheel either left or right until wheel appears centered, then close skewer. The quick-release skewer must be fully engaged on the dropout surfaces.

j. Inspect brake pad alignment and centering by closing and opening pads with brake lever. If brake pads are not centered to wheel, see page 162, Caliper Rim Brakes. If wheel fails to adequately center in frame, either the frame or wheel may be misaligned.

k. Spin wheel and check pad alignment to rim.

FIGURE: 2.45

Pivot derailleur back to clear wheel and cogs

FIGURE: 2.46

Place lever just in front of fork blade if possible

FIGURE: 2.47

Skewer must be oriented to allow lever to fully close, even with wide fork ends

FIGURE: 2.48

Rear lever alignment

View centering of wheel between chain stays and seat stays. Open skewer and adjust as necessary to center wheel in frame. If rim brake pads are not centered to wheel, see Chapter 12, Rim Caliper Brakes. If further attempts to align the wheel fail to adequately center it in frame, either the frame or wheel may be misaligned. Seek professional help.

If it is difficult to maneuver the wheel into the dropouts, install the front wheel when the bike is standing on the ground. By placing the bike on the ground, the axle will seat fully up in the dropouts.

Installing Front Wheels with Disc Brakes

Bikes using disc brake calipers and rotors follow the basic process as described above. The rotor should be placed between the pads of the caliper as it is installed. Use care not to displace the brake pads (figure 2.49).

FIGURE: 2.49

Guide rotor between brake pads

It is important for front wheels using a disc brake to be properly secured. The caliper disc brake applies a load to the disc rotor, which applies a pulling force on the hub in the dropout. This force tends to pull on the wheel in a direction to remove it from the bike. If the wheel is poorly mounted, it may result in the wheel coming out of the fork during use.

Solid Axle Types

For non-quick-release wheels with axle nuts, washers go to the outside of the dropouts (figure 2.50). Secure axle nuts fully and then double check alignment. Front wheels may use a special washer that acts as a wheel retention redundancy.

FIGURE: 2.50

Solid axle system

Through Axle System

The through-axle system uses a hub design that allows the axle to be pulled from the hub. This allows the wheel to be installed into a frame or fork design with ends that are completely enclosed, providing a very rigid and secure interface (figure 2.51).

FIGURE: 2.51

20mm through-axle hub system

The axle and frame will locate the wheel in the frame. There is no room to move the wheel to center the bike as with open-type dropout systems. These systems may use a pinch bolt system to secure the axle. Another option is a quick-release system that requires no tools (figure 2.52).

The Maxle® quick-release system

Quick-release through-axle systems are similar to conventional system in that they use a cam system. The axle has threading on one side and is fit through the dropout and through the hub. A lever system rotates the axle and threads, snugging it in the dropout. The axle is then held secure by the cam. The cam (or in some brands a double cam) is adjusted so there is resistance approximately halfway through the swing from open to closed.

Tubeless Systems

The tubeless tire and wheel systems for off-road and road bicycles are similar to automotive or motorcycle tubeless tire systems. The rim interior is sealed airtight. A specially-designed tire bead then seals the tire to the rim. A common cause of flat tires (especially for off-road riding) is a "rim pinch." The inner tube is pinched when the tire strikes a rock or other object. Tubeless tire systems can be run at lower pressures because there is no inner tube to be pinched. They're more resistant to these types of flats while increasing the contact area of the tire to the ground, which can improve the ride feel. The tubeless tires, however, are still susceptible to punctures from nails, glass, etc. Additionally, the system is susceptible to leaks if the tire bead or rim seat has become damaged or disengages. The tubeless system is also available in a road bike version and is run at high pressure to reduce rolling resistance between tire and tube.

To remove tubeless tires, begin by fully deflating the tire. Push only one tire bead all around to free it from the rim. On some tire/rim combinations, it is possible to pull the bead off the rim without tire levers. If tire levers are necessary, then take care to use only plastic levers. Pull one bead over the rim edge. Push the second bead from the tire seat and pull the tire from the rim.

Tubeless systems may use either a special Presta or Schrader valve secured into the rim and held in place by a nut (figure 2.53). The valve is an air-tight fit to the rim.

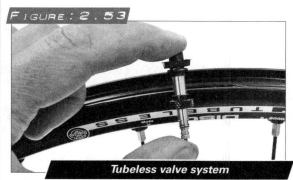

Tubeless valve system

The procedure for installing the tubeless tire:

a. Check that valve is fully seated inside of the rim. Clean the tire bead and rim seat as needed.

b. Insert one bead over the rim wall and into the center of the rim. The first bead must be fully installed before inserting the second bead over the rim.

c. Special tubeless tire seating compounds can be useful to help bead seat properly and seal to the rim. Soapy water on the bead of the tire can also help (figure 2.54).

d. Inflation is best done with an air compressor. This allows the air pressure to quickly force the bead to the rim, creating a seal. If no compressor is available, quickly pump to form a seal. It's helpful to have a friend assist by holding the tire centered to the rim during inflation.

e. Over inflate the tire if the bead is not fully seated. Bead will often seat with a popping sound. Inspect for bead leaks using soapy water at the bead and look for any bubbles. Deflate and re-seat as necessary.

f. Set tire to desired riding pressure.

FIGURE: 2.54

Soapy water can help bead seat into rim

The tubeless tire relies on a volume of air to push bead to rim. If it does not seem possible to seat the bead well enough to inflate the tire, one trick is to use a long strap around the tire. Place the strap around the circumference of the tire. Tighten the strap to help hold the bead to the rim and inflate the tire (figure 2.55). This helps the bead hold to the rim while tire is inflated.

The beads will lock into place. Listen for the popping as they do. Inflate to full inflation and inspect the bead for leaks. Use water at the bead and look for any bubbles. Deflate and re-seat as necessary.

FIGURE: 2.55

Use a strap to apply even pressure on tubeless tires that are difficult to inflate

The tubeless system is best patched by removing it from the rim. The inner surface of the tire is butyl rubber and similar to an inner tube. Locate the hole and clean an area inside the tire body. Use a vulcanizing patch with similar procedure as described for the inner tube repair. There are also "plug" systems to patch a tire without removal. The plug systems attempt to fill the hole with a fibrous rubber material. Irregular shaped holes such as from nail or glass cuts can be difficult to repair using the plug system.

Liquid sealants for tubeless tires are available from various manufacturers and are intended to seal small holes in the tire. These are best applied to the tire before mounting.

The procedure for tubeless tire sealant installation:

a. Install one tire bead on the wheel.
b. Hang the wheel vertically with valve at either the three or the nine o'clock position (figure 2.56). If the bike is mounted in a repair stand, the handlebar ends can be used as a hanger.
c. Pour sealant into the tire at the six o'clock position. Consult the sealant manufacturer's instructions for amount of sealant to be applied.
d. Leave the tire and wheel hanging. Carefully engage the second bead while working from the bottom upward on both sides (figure 2.57).
e. Remove the wheel from the hook and inflate tire and seat bead.
f. Inflate wheel to full a pressure and inspect seating. Spin wheel to distribute fluid.

FIGURE: 2.56

Hang wheel with tire in place

FIGURE: 2.57

Work bead onto rim

Tubular Tires

The tubular tire uses casing that is sewed to enclose an inner tube. The complete tire is then glued to the tubular rim. The gluing process is very important to the performance and safety of the wheels. A poorly bonded tire may roll off of the rim during use and cause the rider to fall.

The tubular rim does not have the sidewalls that act as the bead seat of the clincher rim. Tubular rims have a concave radius surface to accept the tubular tire. The tubular tires do not interchange with clincher rim systems.

Like any bonding or gluing process, preparation is important. The tubular rim surface should be cleaned with a strong solvent that does not leave an oily film. Use proper hand protection and work with good air ventilation. If using a typical 25g tube of adhesive glue, it will take one tube per wheel for rims without a previous base coat.

Because the tire can be difficult to stretch on to the rim, it is best to begin by mounting the unglued tire on the clean rim. Inflate the tire fully to allow it to stretch for several hours.

CAUTION!

The tubular tire system, even when mounted properly, is still susceptible to failure during use. Every precaution should be taken when bonding the tubular to the rim. At this time there are no industry standards for tubular mounting.

The procedure for mounting the tubular tire:

a. Clean the rim tire seat using a solvent such as acetone.

b. Inflate the tire fully. This will roll the bead outward and make it easier to base coat.

c. Using a brush, apply a thin coat to the tire's base strip. Cover the strip side to side with an even coat. Allow this coat to completely dry. This will make handling the tire less messy when mounting (figure 2.58).

d. Apply a thin coat to the rim surface. Allow this coat to completely dry. This may take up to an hour or more. The solvent from the glue needs to evaporate. For new rims with no base coat, apply at least 3 to 4 base coats in this method (figure 2.59).

e. Apply one last coat to the rim before mounting. Do not allow this coat to fully dry or centering the tire will be very difficult. Mount the tire soon after finishing this last coat.

f. Deflate the tire, but leave enough air inside to hold the tire body shape.

g. Place the rim vertically on a clean surface. Do not mount on grass, carpet, etc. Any contamination of the rim glue will weaken the bond.

h. Place and align the valve inside the rim valve hole. Grab the tire firmly on either side of the valve and pull outward with force. Lay the tire down into the rim bed. Continue to apply pressure as the tire is worked on the rim. (figure 2.60)

i. The last section of tire is always the most difficult to mount. Use your thumbs to push tire up and onto rim (figure 2.61).

j. Mount wheel in bike or in truing stand and spin wheel. Inspect top tread of tire relative to rim. Grab sections of tire that appear to wobble and push and twist the tire straight (figure 2.62). Better quality tires will align, while lesser quality tires may not have been initially made straight.

k. Inflate the tire fully to press it into rim bed. Allow tire to sit at least 24 hours before use. Tubular glues are typically contact cements that require drying.

FIGURE: 2.58

Inflate the tire and apply a single base coat

FIGURE: 2.59

Base coat rim with thin even coats

FIGURE: 2.60

Stretch tire as it is mounted

FIGURE: 2.61

Push tire up onto rim

FIGURE: 2.62

Roll tire on rim to center and true

It is possible to mount on rims that have a previous bed of glue. It will require at least one coat of fresh glue, but additional thin base coats may be required if the base coat is thin or provides inconsistent cover.

Old glue bases or dirty glue bases should be cleaned off the rim. For aluminum rims, it is possible to use heavy-bodied paint removers. Use a biodegradable remover when possible and follow stripper directions.

CAUTION:

Do not use paint stripper on carbon rims. Many manufacturers recommend acetone to cut old glue. Contact manufacturer for their recommendations.

It is impossible and impractical to fully inspect the mounting of a tubular without its removal. Roll the tire back away from the rim to inspect the glue at the rim/tire interface (figure 2.63). If popping and cracking is heard, it is an indication the bond is old or there was an inadequate amount of glue in the bond. The tire would be suspect to rolling off the rim.

FIGURE: 2.63

A poorly bonded tire with inadequate glue at edge of tire and rim

CHAPTER 3

Rear Sprockets

The rear sprockets, also called cogs, mesh with the chain, and drive the rear wheel and the bike forward. There is seldom a need to remove the sprockets, but they must be replaced when worn. Sprockets must also be removed in order to service the axle bearings.

The clutch or ratchet systems used on derailleur and some one-speed bikes allow the rider to coast. The sprockets will spin when the rider stops pedaling but will lock and drive the wheel when the pedals and chain are turned forward. The bearings fitted in the system allow the gears to turn freely. There is typically some play between the inner and outer parts of the bearing system. When the wheel turns during coasting, the rear sprockets may appear to wobble slightly side to side. This is common and not usually a problem, because when the bike is pedaled, the inner and outer parts lock together as they drive to eliminate the wobble.

The rear sprockets are attached to the hub in one of two ways. Bikes may use a "freehub," which is ratchet system mounted to the body of the hub (figure 3.1). This cylindrical mechanism acts as a clutch that ratchets for coasting and locks for driving the bike when pedaling. The freehub body has a series of splines on the outer shell. "Cassette" sprockets, also called the "cassette stack," slide over these splines. Note the design and spacing of the splines. The pattern, spacing, and size of the freehub and cassette splines may vary between component manufacturers, making some brands non-interchangeable.

FIGURE: 3.1

Freehub body and hub with cassette sprockets

A lockring threads into the freehub and holds the sprockets (figure 3.2). When the sprockets are removed, the ratcheting freehub remains on the hub body. Most modern derailleur-equipped bicycles use the freehub system, and some models of single speed hubs also use the freehub system.

FIGURE: 3.2

Lockring holds cassette sprockets secure to freehub body (A) Lockring

Alternatively, the rear wheel may have a large thread machined onto the hub (figure 3.3). Sprockets are fixed to a ratcheting mechanism called a "freewheel," which threads onto the thread of the hub shell. The entire unit-sprockets and ratcheting mechanism-comes off when the freewheel is removed. Freewheels are available with single or multiple cogs.

FIGURE: 3.3

Rear hub threaded for freewheel

Cassette Sprocket Removal & Installation

Cassette systems use a lockring sitting outward from the smallest sprocket, which may be marked with the word "LOCK," and an arrow on the lock ring indicating direction to turn for locking. Pressure from the lockring prevents the sprockets from moving side to side on the freehub and also helps prevent the sprockets from damaging the freehub body. Cassette systems are used for both single speed and multiple cogs, such as 9 and 10 speed cassettes.

There are two non-interchangeable lockring tool standards. Cassette systems by Shimano®, SRAM®, Chris King®, Sun Race®, American Classic® and others require a lockring tool with 12 splines. The tool fitting is approximately 23.5mm diameter (figure 3.4). Use the ParkTool FR-5 (figure 3.5). Another option is the ParkTool FR-5G, with built-in guide pin to keep the tool engaged in the lockring while removing it to avoid slipping.

Cassette lockring for Shimano® and others

FIGURE: 3.4

FIGURE: 3.5

Park Tool FR-5

Campagnolo® cassettes require a lockring tool with 12 splines. The tool fitting is approximately 22.8mm in diameter (figure 3.6). Use the Park Tool BBT-5 (figure 3.7). Although the both the FR-5 and BBT-5 lockring removers look similar, the two are not interchangeable.

FIGURE: 3.6

Campagnolo® cassette lockring

FIGURE: 3.7

Park Tool BBT-5

The procedure for cassette sprocket removal:

a. Mount bike in repair stand and remove rear wheel.

b. Remove quick-release skewer or axle nut of solid axle.

c. Inspect cassette and select correct type of cassette lockring remover.

d. Engage remover into splines of lockring.

e. Install quick-release skewer (or axle nut) and install skewer nut on outside of remover (figure 3.8).

f. Snug skewer nut against remover. Skewer acts as a holding device for remover.

g. Hold sprockets in clockwise direction with chain whip tool. Turn remover counter-clockwise with a large adjustable wrench, the hex end of another Park Tool Sprocket Removing Chain Whip Tool SR-1, or the Park Tool Freewheel Wrench FRW-1 (figure 3.9). It should require some force to remove the lockring. Expect to hear a loud clicking sound as the locking teeth of the lockring separate.

h. Turn remover only 1 full revolution counter-clockwise. Loosen and remove skewer before continuing to remove lockring.

i. Continue to hold sprockets and turn remover counter-clockwise until lockring is unthreaded from freehub body.

j. Remove lockring and sprockets. Note orientation of spacers behind sprockets. Spacers should be replaced in same order as removed.

FIGURE: 3.8

Use skewer to hold tool firmly in place

For installing cassette sprockets and lockring, the chain-whip tool is not required. The cassette ratcheting mechanism will hold the freehub body and keep the sprockets from rotating. For cosmetic corrosion protection, grease or anti-seize may be smeared on the freehub body.

Park Tool

Loosen lockring while holding cassette sprockets

The procedure for cassette sprocket installation:

    a. Inspect splines of freehub body. Look for a wide space between splines.

    b. Inspect internal splines of sprockets. Look for a wide spline to mate with wide space on freehub body (figure 3.10).

    c. Align splines and engage all sprockets. Install spacers in same orientation as when removed.

    d. Grease threads of lockring and thread lockring into freehub body.

    e. Insert cassette lockring tool into splines of lockring. Install quick-release skewer and thread skewer nut on outside of lockring tool.

    f. Snug skewer nut against remover. Skewer acts as a holding device for remover.

    g. Turn cassette lockring tool clockwise until lockring is fully tight (figure 3.11).

Align the wide spline inside sprocket with wide space on freehub body

Tighten lockring

Freewheel Sprocket Removal & Installation

Freewheels will have either recessed notches or splines in the body, usually recessed inside the smallest sprocket. To remove freewheel begin by determining type or brand of freewheel and the removal tool required. The removal tool must fit the part correctly, or both may become damaged. To determine the type or brand of freewheel, remove the wheel from the bike and look at the flat surfaces of freewheel near the axle for a brand name. (See Table 3.1 Freewheel Removal Tools for the matching freewheel tool.)

The procedure for freewheel removal:

    a. Mount bike in a repair stand and remove rear wheel from bike.

    b. Remove quick-release skewer or drive side axle nut.

    c. Inspect freewheel center and select correct type of remover.

    d. Engage remover into splined notches of freewheel.

    e. Install quick-release skewer. The skewer nut should be on the outside of the remover.

    f. Snug skewer nut or axle nut against the remover. Nut acts as a holding device for the remover.

    g. Turn the remover counter-clockwise using a large adjustable wrench (figure 3.12). Park Tool removers will also fit the hex end of the Park Tool Sprocket Chain Whip Tool SR-1, or the Park Tool FRW-1 Freewheel Removal Wrench. It will require some force to turn the freewheel. Another option is to mount remover flats in the jaws of a vise and turn the rim counter-clockwise.

    h. Turn the remover only 1 full revolution counter-clockwise. Loosen and remove skewer or axle nut before continuing to remove freewheel.

    i. Turn remover counter-clockwise until freewheel is unthreaded from hub. Lift the freewheel from the hub.

Turn tool counter-clockwise to remove freewheel from hub

TABLE : 3.1   Freewheel Removal Tools

FREEWHEEL BRAND	FREEWHEEL FITTING	APPROPRIATE TOOL	TOOL & DESCRIPTION
Shimano®, Sun Race®, and Sachs®			Park Tool FR-1 12 splines 23mm approx. diameter
Suntour® two notched			Park Tool FR-2 2 notches 25mm across
Suntour® four notched			Park Tool FR-3 4 notches 24mm across
Atom®, Regina®, some "Schwinn® approved"			Park Tool FR-4 20 splines 21.6mm approx. diameter
Single speed, BMX			Park Tool FR-6 4 notches 40mm across
Falcon®			Park Tool FR-7 12 splines 23mm approx. diameter (slightly larger than FR-1)
Compact single speed (30mm thread, "flip-flop hub")			Park Tool FR-8 4 notches 32mm across

Park Tool

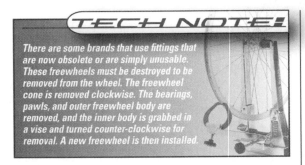

The thread standard for modern bicycle is standardized to 1.37" x 24 tpi. However, there are some double-sided "flip-flop" hubs that have a thread on each side of the hub, with a much smaller 30mm x 24 tpi thread on one side for special single speed freewheels.

The procedure freewheel installation:

a. Apply grease or anti-seize heavily inside mounting threads of freewheel (figure 3.13). Lack of thread lubrication may seize freewheel to the hub.

b. Lay wheel on bench and hold flat. Hold freewheel sprockets parallel to wheel and lower freewheel onto threads.

c. Axle should be centered in hole of freewheel. If axle appears off center, freewheel is cross-threaded on hub threads (figure 3.14). Remove and re-align.

d. Begin threading freewheel clockwise by hand until freewheel feels fully threaded.

e. Use chain whip tool to fully seat freewheel against hub. You may also replace the wheel on the bike and ride it to seat the freewheel.

f. If a new freewheel is installed or if new wheel is installed, check rear derailleur limit screw settings and indexing. See Chapter 9 Derailleur Systems.

FIGURE: 3.13

Freewheel internal threading

FIGURE: 3.14

If axle appears off center, freewheel is cross-threaded

Rear Sprocket Inspection & Cleaning

Rear sprockets will eventually wear out. The teeth are cut to fit chain with a one-half inch pitch. As the chain is ridden it loads only one side of the teeth, and material is ground away, changing the shape and widening the space between the teeth (figure 3.15). The chain rollers will then not properly engage the teeth and, on derailleur bikes, the chain will skip over the cog when load is applied, such as going up a hill.

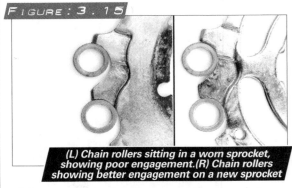

FIGURE: 3.15

(L) Chain rollers sitting in a worn sprocket, showing poor engagement.(R) Chain rollers showing better engagement on a new sprocket

It is possible to visually inspect the sprockets from behind where the chain would engage. Look at various sprockets and notice any that are shiny and smooth compared to the rest (figure 3.16 and figure 3.17). The best test for a worn cog is to ride it with a new or unworn chain. If the cog does not skip under load, it is not worn out.

FIGURE: 3.16

Look for smooth and shiny surface of worn sprocket

This sprocket shows signs of original stamping marks, called "breakage." It has had very little use

Clean the debris between sprockets

Cyclists tend to use two or three rear sprockets more than the others. These favorite gears will wear out first. Commonly, these tend to be the 15- to 18-tooth sprockets. Individual sprocket replacements are not typically available. The entire sprocket set is replaced as a unit.

One-speed bikes will also wear at the rear sprocket. The chain will not skip under load like a derailleur bike, but it will begin to make noise and become less efficient as the teeth become hooked.

The rear sprockets and front chainrings require cleaning if the entire drive train is to be maintained. Use care not to get solvent into the bearings of the freewheel/freehub or the bearings of the bottom bracket. Freehub mechanisms and freewheel bodies use ball bearings running on bearing surfaces and small springs and pawls. These component parts are not typically "overhauled" by disassembly. The unit may be removed from the hub, flushed, and scrubbed clean in solvent. The solvent will then be blown out with compressed air or allowed to evaporate. Lubrication is then dripped into the mechanism. Grease is not recommended for freehubs or freewheel internals because it may cause the small springs and pawls to stick. If the freewheel/freehub spins rough after cleaning, the bearing surfaces are worn out, and unit should be replaced. There are no internal parts available for freehubs or freewheels from manufacturers. See page 48, Freehub Removal & Installation.

Rear sprockets can be cleaned while still mounted to the wheel. Begin by scraping between sprockets with the comb part of the Park Tool GearClean® Brush (figure 3.18), or a thin screwdriver, to remove dirt and debris. Hold wheel so sprockets are tilting downward, then use a dry stiff bristle brush between sprockets. Dip brush in solvent, and scrub sprockets while holding sprockets facing downward. This helps to keep solvent out of bearings. Use a rag to wipe solvent off sprockets, rim, and tire. Grab two corners of rag and pull taut. Use this section to "floss" between sprockets.

Fixed Gear

A fixed gear is a single speed sprocket that is locked to the hub shell. When the rear wheel is turning, the cog must turn, and consequently, the chain and cranks must turn. Fixed gear bikes are used for velodrome racing bikes (track bikes) and some street bikes. It is possible to modulate the speed by changing leg speed, but for street use, this should not be considered a substitute for a caliper braking system with a hand lever.

The fixed gear cog threading is the same pitch and diameter of the common threaded freewheels and will fit hubs threaded for freewheels. However, the fixed cog is intended for hubs designed with a lockring (figure 3.19). The lockring of a fixed gear hub is slightly smaller then the cog and is left hand threaded. Because of the left hand thread of the lockring, it would be self-tightening if the rear cog were to begin loosening. Lockrings only need to be snug, do not over tighten.

Lockring and single speed fixed cog

Fixed gear cogs come in a ⅛" width and ³⁄₃₂" widths (nominally 3mm and 2.4mm, respectably) and must match the chain roller width. Grease threads of both the cog and lockring before installing. Thread cog onto hub and tighten with chain whip. Install lockring and snug. Chain length and tension is determined the same as a single speed bike.

Park Tool

CHAPTER 4

Hubs

Hubs are the center of the wheels, which allow the rim, spokes, and tires to rotate around the axle. The hub axle is fixed to the front or rear forks, while the hub shell rotates with the tire and spokes. On derailleur bicycles, multiple rear sprockets are affixed to the rear hub with a clutch mechanism that allows the rider to drive the wheel or to coast. On disc brake bikes, the hub will also hold the disc rotor used for braking. Hubs may also hold an internal gear system. For internal gear hub systems see Chapter 9 - Internal Gear Hubs.

Bearing Service-cup and cone adjustable

Adjustable-type hubs use a cone-shaped race threaded onto an axle. The hub shell holds a cup-shaped race. Ball bearings are trapped between the cone and cup. Rear hubs must allow for the sprockets and tend to be more complex than front hubs. The modern freehub or cassette hub uses a separate freehub mechanism that may be removed in a separate operation. The procedures below are written primarily for cup and cone hubs, such as Shimano® hubs, but they are also applicable to other adjustable-type hubs.

The hub bearing system uses round ball bearings trapped between two bearing surfaces. The bearing surfaces and balls are greased to minimize wear. These systems are shielded from dirt by covers and seals. Excessive exposure to the elements will increase wear on the bearing surfaces and shorten ball bearing and bearing surface life.

Bearing surfaces are made from hardened steel and are cut by grinding. Even the highest quality bearing surfaces will have slight grinding marks. Better quality bearing surfaces are ground smoother and will have less friction and resistance to turning. All bearings, however, will have some friction as they rotate. This is normal and does not affect the ride. Generally, the lighter load a bearing is expected to experience, the "smoother" the feel. Bearing systems experiencing more stress and pressure will seem to have more drag, even when the adjustment is correct. For example, a bearing for a rear derailleur pulley, which is designed for lower loads, will seem to have less spinning resistance compared to a bottom bracket bearing, which is designed to experience more load.

Hub cones have narrow wrench flats that require a special, thin wrench called a cone wrench. The common cone wrench size for front hubs is 13mm and 15mm for rear hubs. If the locknut is a simple hex nut, use a combination wrench or even an adjustable wrench. Hex locknuts are commonly 17mm or 16mm. Some locknuts will accept only a cone wrench.

Freehub bodies on rear hubs are lubricated internally with a light lubricant. Soaking the freehub body with a solvent will remove lubrication. Avoid getting solvent into the mechanism during the hub disassembly and cleaning. Wipe freehub clean of old grease. Freehubs can be removed in a separate operation for cleaning. See page 48, Freehub Removal & Installation.

Disassembly-cup and cone adjustable hubs

On any disassembly, it is a good idea to take notes on parts orientation. Note especially any differences between left and right side parts. For example, an axle may appear asymmetrical with more threading on one side than the other. The parts arrangement of a typical Shimano® hub is seen below (figure 4.1). NOTE: The oversized axle Shimano® XTR M970 and M975, Dura Ace 7850 hubs use the same design and service concepts as the hub described below.

FIGURE: 4.1

Parts of a common Shimano® rear hub (A) Hub shell, (B) Ball bearings, (C) Axle, (D) Locknuts, (E) Cones, (F) Washers, (G) Rubber seal

The procedure for cup and cone adjustable hub disassembly:
   a. For rear hubs, begin by removing rear sprockets (See Chapter 3, Rear Sprockets, page 31).
   b. For front or rear hubs, remove the quick-release skewer. For solid axle-type hubs, remove axle nuts. If the hub has a disc brake rotor, it should be removed to avoid contamination by grease.

c. Inspect axle ends. Measure and note the amount of axle protruding past locknut. For quick-release hubs, counting the number of threads is an adequate measurement (figure 4.2).

d. Begin dismantling from the left or non-drive side. If available, mount hub in an axle vise. Mount right side of hub down with left side facing upward.

e. Remove rubber covers or seals, if any.

f. Hold cone using cone wrench and loosen locknut counter-clockwise. For the Dura-Ace 7850, XTR 950 oversized axle hubs, use a 5mm hex with cone wrench to loosen left-side locknut (figure 4.3).

g. Remove locknut and washers. Place parts on a string, piece of wire, or zip-tie in the same orientation as they came off hub. This makes re-installation easier (figure 4.4).

h. Remove cone by turning counter-clockwise and place on tie.

i. Place hand below right side of hub and lift wheel slowly. Be prepared to catch loose bearings that fall from hub. Place wheel on bench.

j. If inspecting for a bent axle, remove right side locknut and cones. Note that left side and right side cones, washers, and locknuts may be different. Do not confuse left and right side parts. Use tie method to keep track of parts. Also note axle thread may be asymmetrical. The side with more axle spacers gets more axle thread.

k. Count the number of bearings on each side and then use pencil magnet to remove bearings from hub shell. Measure ball bearing size. Hub bearing size may be ¼ inch, ³⁄₁₆", or ⁵⁄₃₂" depending upon model.

l. Leave dust cap in place. This may slow the overhaul, however, as dust caps tend to be fragile and removal may result in damage. Use a small brush or a rag used over a small screwdriver to clean inside and under dust caps.

m. Clean all parts. Parts must be dry for assembly. Wipe freehub mechanism using damp rag. Do not soak freehub in solvent unless it is to be removed.

FIGURE: 4.2

Count or measure the amount of axle protrusion past locknut face

FIGURE: 4.3

Loosen left side locknut

FIGURE: 4.4

Hold parts in order with tie or string

Parts Inspection-cup and cone adjustable hubs

View hub cups and cones for pitting or damage. Use a ballpoint pen to trace the bearing path. Roughness and wear will be felt as the small ball of the pen passes over pits (figure 4.5). Inspect ball bearings for brightness. If balls are dull-looking, they should be replaced. If the cup is damaged, it typically cannot be replaced. The hub must be replaced. To inspect the axle, roll it on a flat surface and watch for a gap along the axle-to-flat surface area appearing as axle rolls. Bent axles cannot be straightened and should be replaced.

Pitted cone showing wear

Assembly-
cup and cone adjustable hubs

Refer to any notes you made from the disassembly procedure. For example, the axle thread length may vary between left and right side. Do not take apart the cone, spacer, and locknut tie until ready to install.

It is important the threaded axle of the quick-release hub not protrude past the face of the dropout (figure 4.6). The quick-release skewer must press on the dropout, not the axle end. Check alignment of axle between left and right locknuts or shorten axle end by grinding.

Axle protruding past dropout will not properly secure with quick release skewer

The procedure for cup and cone adjustable hub assembly:

a. Grease axle threads.
b. Grease heavily inside hub shell cups. Place ball bearings in both cups and cover with more grease. Make sure balls are seated flat in cup. The balls should be covered in grease.
c. If all parts were removed from axle, install right side parts. Use care to install in the same orientation as they came off. Note rear axle threads may be asymmetrical. Refer to earlier notes.
d. Return axle protrusion to the original measurement past locknut face, as noted in disassembly. Tighten right side locknut fully against cone.

e. Install axle through right side of hub.
f. Install left side axle parts using care to install in the same orientation as they came off. Do not set axle protrusion on this side and do not tighten locknut at this time.
g. For quick-release type hubs, snug the cone down until it contacts the ball bearings, then turn back counter-clockwise one-quarter turn (90 degrees). This will purposely make the bearing adjustment too loose. Hold the cone with the cone wrench without turning it any farther, and, while holding the cone one-quarter turn from snug, fully tighten the locknut. Proceed to Hub Adjustment-cup and cone.

Hub Adjustment: cup and cone

The convex bearing race (cone) and concave bearing race (cup) oppose one another with ball bearings trapped between them. The races can be moved relative to one another and then locked in place. If the adjustment is overly tight there will be too much pressure of the balls on the bearing surfaces and the system will quickly wear out. A rear hub bearing that is too tight can also result in freehub drag. This is a precise and sometimes time-consuming adjustment. Several attempts at adjustment may be required.

If the adjustment is too loose there will be movement or "play" between the parts. This causes a knocking in the bearing surfaces, and, again, they will wear out prematurely. Generally, the bearings should be adjusted as loose as possible but without play or knocking in the system.

For adjustable-bearing systems, the bearing surfaces move on threaded parts. It is normal for threaded parts to have play between the internal and external threads. A hub cone will wiggle on the axle thread until the cone locknut is tightened down against the cone. When checking bearing adjustments, the locknut must be tight against the cone.

The goal for adjustable bearings is to have the bearings rotate as freely as possible without any knocking or play. When beginning a bearing adjustment, start with it loose and then proceed to tighten the adjustment in small increments until the play disappears. This ensures the adjustment is as loose as possible but is without play. In most cases, try to make small changes, in increments of $\frac{1}{32}$ of a complete rotation (figure 4.7). Imagine turning the cone wrench spoke to spoke while making adjustments.

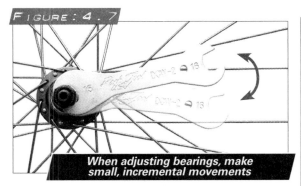

FIGURE: 4.7

When adjusting bearings, make small, incremental movements

Quick-release hubs have hollow axles that allow for the quick-release skewer shaft. These axles flex slightly when the quick-release lever is closed and pressure is applied to the dropouts. Hub bearing adjustments must account for this extra stress. For adjustable-type hubs, when not clamped tight in the frame, there should be a slight amount of play in the axle. This play should disappear when the hub and wheel are clamped in the frame.

To adjust the bearings, the wheel is out of the bike. However, to test the adjustment, it is necessary to re-install the wheel and close the skewer fully tight.

If a quick-release hub has an acceptable adjustment, grab the wheel while it is still in the frame and pull it side to side laterally. Rotate wheel and test again, feeling for a knocking sensation (figure 4.8). If no play is felt, remove the wheel. Grab the axle (not the skewer) and rock it up and down to check for play. If the axle has play when the wheel is outside the bike, but no play inside the bike, the hub is properly adjusted. If there is no play in the axle when the wheel is outside the bike, the adjustment is too tight, even if the axle seems to turn smoothly when out of the bike.

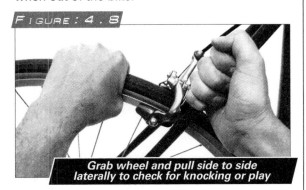

FIGURE: 4.8

Grab wheel and pull side to side laterally to check for knocking or play

Adjusting cones, replacing the wheel on the bike, and testing for play can be time-consuming and frustrating. The following procedure speeds the process by simulating the on-the-bike compression while still allowing access to a cone and locknut for adjustment. This procedure requires the use of a spacer or washers to simulate the dropout thickness. For example, a 10mm box end wrench (forged type) can be used as the spacer. The wrench offers a lever to hold while adjusting the opposite cone. Do not use larger wrenches, because the wrench surface must support the skewer housing. The adjustment is made on the side of the axle opposite the wrench/spacers. On a rear wheel, the wrench/spacer will go on the sprocket side (right side) of the hub. On a front wheel, the wrench/spacer can go on either the left or right side.

NOTE: This procedure only works for threaded axles that extend past the locknut. Do not use this procedure if the locknut is also an axle end cap (figure 4.9). Adjust these hubs with slight amount of play. Secure hub in frame with quick-release and check for bearing play. Remove and correct adjustment as needed and re-install to test. Repeat adjustment as necessary.

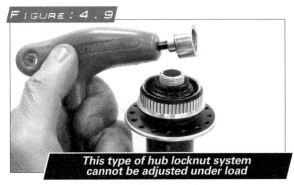

FIGURE: 4.9

This type of hub locknut system cannot be adjusted under load

The procedure for hub adjusting:
  a. Remove wheel if still on bike.
  b. Remove quick-release skewer and springs. Remove any rubber boot covering cones and locknuts on side being adjusted.
  c. Insert skewer through wrench/spacers and then through axle. Skewer should pass through right side of either the front or rear hub (figure 4.10). Install quick-release adjusting nut on left side. The quick-release nut must press only on the axle end, not on the axle locknut (figure 4.11).

d. Use the same pressure to close the quick-release lever as you would use when normally clamping wheel in bike. If in doubt see Chapter 2, Tires and Tubes.

e. Place the wheel on your lap. Use the cone wrench to hold the "adjusting side" cone. Note position and angle of "fixed wrench" on right side relative to cone wrench on "adjusting side." Use a second wrench to loosen locknut counter-clockwise (figure 4.12).

f. Loosen cone counter-clockwise about ⅛ to ¼ turn. The purpose is to first create play, then remove it incrementally.

g. Hold cone from moving with cone wrench and tighten locknut. Locknut must be fully tight before play can be checked. Do not check for bearing play until locknut is fully secure. The locknut pushes on the cone and will affect bearing adjustment.

h. Test for play by grabbing lever (wrench) and pulling side-to-side laterally (figure 4.13).

i. When play is felt, adjustment is too loose. To tighten adjustment:

1. *Use a cone wrench and hold "adjusting" side cone from moving. Note the position and angle of adjustable side wrench relative to the "fixed" side wrench.*

2. *Loosen locknut, using care not to allow cone wrench to turn.*

3. *Recall angle of cone wrench and tighten adjustment by turning cone clockwise ¹⁄₃₂ of a turn.*

4. *Hold cone from moving with cone wrench and tighten locknut.*

j. Test again for play. Rotate axle and check for play at various points of rotation.

k. If play is still present, repeat step "i" until play just disappears. Remember to make small adjustments clockwise one at a time. Check for play after each adjustment. It may take several small adjustments before play is gone.

l. Once play has disappeared, test that final adjustment is not overly tight. Open skewer lever and check for axle play by pulling axle laterally.

m. If no play is felt when skewer is released, hub adjustment is too tight. Tighten skewer as before. Loosen locknut and loosen adjustment only slightly. Check for play while axle is still clamped. If no play is detectable, test again as in "l".

n. Adjustment is finished when there is no play felt when skewer is closed, but some play is felt when axle is not secured by quick release.

o. Remove skewer and any extra adjustment spacers (wrench). Re-install rubber covers over axle ends. Remount sprockets, if removed. Install skewer springs and install skewer to normal position.

p. Install wheel on bike. Use same skewer clamping pressure when mounting the wheel as was used when making adjustments.

FIGURE : 4 . 10

Secure spacers such as a wrench to act as dropout on non-adjustable fixed side

FIGURE : 4 . 11

Quick-release nut must press only on axle end, not on adjusting side locknut

FIGURE : 4 . 12

Loosen locknut and make adjustment to cone

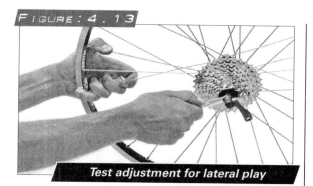

FIGURE: 4.13

Test adjustment for lateral play

If an adjustment cannot be found to allow smooth rotation of the axle, the bearing surfaces may be worn out. If play does not disappear until bearing adjustment is very tight, a locknut may not be tight against cone, which will allow movement. It can also occur that the bearing cups inside hub shell have come loose. It may be possible to get a retaining compound or a thin thread-locker behind the cup to re-secure it. However, a hub or wheel replacement is the best option.

Hub Adjustment-Solid Axle-Cup and Cone

Non-quick-release hub systems use axle nuts and washers on the outside of the dropouts to hold the wheel in place (figure 4.14). Adjustment of solid axle hub bearings is similar to the hollow axle quick-release type, but there is no need to allow for axle flex. Remove the wheel from the bike. The adjustment for solid axle hubs does not change when mounted in the bike. It can be useful to mount a "fixed wrench" to act as a lever on the right side when adjusting. This allows you to tighten or loosen relative to the fixed cone. If no play is present, create play by loosening bearing adjustment. Proceed to adjust tighter in small increments until play is gone. The goal is to find the loosest adjustment that has no play.

FIGURE: 4.14

Solid or non-quick-release
axle on derailleur type bike

Campagnolo® and Shimano® Dura-Ace 7800 and 7801 Oversized Hub Service

There are several generations and designs of the Campagnolo® hub. The older "hour glass" type used a traditional cup and cone design with a threaded axle, similar to conventional Shimano® hubs. Since 2001, the oversized shell types of the Campagnolo Record®, Centaur® and Chorus® models since 2001 share the same basic design and service procedures described here (figure 4.15).

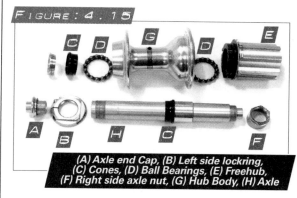

FIGURE: 4.15

(A) Axle end Cap, (B) Left side lockring,
(C) Cones, (D) Ball Bearings, (E) Freehub,
(F) Right side axle nut, (G) Hub Body, (H) Axle

Additionally, newer Campangolo® and Shimano® Dura Ace 7800 hubs share many service features. Each uses an oversized aluminum axle with end caps. The drive-side hub axle bearings are inboard of the freehub on each.

While Campagnolo® lists the hub shell cups as replaceable, this should be done by a Campagnolo® service center.

Campagnolo® oversized hubs use unthreaded cones and are similar in concept to threadless headsets. These are locked in place by a compression ring and a lockring with a pinch bolt. The front hub is a simple version of the rear, with bearing adjustments made from the lockring side.

Both the Shimano® 7800 and Campanolo® hubs use ball bearings for the axle rotation and cartridge bearings inside the freehub body. Campagnolo® freehub bearings can be greased by removing a setscrew in the freehub body. Both freehubs can be left on axle for axle bearing overhaul.

The procedure for hub adjusting:

a. Remove skewer and cassette cogs.

b. Remove freehub from axle. Right side locknuts are left hand threading. SHIMANO®: Insert a 5mm hex into each side of the axle and turn right side axle locknut clockwise to remove (figure 4.16).
CAMPAGNOLO: Hold axle by inserting 5mm hex wrench into right side. Loosen and remove right side locknut turning clockwise. Freehub will now slide off axle. Note any spacers, washers, or seal orientation.

c. Remove left side locknuts. SHIMANO®: hold cone and loosen locknut.
CAMPAGNOLO®: insert 5mm hex wrenches into right end of axle and left side locknut. Loosen counter-clockwise and remove the left side axle end cap.

d. Remove left side cone or lockring. SHIMANO®: loosen and remove cone (figure 4.17).
CAMPAGNOLO®: loosen the binder bolt on the left side lockring. Use either a 2.5mm hex wrench, #2 Phillips, or small straight blade screwdriver, as appropriate (figure 4.18). Unthread and remove lockring counter-clockwise. It may be finger-tight at this time, use an adjustable wrench if necessary.

e. Remove ball bearings from hub shell. SHIMANO®: use magnet to extract balls.
CAMPAGNOLO®: ball bearings are held in retainers. Use a thin-tipped screwdriver and gently pry upward on the seal while keeping bearings in the retainer (figure 4.19). Note orientation of seal and bearing retainer for assembly.

f. Clean, dry, and inspect parts. However, do not soak freehubs with degreaser. Clean pawls and spring with solvent but use care not to contaminate freehub bearings. Freehub cartridge bearings are considered non-replaceable.

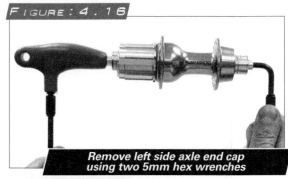

FIGURE: 4.16

Remove left side axle end cap using two 5mm hex wrenches

FIGURE: 4.17

Remove locknut counter-clockwise

FIGURE: 4.18

Loosen the lockring binder and turn lockring counter-clockwise

FIGURE: 4.19

Carefully pry up the bearing covers

Parts Inspection

View cups and cones for pitting or damage. Use a ballpoint pen to trace the bearing path. Roughness and wear will be felt as the small ball of the pen passes over pits. To check for a bent axle, roll axle on a flat surface. Watch for gap appearing as axle rolls. Bent axles cannot be straightened and should be replaced.

Assembly- Campagnolo® oversized axle and Shimano 7800/7801

The procedure for hub assembly & adjustment:

a. Grease axle threads and ends of axle. Slide freehub body with any seals and washer in place over right side of axle.

b. Install and secure right side axle nut. SHIMANO®: hold left side of axle with 5mm hex wrench and secure right locknut.
CAMPAGNOLO®: turn nut counter-clockwise while holding axle with 5mm hex wrench.

c. Pack grease into both bearing cups of hub body.

d. SHIMANO: install bearing into cups and cover with grease.
CAMPAGNOLO®: place both bearing retainers into cups with bearings facing cone. Cover bearings with seal and press seal into place by hand.

e. Lightly grease pawls of freehub and hub ratchet gear inside hub body.

f. Place freehub with axle assembly through right side of hub body and engage freehub pawls into hub ratchet gear (figure 4.20). Rotate freehub counter-clockwise to assist engagement of pawls into the gear of the hub body. It may be necessary to use a thin-tipped screwdriver and gently push each pawl inward while pressure is applied to the freehub.

g. SHIMANO®: thread cone onto axle.
CAMPAGNOLO®: slide left side cone on axle. Slide compression ring onto axle and engage into cone.

h. For quick-release type hubs, snug the cone down until it contacts the ball bearings. Then turn back counter-clockwise.

i. Install left side locknut.
SHIMANO®: install washer and locknut onto axle.
CAMPAGNOLO®: thread left side locking collar onto axle until it contacts compression ring and cone. Turn back approximately ⅛th turn counter-clockwise and snug binder bolt.

j. CAMPAGNOLO®: Hold axle from right side with 5mm hex wrench inserted into axle. Install washer and end cap onto axle. Secure end cap using a second 5mm hex wrench.

FIGURE: 4.20

Install freehub body and rotate to engage pawls into ratchet gear

Adjustment

Adjust hub bearings in small increments so the bearings are as loose as possible without lateral play or knocking. Oversized axles have very little effective flex when loaded by the quick-release skewer. Allow only a small amount of play when the wheel is out of the dropouts.

The procedure to adjust the Campagnolo® Record hub:

a. Install cassette sprockets and quick-release skewers.

b. Install wheel into bike and close skewer with full pressure.

c. Adjust bearings using lockring on left side. Grab wheel and pull side-to-side. If play is present, loosen binder in locking collar and turn the collar clockwise 1/32 to 1/16 of a turn (figure 4.21). Snug lockring collar binder and check play again.

d. Repeat as necessary to remove play.

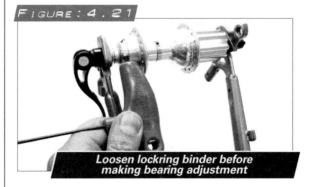

FIGURE: 4.21

Loosen lockring binder before making bearing adjustment

ParkTool

The procedure to adjust the Shimano® 7800/7801 hub:

a. Adjust bearings from left side. Hold cone and secure locknut.

b. Adjust for only a slight amount of play in axle.

c. Mount axle in frame and grab wheel, pulling side to side.

d. If play is present, remove wheel and tighten hub adjustment slightly.

e. Retest wheel and repeat until no play is felt when wheel is secured in a frame.

Freehub Removal & Installation

The ratcheting mechanism of the freehub may eventually wear out. There are no serviceable parts inside most freehubs. The freehub may be removed on many models for cleaning or replacement. Dust caps in many freehubs can be easily damaged if removed. Work around dust caps to avoid damage as replacement caps are difficult to obtain. The procedures below are for Shimano® and similar freehubs.

The procedure for freehub removal and installation:

a. Remove skewer and cassette.

b. Remove axle as described on page 40, under Cup and Cone Service.

c. Inspect inside freehub body for bolt fitting. If no fitting is apparent on right side, inspect through left side.

d. Insert hex wrench and turn counterclockwise. Hex wrench size may vary from 10 to 14mm (figure 4.22).

e. Remove freehub. Inspect for any washers or spacers behind freehub and remove.

f. Use a seal pick to remove any dust seal that may be behind the freehub body (figure 4.23).

g. Flush freehub with solvent. Scrub the bearing cup clean.

h. Blow dry freehub. If no compressor is available, allow freehub to dry until no solvent is left inside.

i. Drip lubricant inside the freehub body from the backside and front side. Install dust seal.

j. Grease freehub installation bolt.

k. Install washers or spacers as necessary.

l. Install freehub onto hub body.

m. Install and secure freehub bolt.

n. Assemble axle assembly into hub and adjust.

FIGURE : 4 . 22

Loosen and remove freehub bolt

FIGURE : 4 . 23

Remove seal (if present) behind freehub body

Cartridge Bearing Hubs

The cartridge-type hub uses an industrial or rolling element bearing. These tend to be non-serviceable bearing units that are simply used until they wear out. Ball bearings are trapped between inner and outer rotating races (figure 4.24). There should be no play between the inner and outer races of the cartridge. With use, play will develop between these two races and the entire cartridge unit will require replacement.

FIGURE : 4 . 24

Cut away of cartridge bearing showing inner races and ball bearings

Most cartridge hubs are not serviceable in the sense that they are overhauled and adjusted. The bearing units use rubber covers. The bearing, however, is not fully "sealed" and is susceptible to dirt and water. The bearing is removed as a unit, and a new one is pressed in. Some hub models require specialty tools and service of these hubs is best left to professional mechanics.

Cartridge hub designs typically press the outer race of the cartridge bearing into the hub shell. Removal of the bearing from the hub shell may involve impact or pressing of the bearings. It is likely that the impact will damage the bearing. If a bearing is being removed, it is assumed it will be replaced with a new bearing.

The hub axle may be threaded or non-threaded. The axle holds the inner race of the cartridge bearing secure. Threaded axles typically use a "sleeve nut" system. The nut will be tightened until it touches the bearing, then should be backed away ¼ turn. A locknut then secures the sleeve nut. This prevents the sleeve nut from pressing on the inner bearing race. The inner and outer cartridge races align vertically for smooth operation. If the inner race is pushed inward, the bearing tends to wear out quickly (figure 4.25).

FIGURE: 4.25

Threaded sleeve nut holding axle to cartridge bearing

Bearings of the threaded axle system are commonly removed by impact. A punch is placed through the hub, and the bearing is struck first on one side and then the other. This tapping "walks" the bearing out of the hub shell (figure 4.26).

FIGURE: 4.26

Removing pressed races

Non-threaded axles are typically made with a collar (figure 4.27). These axles use end-caps and come either in threaded or push-on fit. Look for wrench flats either on the cap or inside the axle. After end-caps are removed, the axle is struck with a mallet, and acts as the punch to drive out the bearing.

FIGURE: 4.27

Non-threaded axle with a cartridge bearing

The installation of cartridge bearings typically involves an interference fit. The bearing will be slightly larger than the hub shell. Hub manufacturers provide pressing and impact tools. It is possible to use steel sockets that match the diameter of the bearing race at the interference fit (figure 4.28). For example, if the interference fit is on the outer race of the bearing, the diameter of the driving tool must match the diameter of the outer race of the bearing.

FIGURE: 4.28

Driving in a cartridge bearing with a socket

Mavic® Hub (Level 1 Type)

There are several versions of the Mavic® hub system, and exact procedures may vary with each model. Mavic® cartridge bearings are pressed into the hub shell. The axle must be removed to drive the bearings out with a punch. Bearing service tools are available from a Mavic® retailer. It is possible to substitute punches and sockets of the correct outside diameter. Service of the rear hub is typically more complex due to the freehub. The service procedures below for the "level one" hubs using the "Force Transfer System Light."

The procedure for service of the rear Mavic® Level One hub:

    a. Remove skewer, cassette cogs, and rotor, if applicable.

    b. Remove left side end cap by pulling on it.

c. Insert 5mm hex wrench right side of axle. Insert 10mm hex wrench in left side of axle. Turn either side counter-clockwise to loosen and remove axle from both sides of hub (figure 4.29).

d. Pull freehub body from hub shell. Note any washer under freehub (figure 4.30).

e. There is a seal on hub shell beneath freehub that may be left in place. Use care to not cut or damage seal if removing it.

f. It is not necessary to removal pawls from hub shell. If pawls are removed, work careful and pull pawl away from body. Use care not to lose pawl springs or parts.

g. First remove right side and then left side cartridge bearing using drift punch. Tap side to side gradually to remove (figure 4.31).

h. To replace bearing in freehub, remove threaded right side cap counter-clockwise. Use cassette cogs and chain whip to hold freehub body while removing cap (figure 4.32). Cassette lockring is not required.

i. Drive bearing from freehub.

j. Install drive-side bearing using driver tool (figure 4.33). Center bearing to hole and tap into place to fully seat bearing.

k. Install opposite bearing using driver tool. Center bearing to hole and tap into place.

l. Install bearing in freehub using driving tool and re-install threaded cap.

m. Install seal if removed. Lubricate seal, pawls, and inside freehub with mineral oil or light chain lubricant.

n. Install right side axle into freehub. Place washer on axle inside freehub body.

o. Engage freehub body onto hub. Squeeze pawls inward while turning freehub counter-clockwise.

p. Install axle through left side and thread into right side axle.

q. Hold right side axle using a 5mm hex wrench and tighten left side axle with 10mm hex wrench.

r. Install left side axle end cap by pushing on axle end.

s. Install cassette stack and rotor, if applicable. Install wheel in bike.

t. Hub adjustment is done on left side at lockring. Use a pin spanner such as the Mavic tool, or Park Tool SPA-2.

u. Grab rim and pull side to side. If play exists, turn adjusting nut clockwise in small increments until play is gone (figure 4.34).

enough lube covers ('½-'½ bearing uncovered)

FIGURE: 4.29
Remove axle from hub with hex wrenches

FIGURE: 4.30
Remove freehub body from hub shell

FIGURE: 4.31
Drive bearings from hub shell

FIGURE: 4.32
Remove right side cap by holding freehub body and turning cap counter-clockwise

Drive bearing fully into hub shell

Adjusting bearing play at lockring

The front hub of the Mavic® Level One series wheels have two bearings pressed into the hub shell. Look for 5mm hex fitting in the axle and hold the opposite side bearing adjusting nut with a pin spanner (figure 4.35). Loosen and remove adjustable cap. Bearings are tapped out and pressed back as with the rear hub. Tightening the one bearing adjustment lockring on the bike as with rear hub makes the adjustment complete.

Removing the axle from a front hub

Park Tool

CHAPTER 5

Wheel Truing

icycle wheels act as the "ball bearings" between the frame and the ground and allow the bike to roll forward as we pedal. Straight, round wheels add to the bike's performance. Some adjustment to the wheel run-out (trueness) is possible by making adjustments to spoke tension. Non-serviceable bladed wheels or a large carbon discs have no truing adjustment or repair options like traditional spokes.

The bicycle wheel is composed of a hoop or rim that is suspended by spokes around the hub. Each spoke is under tension and pulls on a limited section of rim. Spokes coming from the right-side hub flange pull the rim to the right. Spokes coming from the left-side hub flange pull the rim to the left. Spokes are oriented at the rim in a left-right-left-right pattern to counter the pull from each side or flange. Having spokes tight, with relatively even tension, makes the wheel spin straight. Changes to spoke tension will change the amount of pull on the rim where the spoke attaches and affect its position or "true." This process of changing spoke tension is called "truing." Professional mechanics will use tools such as truing stands, centering gauges (dishing tools), spoke wrenches, spoke tension meters, and their experience to adjust spoke tension and produce a durable and strong wheel (figure 5.1).

FIGURE: 5.1

Equipment used by professional mechanics

Wheels are under constant stress when used, and occasional truing will keep the rim running straight. Spoke tension is adjusted by tightening or loosening a threaded nut, called the "nipple," at the end of the spoke. Although a common phrase among mechanics is to "tighten the spokes," it is the nipples that are turned, not the spokes. The nipples are turned with a spoke wrench (figure 5.2).

FIGURE: 5.2

Spoke wrenches for various-sized spoke nipples

Wheels not only help us go, they also help us slow. Caliper brakes such as linear pull, cantilever, side pull, and dual pivot brakes use the rim sidewall as the braking surface. Brake pad adjustment is difficult and often futile with an out-of-true or wobbly wheel.

Wheel Truing Overview

When truing, it is especially important to use the correctly sized wrench. Spoke nipples are typically made of brass or aluminum, and both are relatively soft materials. Nipples are typically square and come in different sizes. A wrench that is even slightly too large easily damages the nipple by rounding the corners (figure 5.3). Use a caliper to measure across the nipple flat and purchase the correct-sized wrench. There is no correlation between spoke diameter and nipple size. See Table 5.1, Spoke Wrench Fit. If you own spoke wrenches of different sizes, use the smallest that will fit, even if it seems slow putting the wrench on the nipple (figure 5.4).

FIGURE: 5.3

If spoke wrench is large for the nipple, damage may occur

F IGURE : 5 . 4

A proper fitting wrench will help ensure properly tightened spokes

T ABLE : 5 . 1   **Spoke Wrench Fit**

SIZE OF NIPPLE	PARK TOOL SPOKE WRENCH MODEL & COLOR OF HANDLE
3.23mm (0.127")	SW-0, or SW-40 black
3.3mm (0.130")	SW-1, green
3.45mm (0.136")	SW-2, or SW-42 red
3.96mm (0.156")	SW-3, blue
4.4mm (0.173")	SW-14
Internal hex nut, 5mm	SW-15
Internal hex nut, 5.5mm	SW-15
Internal square 3.25mm	SW-15
Round- 9mm spline	SW-13
Round-5.7mm spline	SW-13

There are some styles of nipples made with a special pattern or size. Wrenches may be available only from the manufacturer. There are also some styles of nipples that are internal to the rim. It is necessary to remove the tire and rim strip to access the back of the nipple. The nipple head may be square or hex shaped. Use a spoke wrench such as the SW-15 (figure 5.5). This is not industry standard for internal nipple size or shape.

F IGURE : 5 . 5

Truing internal nipple wheel with bladed spokes. Note adjustable wrench holding blade.

There are four basic aspects of wheel truing: lateral true, radial true, rim centering over the hub (dish), and spoke tension. A properly trued wheel will have all four aspects adjusted evenly for best performance.

Lateral True: Also called "rim run-out," this is the side-to-side wobble of the rim as the wheel spins (figure 5.6). This aspect is the most critical to rim brake caliper settings. Too much run-out will make it difficult to set the rim brake pads without the pads rubbing the rim. Extreme run-out problems will result in the tire hitting the frame or fork.

F IGURE : 5 . 6

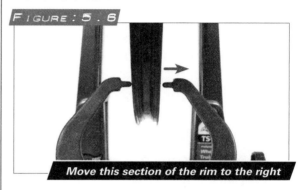

Move this section of the rim to the right

Radial True: This is the amount of vertical run-out or hop (figure 5.7). If the wheel becomes out-of-round, it moves or hops up and down with each revolution. In severe cases this will affect brake pad placement and can be felt by the rider as a bump every wheel revolution.

F IGURE : 5 . 7

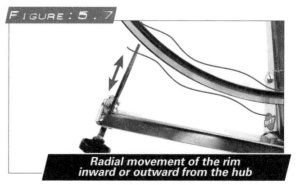

Radial movement of the rim inward or outward from the hub

Rim Centering or Dish: This is the centering of the rim in the middle of the front fork or rear frame. If the rim is offset left or right within the forks or dropouts, it may be difficult to adjust the brakes. Severe cases of poor centering can also cause handling problems because the front and rear wheel won't track in a straight line (figure 5.8).

This rear wheel is off-centered to the right side of the frame

Use zip-ties for reference indicator if truing stand is not available

Tension: This is simply the tightness of the spokes. Spokes are tensioned just like other fasteners. Spoke tension is best measured using a tool called a spoke tension meter (tensionometer) such as the Park Tool TM-1, which flexes the spoke using a calibrated spring (figure 5.9). With experience, spoke tension can be roughly estimated by squeezing pairs of spokes and feeling the deflection.

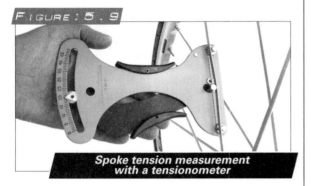

Spoke tension measurement with a tensionometer

Truing Procedures

It is useful to use a steady pointer as a reference, such as one found on a truing stand, when sighting rim movement and deviations. Park Tool truing stands allow easier and faster work when truing. The truing stand uses a caliper indicator as a reference to gauge the rim run-out. If no truing stand is available, it is possible to use anything that will hold the wheel as steady as a truing stand or even the bicycle frame itself. Use the brake pads or a zip-tie to create an indicator as a reference gauge. Secure and snug a zip-tie at braking surface height on each side of the seat stay or fork blade. Cut zip-tie to a length able to touch the rim (figure 5.10).

When truing, it is critical to get the spoke wrench fully engaged on the nipple before turning. A wrench that is only partially engaged may damage the nipple and make truing difficult. When truing a wheel, the wrench and nipples may end up being viewed upside down. This happens if the wrench and nipple are viewed below the axle center. The wrench will appear to the mechanic as turning to the left when tightening the nipple. Do not allow this to confuse you. Keep in mind that the nipple is rotating around the fixed spoke. Imagine a screwdriver at the nipple end and turn it clockwise or counter-clockwise as required (figure 5.11).

Visualize turning the wrench as if a screwdriver is turning the nipple

There are some models of wheels where the nipple is located at the hub flange. These wheels true the same as conventional wheels. Tightening a spoke will draw the rim towards the hub flange side where it connects. The threading of the spokes and nipples is still a right-hand thread, and nipples tighten clockwise as seen from the orientation of the nipple.

The image below is a "mechanic's eye" view of the rim (figure 5.12). The spoke nipples labeled A, C, and E, are on the left side of the rim and come from the left side hub flange. Spoke nipples B, D, and F are on the right and come from the right side hub flange. Left side spokes pull the rim toward the left. Their pulling is offset by the pull of spokes on the right. Each nipple affects a relatively wide area of the rim. For example, spoke C pulls mainly at the nipple hole of the rim, but this spoke also affects the rim up to and even past A and F. Turning nipple C to increase spoke tension will move that section of rim to the left. Turning nipple D to increase tension will move that section of rim to the right. Loosening nipple C will also move the rim to the right, because of the constant pull of D and B.

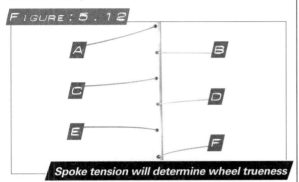

FIGURE: 5.12

Spoke tension will determine wheel trueness

Before making any adjustments to spoke tension, use a light lubricant and oil the threads of the spokes and the hole where the nipple exits the rim (figure 5.13). This will reduce the effort of turning the nipple to tension the spoke.

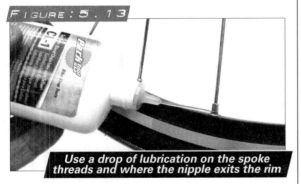

FIGURE: 5.13

Use a drop of lubrication on the spoke threads and where the nipple exits the rim

Lateral Truing

Lateral, or side-to-side truing, is the most common required truing procedure. The lateral run-out shows up relatively easily when viewed at the rim caliper brake pads. Tightening or loosening spokes at a section of rim can change lateral movements of the rim. Inexperienced mechanics should generally tighten nipples when correcting deviations. Tightening the spoke tension will typically produce more rim movement while making these corrections.

Wheel rims do not need to spin perfectly straight with zero run-out in order to be completely serviceable. Most wheels will be adequately true if they wobble laterally less than 1/16" (1.0mm), and if the rim does not strike the brake pads.

The procedure for lateral wheel truing:

a. If a truing stand is available, remove wheel from bike. Alternatively, mount the wheel in the bike and attach zip-ties on each side of the rim at the seat stays or fork blades. If the wheel requires extensive truing, remove the tire.

b. Place wheel in truing stand. Move indicators close to rim.

c. Spin wheel and inspect for left-right deviations.

d. Adjust indicator of truing stand (or zip-tie end) so that it lightly touches the rim in one area. Work off of either left or right side.

e. Stop wheel where rim and one indicator are closest or touch. This area is the largest lateral deviation of the rim run-out and should be corrected first.

f. Rotate rim back and forth past indicator and find center of rim deviation. It is easier to see the run-out as it moves toward an indicator or rubbing it, rather than as a deviation that moves away from an indicator (figure 5.14).

g. If rim deviation moves toward the left side, find the right flange nipple at the rim closest to center of deviation. If rim deviation moves toward the right side, find the left flange nipple closest to center of deviation. Tightening this spoke will move rim deviation in this section of rim.

h. Tighten appropriate spoke nipple 1/4 to 1/2 turn. A 1/4 turn is a 90-degree turn of the nipple, while a 1/2 turn is a 180-degree turn. Spin the wheel and check deviation again. It is often necessary to repeat the process at one area. Do not tighten more than 1/2 turn at a time. It is better to proceed in small increments and to check progress between each tightening by spinning the wheel.

i. Locate another side-to-side deviation using indicator. Repeat process of finding center of deviation and correcting deviation by finding and turning nipple from spoke of opposite flange.

j. After making three corrections on one side of the rim, switch to other side indicator or zip-tie. This will help maintain previous wheel centering.

k. Continue making corrections. To check tolerance, use indicator so it just barely rubs the rim in one area. Spin wheel slowly from this point and inspect for the largest gap between indicator and

ParkTool

rim. This area is the worst left to right lateral deviation. If this gap appears less than 1mm (approximately the thickness of a dime), wheel is adequately trued laterally. In some cases, it will be necessary to continue truing for tighter tolerances.

l.   If only lateral true is being adjusted, clean the rim's braking surface with a solvent such as rubbing alcohol or window cleaner. If used, cut zip-ties from frame. Remount tire if removed and re-install wheel into bike.

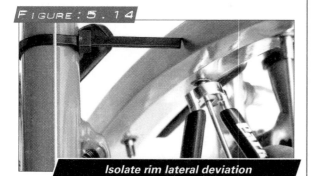

FIGURE: 5.14

Isolate rim lateral deviation

Radial Truing

The wheel rim may appear to move in and out toward the center as it rotates around the hub. This can also be viewed as an up-and-down movement. This radial aspect of the wheel can be affected by spoke tension. Sections of rim moving away from the hub are called "high spots." Sections of rim moving toward the hub are called "low spots." Sections of rim can be moved toward the hub by tightening spokes from both flanges at high spots. Loosening spokes from both flanges will tend to move a section of rim slightly outward at low spots. In correcting radial run-out, it is necessary to correct both high spots and low spots. It is typically best to work using pairs of spokes, one from the left side and one from the right side. By working with adjacent left-right spokes there is less of a tendency for the wheel to become laterally out of true. It is necessary, however, to always double check the lateral true after making radial corrections.

The procedure for radial wheel truing:

a.   Remove tire from wheel.

b.   Mount wheel in a truing stand or mount wheel in bike frame and attach zip-tie indicator to frame. Attach tie close to outer edge of rim.

c.   Bring indicator (zip-tie) close to outside edge of rim.

d.   Spin rim and bring indicator (zip-tie) slowly closer to rim until there is a very light rub. This point is the largest high spot or radial deviation away from the hub.

e.   Stop rim at light rub. Move rim back and forth through rub and locate center of deviation. This section of rim needs to move closer to hub (figure 5.15).

f.   Tighten the two spokes in the middle of the deviation. Tighten one left side and one right side spoke, each the same amount, beginning with ½ turn.

g.   Move the rim back and forth through the selected area. Repeat tightening if necessary.

h.   Spin the wheel and move the calipers (zip-tie) slightly closer to the rim to find next deviation. Correct the rub by tightening a left-right pair of spokes at the center of the rub.

i.   After making three radial corrections, stop and double-check lateral true. Correct the lateral true as needed before proceeding with further radial adjustments.

j.   After making several radial corrections to high spots, the rim may show only areas moving toward the hub or low spots. It will be necessary to loosen the low spot areas. Spin the rim and move caliper (zip-tie) to create a light continuous scrape. The areas not scraping are low spots and need to move away from the hub to be corrected. Isolate the center of the worst low spot.

k.   Loosen two spokes on either side of the center of the low spot. Spokes should be adjacent left-side and right-side pairs.

l.   Repeat procedure on other low spots. Occasionally check and correct lateral true.

m. Check for acceptable radial tolerance. Adjust indicator so it just barely rubs the rim in one area. Spin wheel slowly from this point and inspect for the largest gap between indicator and rim. This area is the largest radial deviation. Wheel is adequately trued for round when the deviation from the highest to lowest is less then 1mm (1/16 inch).

n.   Check and correct lateral true as needed.

o.   If no other truing is to be done, clean the rim's braking surface with a solvent such as rubbing alcohol or window cleaner. Cut zip-ties from frame. Re-install tire and re-install wheel to bike.

FIGURE: 5.15

Isolate the radial run-out and select a left-right pair of spokes to correct problem

If the wheel rim has been damaged and deformed from impact, such as during riding or even during shipping, it may not be possible to correct the rim to a tight tolerance. If the rim shows an inward movement in one section toward the hub and the spokes in that area are already loose, the rim has been bent. This type of damage is not repairable. Replacement of rim or wheel is recommended. Contact a professional mechanic.

Wheel Centering (Dishing)

The rim should be centered in the frame, front fork blades, or the rear stays. Use a ruler and measure from the left and right stay or fork blade to the rim. If the distances are equal and the rim looks centered, it is centered. If there is a greater distance from one stay or blade compared to the other, the wheel is off-center, or "misdished."

The rim can be moved over to the frame center by adjusting spoke tension. Remember, spokes from the left flange pull the rim toward the left, while spokes from the right flange pull the rim toward the right. Tightening all left side spokes evenly will move the rim to the left. Tighten all right side spokes evenly moves the rim right. Alternatively, loosen all left side spokes to move the rim right. Loosen all right side spokes to move the rim left.

The most accurate method to check rim centering over a hub is with a centering gauge called a dishing tool, such as the Park Tool WAG-4 Wheel Alignment Gauge, or WAG-3 Portable Wheel Dishing Gauge. The Park Tool WAG-4 comes with two sliding blocks on the feet. These blocks allow the tool to measure off the wheel rim even when a tire is still mounted.

The procedure for checking wheel centering with a dishing tool:

   a. Note which side of the wheel is being checked. In this example, we will assume the right side is being checked first and use this as a reference for the left side.

   b. Lower the sliding gauge until the end rests on the face of the right side locknut (figure 5.16). Do not rest gauge on end of axle. The wheel will reference the locknut face when mounting in the frame.

   c. Turn wheel over to check opposite side. Place feet of dishing tool on rim. Note indicator relative to locknut face. There are three possible results.

Situation A:

Both feet of dishing tool rest on the rim and the indicator pointer lightly contacts left locknut face, or is within 1mm of the face. This rim is adequately centered to the locknuts. No correction of centering is required (figure 5.17).

Situation B:

Both feet of the dishing tool rest on the rim, but there is a significant gap between the indicator and locknut face (figure 5.18). This situation shows rim is off-center toward left side. If the gap is greater than 1mm, the wheel should be recentered. This rim in this example should be moved to right. Caution: a rim is off-centered in the bike only half the distance from the dishing tool indicator to the locknut. For example, if the indicator is 3mm from locknut, wheel is off centered to mid plane of the bike by 1.5mm. In Situation B, it is better to view the error (if any) at the rim rather than at the hub. If after checking the wheel you find Situation B described above, it is best to reset the indicator using the left side as a reference then recheck the opposite side. You will find there is now a gap between rim and dishing tool foot where the indicator rests on the locknut face. This method makes it more obvious that the rim should be moved toward the leg of the tool. If you see the error or gap at the hub, the rim is actually pulled toward the opposite side to close the gap of the locknut face to indicator.

Situation C:

Three-point contact of both feet and indicator at locknut is impossible. If indicator rests on locknut face, only one foot will contact rim, with other foot higher than rim (figure 5.19). If both feet are on rim, indicator will be below level of locknut face. This situation indicates the rim is off center toward right side. The rim should be moved to the left.

   d. Correct centering error by tightening spokes from the flange on the same side as the gap between the rim and the foot of the dishing gauge. Tighten each spoke on one side only ¼ turn.

   e. Double check and correct lateral true as necessary. The dishing tool assumes the rim is laterally true.

f. Use a dishing tool and check wheel again, starting with step "a" above. Keep in mind that the original reference side has changed the position of the rim to the locknut face. Repeat corrections if necessary. If the rim to dishing tool gap is less than 1mm, wheel is adequately centered.

g. If no other truing is to be done, clean the rim's braking surface with a solvent such as rubbing alcohol or window cleaner.

FIGURE: 5.16

Dishing gauge set to
reference right side of wheel

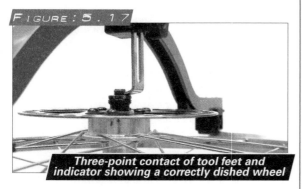

FIGURE: 5.17

Three-point contact of tool feet and
indicator showing a correctly dished wheel

FIGURE: 5.18

Dishing gauge indicator
showing rim is off center

FIGURE: 5.19

Dishing gauge indicating
wheel is off center

When making corrections to dish, keep in mind that it will also make changes to overall tension. Corrections by tightening one side will increase overall tension of both sides, while corrections by loosening will decrease overall tension of both sides.

Spoke Tension

Consider that spokes are really just long thin bolts with nipples as the nuts. They're no different than fasteners. Like any threaded fastener, there is an acceptable range of tightness, which is called tension. Spoke tension is the amount of force pulling on the spoke.

As the wheels rotate while you ride, the spokes that are on the bottom, next to the ground, will momentarily lose their tension level then regain tension as they rotate past this low point. This change of tension in each revolution is called a "stress cycle." Wheels with a relatively low overall spoke tension actually see a greater swing in tension as compared to wheels with greater overall tension. Stress cycles, this tightening and then loosening of tension, fatigue the metal and lead to spoke breakage. Wheels with low overall spoke tension will continue to loosen even more as the bike is ridden. This results in shortened spoke life, more spoke failure, and a wheel that requires continuous truing.

While low overall spoke tension can result in problems, too much tension can also develop issues. Spokes with too much tension can deform or crack the rim near the nipple holes (figure 5.20). Too much tension can also lead to failure of the hub flange. Spoke nipple wrench flats can become deformed and rounded by forcing the nipple to turn when the spoke tension is too high. However, the spoke itself can typically take more stress then rim, nipple, or hub flange.

FIGURE: 5.20

Crack in rim from excessive spoke tension

When adding or subtracting tension, work slowly and in relatively small increments. For example, to add tension to a wheel, begin with a spoke next to the tire valve hole and add only ¼ turn to each spoke. After adding this tension, double-check the lateral trueness. It is common to make corrections to the other aspects of truing after adding overall tension. If more tension is desired, add another ¼ turn to each spoke and again check the other aspects of truing. Repeat the process until the desired tension is achieved.

It is common for the spokes to become twisted along their long axis as the nipples are turned. The is called "spoke wind-up." The safest method to relieve this torsional stress on the spoke is to simply ride the bike. You may hear an initial popping or pinging sound while the spokes untwist. In some case, it may be necessary to true the wheel again laterally.

Spoke tension is best measured with a spoke tension meter (also called a tensionometer), such as the Park Tool TM-1 Tension Meter. It is possible to some degree to "feel" the tension by squeezing crossing or parallel spokes. The squeezing technique can be quite deceiving and inconsistent. The stiffness of the rim and thickness of spokes vary widely. A tension meter allows the user to determine both relative spoke tension between spokes and the tension force of each spoke measured in kilograms force, abbreviated here as "kgf." The TM-1 is calibrated to read tension for sixteen different types of spokes, including bladed, titanium, and aluminum (figure 5.21).

FIGURE: 5.21

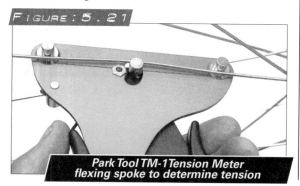

Park Tool TM-1 Tension Meter flexing spoke to determine tension

Rim manufacturers have set tension recommendations from as low as 60 kgf to as high as 200 kgf. However, 100 kgf is a common tension recommendation. It is the rim, not the spoke type or diameter, that determines the limits of tension. Generally, the heavier and stronger the rim, the more tension it can handle. A light rim may weigh from 280 grams to 350 grams. A relatively heavy rim may weigh 450 grams or more. Additionally, rim eyelets may help distribute the load on the rim wall. A lack of eyelets on a light rim implies that less spoke tension should be used. There is a wide range of tension possibilities, and it is always best to consult the rim manufacturer for the most up-to-date specifications.

Manufacturers typically give specifications for the wheel with no tire pressure. Tire pressure will have the effect of lowering the tension slightly. Generally, do not try to account for this drop by adding more tension than recommended by the manufacturer. Parts makers list tension for the tight side of the wheel. For rear wheels, this will be the sprocket side or right side. For front wheels with a disc, the tighter side is the disc side. If the flanges are equally spaced from the hub center, then either side can be measured. This is the case for most front wheels made without a disc rotor mount.

The procedure for measuring tension with Park Tool TM-1 Tension Meter:

   a. Measure the diameter of the spoke using the included spoke diameter gauge. The smallest slot the spoke fits into determines the diameter. A measuring caliper can also be used to measure the spoke diameter. The diameter at the middle section of spoke will determine the appropriate spoke-type column on the Conversion Table.

   b. Squeeze the TM-1 at the handle grips. Place the spoke between the two fixed posts and the moveable post. With butted spokes, position the posts so they rest on the narrowest portion of each spoke. With aero/bladed spokes, position the posts so they rest against the wide, flat side of the spoke.

   c. Gently release the handle. Releasing the tension rapidly will cause erratic reading results.

d. With the TM-1 engaged on the spoke, the pointer will be pointing to a number on the tool's graduated scale. This number is a deflection reading. Use that in conjunction with the TM-1's conversion table to determine the actual tension of the spoke.

e. For the most accurate measurement, measure all spokes on one side and take the average reading, but measuring approximately ¼ of the wheel will give you a good idea of the overall tension. If you have a 32-spoke wheel, measure eight spokes and take the average.

f. Using the conversion table, find the column corresponding to the material and diameter of the spoke being measured. Follow the column down to the row corresponding to the spoke's deflection reading (as determined in step "d"). The number at this intersection is the actual tension of the spoke in kilograms force (kgf).

The spoke tension will vary slightly from spoke to spoke with even a well-trued wheel. A wheel that has the same relative tension for all the spokes on a flange, however, will tend to stay true longer. The use of a spoke tension meter will help get the spokes closer to the same relative tension. Generally, attempt to get the spokes within 20 percent of one another. On wheels with dish (rear wheel or front disc wheels), the left and right side tensions will not be equal. This is normal and will not be a problem for the wheel. Using a tensionometer will also help get the overall tension acceptably high.

Replacing Broken or Damaged Spokes

A broken spoke will cause the wheel to come out of true. It may be possible to correct lateral true enough to keep riding until the spoke can be replaced. However, low spoke-count wheels (28 spokes or less) may develop substantial lateral run-out from a single broken spoke. It may not be possible to correct the run-out enough to safely finish a ride even by opening the brake calipers.

To repair a wheel with a broken spoke, begin by removing the tire. On rear wheels, also remove the rear sprockets. Remove the old spoke from the wheel and hub. The new spoke should be the correct length. If possible, measure the old spoke or remove a second spoke for measurement. Feed the new spoke through the hub in the same orientation as the original spoke. The spoke head should similarly face inward or outward in the flange. It may be necessary to flex and bend the

spoke but avoid kinking it (figure 5.22). Inspect another spoke of the same flange and same orientation and follow the same pattern.

FIGURE: 5.22

Bend spoke to lace into wheel

Replace the nipple as well as the spoke. If possible, use a spoke tension meter to measure spokes on the same side as the broken spoke and average the readings. Tighten the new spoke until it reaches the average. True the wheel with the procedures described above.

Wheel Wear, Damage & Repair

Rims may become damaged from impacts, such as hitting a rock, pothole, or curb. Crashing or impacting the side of the rim in a fall can also create fatal damage. Truing may provide limited repair for crashed wheels. Begin by checking relative tension in the damaged area. For example, if a wheel deviates in one section to the right, check left and right side spoke tension in that area. If the wheel runs right even though right side spokes appear loose and left side spokes appear tight, the rim metal is bent. This indicates the rim has been deformed beyond the point where spoke tension can repair it (figure 5.23).

FIGURE: 5.23

Wheel rim deformed beyond repair

Adjusting spoke tension on a wheel with a badly bent rim is unlikely to help except possibly to get the rider home from a ride. Trying to bash the rim or attempting to rebend the rim back in the problem area is a desperate repair measure. It's unlikely to help return the wheel to a useable condition. Wheel rims can be replaced, and a new rim is easily laced around the old hub. See a professional mechanic for this service or purchase a new wheel.

For bicycles with rim caliper brakes, the pads will grind the rim walls while grabbing the rim and thin the metal. The pressurized tire is held in place by the rim sidewall, which is now weakened. Thin sidewalls may break or fail during a ride cause a tire blowout. Inspect visually and feel the rim-braking surface for a dished, concave surface. If the rim appears worn, remove the tire and place a straight edge along the rim surface. Inspect for a gap between the straight edge and the rim. If the gap is larger than 0.2 mm (approximately the thickness of a business card), the rim should be replaced (figure 5.24).

FIGURE: 5.21

Rim showing unacceptable wear on braking surface

CHAPTER 6

Pedals

Pedals are the platforms we push against for each revolution of the crank arms. Pedals come in a variety of designs for specialty uses. The "platform" pedal may be used with any recreational street shoe. Toe clips can be added to help foot retention to the pedal. "Clipless" pedals require shoes fitted with special cleats. Clipless pedals should be lightly lubricated at cleat engagement pivot points. Regardless of the pedal, occasionally check the security of all threaded fasteners on the pedal body.

Pedal Removal

Pedals need to be removed to service the bearings or to pack a bike for shipment. Most pedals have wrench flats on the pedal axles adjacent to the crank. While they appear similar, use a proper pedal wrench not a cone wrench for the narrow wrench flats of the pedal. A pedal requires much greater tightening torque than a cone wrench can deliver, and attempts to force the cone wrench on the pedal will damage both.

Pedals may also use a hex fitting at the end of the spindle behind the cranks as well as pedal wrench flats. Use a long-handled hex wrench for removal and installation to obtain adequate torque. It is often necessary to rotate the bike to find good leverage (figure 6.1).

FIGURE : 6 . 1

Pedal wrench fitting behind spindle axle

The right side (drive side) pedal has a right-hand thread. It removes counter-clockwise and installs clockwise. The left side (non-drive side) pedal has a left-hand thread. It will remove clockwise and install counter-clockwise. This is to prevent the left side pedal from rotating itself loose. Pedals are commonly marked with an "R" on the right side pedal and an "L" on the left side pedal.

The procedure for pedal removal:

a. Mount bike in repair stand and shift chain to largest chainring. This helps protect against cuts from chainring teeth.

b. Rotate bike until right pedal is easily accessed. Reach over or through frame as necessary for best leverage.

c. Place wrench securely onto pedal wrench flats. For hex wrenches, fully secure wrench into back of pedal. Re-position wrench until crank and wrench form an angle of 90 degrees or less. Use opposite crank for extra leverage. Correct mechanical advantage is critical on pedals, which are often overly tight. If possible, grab opposite crank for second lever. See page 5, Chapter 1, Basic Mechanical Concepts.

d. Turn pedal wrench counter-clockwise (as seen from outboard of pedaling looking inward) to remove right pedal. Use care not to cut hand on crank or chainring. Loosening both the right and left side pedal can be seen as pedaling forward while the wrench engages the pedal flats. (figure 6.2).

e. Remove pedal completely from crank.

f. Rotate bike as necessary until left pedal is easily accessed.

g. Engage pedal wrench onto left pedal and grab right crank for second lever. Position wrench and crank for good mechanical advantage.

h. Turn pedal wrench clockwise to remove left pedal or turn crank so the pedal is pedaling forward. Remove left pedal completely from crank.

FIGURE : 6 . 2

Pedal in a forward direction to remove pedals from cranks

Pedal Installation

The common pedal thread for aluminum cranks is $\frac{9}{16}$-inch x 20 tpi. The pedal thread of the steel one-piece crank is ½ inch x 20-tpi. Pedal threads tend to be made of bearing hard steel and are relatively difficult to damage. However, minor pedal thread damage may be repaired with a thread file.

Pedal threads can damage the aluminum threads of the crank if the threads are misaligned. Start initial threading with only your fingers to avoid forcing the pedal into the crank threads. Using a pedal wrench to start the thread will not allow the feel necessary to detect cross threading of the pedal. Pedals are secured to a relatively high torque range, approximately 300 inch pounds. A common pedal wrench may be held 8 inches (20cm) from the pedal. It would require an effort of approximately 35 pounds (16 kilograms). Grease or anti-seize on the threads is recommended to prevent pedal threads rusting and seizing to the crank arm. Pedals installed in carbon cranks should use a pedal washer.

The procedure for installing pedals:

a. Identify right and left pedals. Look for "L" or "R" marking on pedal axle or wrench flats. If no "L" or "R" marking is seen, use pedal thread direction to identify pedals. Left-threaded pedals (threads sloping upward to the left) go to left crank. Right-threaded pedals (threads sloping upward to the right) go to right crank.

b. Apply grease or anti-seize to threads of both pedals. Install pedal washer if appropriate.

c. Thread right side pedal into right crank using only your fingers to avoid cross threading.

d. Engage pedal wrench to flats (or inside hex fitting) and fully thread pedal into arm. For pedals with external wrench flats, hold wrench with one hand while holding pedal with other. Pedal the bike backward to install.

e. Arrange pedal for best mechanical advantage and use opposite arm as second lever (figure 6.3). Tighten pedal fully.

f. Repeat for left pedal by threading pedal counter-clockwise to install.

g. Fully secure left pedal.

FIGURE: 6.3

Good mechanical advantage to securing pedal

Damage to Crank Pedal Threads

If the crank threads are damaged, the pedal may be difficult to install. To repair thread, use an appropriate sized tap, either $\frac{9}{16}$ inch x 20 tpi, or ½ inch x 20 tpi and chase the threads of the crank.

If a pedal has come loose and fallen out, the outer thread of the crank hole may be mangled and damaged. Use a pedal tap to align thread. A tap will not restore metal that has been removed or torn away.

If the pedal threads in the crank are damaged beyond a tap repair, they may be repairable using a thread insert system. Solid aluminum cranks may be repaired by being drilled or tapped to a large thread. A special bushing is then installed with an internal $\frac{9}{16}$-inch thread. This repair is best left to professional mechanics. If the arm is carbon or hollow aluminum, this repair may not be possible.

Pedal Bearing Service

The bearing systems in pedals are similar to other rotational bearings on the bike. The axle is attached to the crank and rotates inside the pedal body. Bearing service is possible on some models, but some models are simply thrown away when bearings become excessively worn. Service only one pedal at a time to avoid getting confused between internal parts and outer pedal bodies.

Shimano® Pedals- axle-bearing assembly type

Shimano® pedal bearing systems may use an axle-bearing assembly unit that is pressed into the pedal body. Examples are Shimano® XTR, XT, DX, and 105 pedals. If the inner pedal bearing mount has only one locking fitting, it most likely uses this system (figure 6.4). The pedal body acts only as housing to the bearings and does not contain race surfaces. It is not necessary to dismantle the bearing assembly unit to add new grease.

ParkTool

FIGURE: 6.4

Pedal bearing assembly unit with Shimano® TL-PD-40 tool

The bearing assemblies in these pedals are removable and adjustable. Tool selection varies with model. Removal will require the Shimano® TL-PD-40 if there are ten points on axle assembly unit. Other models use a hexed-shaped wrench flat such as a cone wrench.

The procedure for service of Shimano® axle-bearing assembly pedals:

   a. Remove pedals from cranks.

   b. Mount pedal in soft jaws of a bench vise. Use rag to protect pedal body.

   c. Remove assembly unit. Left side pedal has an internal right-hand-threaded bearing unit. Remove the assembly unit counter-clockwise. Right side pedal has a left-hand-threaded internal bearing unit. Remove this bearing unit clockwise. Using Shimano® TL-PD-40 tool, turn it with a 36mm wrench such as the Park Tool HCW-4 (figure 6.5). If the fitting is a hex shape, use a 19mm cone wrench.

   d. To adjust bearing, grab the axle threads in soft jaws or the Park Tool AV-4 axle vise.

   e. To test bearing adjustment, grab cylinder section of shaft unit not threaded plastic. Bearing adjustment only affects cylinder section. Play in plastic threaded section will disappear when unit is remounted in pedal body. To adjust, hold cone and loosen locknut counter-clockwise (figure 6.6).

   f. Make adjustment after locknut is loose. Adjust only in small increments. Turn clockwise to tighten bearing adjustment. Turn counter-clockwise to loosen bearing adjustment. Hold cone and secure locknut.

   g. Test bearing adjustment and re-adjust as necessary. Adjust for loosest setting without play at cylinder.

   h. If desired, clean and scrub both body and shaft in solvent. Blow-dry with a compressor. Wipe off and allow dry completely if no compressor is available.

   i. To add fresh grease, fill bottom forth of shaft unit hole in body with grease (figure 6.7). Bearing unit is a press-fit inside body. When installed, new grease is forced inside bearing unit.

   j. Use Shimano® TL-PD-40 tool or appropriate wrench and thread shaft unit into pedal body. Thread until body stops. Do not over torque.

   k. Repeat process on other pedal.

FIGURE: 6.5

Remove axle-bearing assembly with TL-PD-40

FIGURE: 6.6

Adjusting pedal bearing shaft unit

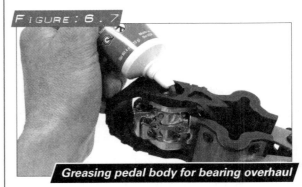

FIGURE: 6.7

Greasing pedal body for bearing overhaul

SHIMANO® Pedals: lockring and cup type

The Shimano® PD-7810 Dura-Ace pedal uses a cup and cone bearing system, which is similar in concept to the adjustable-type bottom bracket with an adjustable side and fixed side. The spindle acts as the axle. The lockring holds an adjustable cup on the inner side of the pedal body. The second cup and axle surface are inside the pedal body itself (figure 6.8).

Loosen pedal lockring

F I G U R E : 6 . 8

Dura-Ace cup and cone bearing assembly

The left side pedal uses a bearing cup with right-hand threading. The lockring and cup unthread counter-clockwise. The right side pedal uses a bearing cup with left-hand threading. The lockring and cup unthread clockwise.

The procedure for bearing adjusting:

a. Remove pedal from bike.
b. Using a cone wrench, loosen lockring adjacent to axle (figure 6.9). The left side pedal uses a bearing cup and lockring with right hand threading. The lockring and cup unthread counter-clockwise. The right side pedal uses a bearing cup with left-hand threading. The lockring and cup unthread clockwise.
c. Turn bearing cup first away from bearings and then gently run cup into the pedal body until it touches ball bearings.
d. Hold cup in position and tighten the lockring against the pedal body. Do not allow the cup to rotate relative to pedal body.
e. Test adjustment by checking for play in axle. Repeat adjustment as necessary by loosening lockring and making small incremental adjustments to cup as necessary.

F I G U R E : 6 . 9

Cartridge Bearing Pedal Service- Crank Brothers®

There are no bearing adjustments on pedals using cartridge bearings. Bearings are replaced when worn. The Crank Brothers® pedals are a typical cartridge bearing design.

The Crank Brothers® pedals use a cartridge bearing system for the outward bearing. The inner bearing is a journal bearing. A journal bearing has no ball or needle bearings, and is usually a simply plastic sleeve. A rebuild kit includes both bearings and rubber seal(s).

The procedure for Crank Brothers® "Egg Beater" pedal bearing replacement:

a. Remove end cap from pedal (pedal may remain on bike).
b. Loosen counter-clockwise and remove nut under end cap (figure 6.10).
c. Pull pedal body from axle.
d. Cartridge bearing placement is a loose fit inside pedal body. Tap body on hard surface to remove bearing or use end of spoke to remove bearing.
e. Remove seal(s) from inner side of pedal body using seal pick or small tipped screwdriver.
f. Journal bearing is a press fit into pedal body. Use a hooked seal pick to pull bearing from body (figure 6.11). Use a spare spoke (cutting the head at the elbow) to create a hooked tool if no pick is available.
g. Clean axle and inside of pedal body as necessary.

FIGURE: 6.10

Remove nut

FIGURE: 6.12

Press inner journal bearing using shaft

FIGURE: 6.11

Remove journal bearing from body

FIGURE: 6.13

Install dust cap

Inspect pedal body and pedal spindle. If the surface for the journal bearing is badly worn or pitted, the pedals should simply be replaced.

**The procedure for Crank Brothers®
pedal bearing installation:**

   a. Press journal bearing into pedal using pedal shaft to drive bearing fully into body (figure 6.12). Pull pedal from body after bearing is pressed.

   b. Install new seal over journal bearing on inboard face of pedal.

   c. Grease pedal shaft and install into pedal body.

   d. Install new cartridge bearing into pedal body and over spindle end. Install and secure nut to end of pedal spindle.

   e. Install and secure dust cap (figure 6.13). Dust cap removes lateral play and must be installed.

   f. Repeat process on second pedal.

CHAPTER 7

Cranksets

Cranks are levers that connect the pedals to the bottom bracket spindle. The cranks are fitted with toothed sprockets called chainrings that drive the chain. The cranks are sometimes removed to replace chainrings, service the bottom bracket bearings, or better clean the rings and arms. Designs include the "three piece" crank and the "two piece" crank. Two removable cranks are bolted to a bottom bracket spindle held by bearings (figure 7.1). These arms are removed to service the bearings. The two-piece design includes the external bearing crankset systems such as Shimano® HollowTech II and other similar systems that permanently fix the spindle to one crank (figure 7.2).

Three-piece crankset, consisting of two arms and one spindle

External bearing system crank with spindle permanently attached to one arm

Crank Removal (three-piece cranks)

The three-piece cranks are fitted and pressed tightly to a spindle. Most systems require a puller to remove the arms. Cranks are commonly made with a 22mm x 1mm thread fitting for the puller.

Some cranks are fitted with the "one-key" release system. The crank puller is effectively built into the crank (figure 7.3). A crank cap acts as retaining ring and is threaded into the crank. The crank cap takes the place of the dust cap and surrounds the crank bolt head. To remove this crank, leave the crank cap in place. Turn the crank bolt counter-clockwise. The bolt backs against the crank cap and pulls the arm from the spindle.

One-key release system crank cap and crank bolt

The one-key system relies on the cap being secure in the arm. The cap should be occasionally tightened (figure 7.4). The thread is normally a right-hand thread. If the cap is a left-hand thread, it is typically marked accordingly and should be tightened counter-clockwise.

Check security of one-key release system cap

For cranks without the one-key system, a crank puller is required to extract the arm from the spindle after the crank bolt is removed. The puller uses a threaded stud to push against the spindle end. This stud threads into a "nut," which then threads into the 22mm thread fitting of the crank. The spindle and arm are pulled apart when the stud presses against the spindle.

The spline system spindles use a larger bolt compared to the square spindles. This means the square crank pullers simply have nothing to push against and will not work on the spline systems. Spline-type cranks may use the Park Tool CWP-6 or CCP-4 Crank Puller when no one-key system is in place. Both pullers are designed for the standard 22mm x 1mm thread in the crank. The CWP-6 Crank Puller includes changeable tips to work on the Octalink®, ISIS Drive®, and square spindle cranks (figure 7.5).

Spline-type arm without one-key release system may use the CWP-6 Crank Puller

Crank Removal:
Octalink or ISIS Drive Spline

The Octalink® and ISIS Drive® splined type cranks have round holes fitted with splines (figure 7.6). The spline pattern of the spindle must match the pattern in the arm. The cranks are held tight to the spindle by the tension from the crank bolt. To confirm the crank type, it may be necessary to remove the crank bolt or cap to inspect inside for a round, splined-shaped hole.

Spline type crank of the ISIS Drive® system

There is more than one spline standard. Shimano® uses two different styles of Octalink® bottom bracket spindle fittings. Both have an 8-spline fitting. The original is called Octalink® V1, and was used on models BB-7700, 6500, 5500, M950 and M952. The Octalink® V2 fits the BB-ES70/71, BB-ES50/51 (figure 7.7). The V2 system uses a thicker and longer spline (approximately 9mm), while the V1 spline is relatively narrower and shorter (approximately 5mm). The V1 and V2 Octalink® standards cannot be interchanged between spindles or cranks.

Shimano® Octalink V1 spindle is seen on the left. The Octalink V2 spindle is on the right. Do not mix standards.

There is only one ISIS Drive® standard for the crank and spindle fitting. The standard uses a 21mm diameter spindle with 10-splines. The ISIS Drive® is a standard, not a particular brand. The ISIS Drive® and Shimano® Octalink systems are not interchangeable for either bottom brackets or cranks.

The procedure for splined crank removal:

  a. Shift chain to largest chainring. This protects hands from chainring teeth.
  b. Remove crank bolt and any washers inside the crank.
  c. Unthread nut from handle stud of CWP-6 or CCP-4 until it contacts the flat, rotating tip.
  d. Turn nut and handle together into crank and tighten with wrench until snug. If nut is not completely threaded into crank, the threads of the arm or nut may be damaged during removal.
  e. Turn stud clockwise into nut. When resistance is felt, continue threading stud into nut until crank is removed.
  f. Remove tool from crank and repeat process on other side.

Crank Installation—Octalink®
or ISIS Drive® Splined

One-key release systems require extra care when installing the arm to the spindle. The one-key release systems make it difficult to see how the arm is fitting onto the splines of the spindle. Cranks and spindles must align and match exactly on the splines as the crank is pressed into place. A forced mismatch can damage the crank. Splined cranks without the one key system allow easy viewing of the spline fit. One key cranksets are installed the same way as other systems. If there is concern about mating the spindle to the arm, remove the one-key system, install the arm, and re-install the one-key system.

The procedure for splined crank installation:

a. Grease threads inside bottom bracket spindle and grease outer splines of bottom bracket spindle.

b. Rotate splined spindle until one narrow spline aligns to the 12 o'clock position or top dead center.

c. Position right crank on spindle until arm points straight down to the six o'clock position (figure 7.8). Carefully thread bolt into spindle. View opposite side of spindle and check that a narrow spline stays aligned to top dead center. Threading should continue without resistance until crank visually covers spindle splines as seen from the bottom bracket side.

d. Tighten bolt fully.

e. Align left arm so it points directly opposite the right arm (figure 7.8). Thread bolt into spindle and tighten bolt fully.

FIGURE: 7.8

With right crank at 6 o'clock position, spline on left is at top dead center

Crank Removal:
3-piece Square Spindle

The square-spindle cranks have a square hole to accept a square-ended spindle. The square-spindle presses tightly into the arm with pressure from a crank bolt. Most square spindles can be seen where the arm meets the spindle. It may be necessary, however, to remove the crank bolt and inspect inside for a square hole (figure 7.9).

FIGURE: 7.9

A square crank hole with square spindle inside

The procedure for square spindle crank removal:

a. Shift chain to largest chainring to protect hands against chainring teeth.

b. Look for bolt or nut inside crank. If no bolt is visible, remove dust caps. Some caps pry out, while others unthread.

c. Turn bolt or nut counter-clockwise and remove. Inspect inside arms for washers and remove if present.

d. Before installing crank puller into crank, turn puller nut away from internal driver as much as possible. If puller nut unthreads from internal driver, thread it back on only 3-4 turns.

e. Thread nut of puller into arm while taking care not to cross thread. Tighten puller nut into crank using wrench (figure 7.10). Failure to tighten nut may result in crank thread failure during removal.

f. Thread internal driver into puller nut. Using handle or adjustable wrench, tighten driver (figure 7.11). When resistance is felt, continue threading stud into nut until crank is removed.

g. Pull arm from spindle and unthread both parts of tool from arm. Use care not to skin knuckles when removing tool.

h. Repeat process on other crank.

FIGURE: 7.10

Tighten puller nut securely into arm before extracting crank

Tighten internal driver of puller to extract arm

Torque wrench use will help assure full pre-load on bolt.

Crank Installation: 3-piece Square Spindle

The square-tapered hole on the crank is pressed tightly to a tapered, square spindle. A crank bolt or nut acts as the pressing tool and forces the arm up the slope of the spindle. The bolt or nut must be tight enough to keep the arm from loosening but not so tight that the arm becomes split and damaged. Aluminum cranks typically do not require lubrication of this press fit. Aluminum by its nature is covered with a thin layer of oxidation, which acts as self-lubrication. When possible, use a torque wrench to secure the bolt. The crank bolt may need 300 to 450 inch pounds, depending upon brand. Adequate torque is typically enough to keep arms from creaking. If a crank creaks even at full torque, remove and grease the pressed surfaces. If a crank bolt comes loose and the arm falls off, the cause is likely to be a lack of torque during installation.

The procedure for square spindle crank installation:

a. Grease under head and threads of bolts/nuts.
b. Install right crank onto right side of spindle.
c. Install bolt/nut and tighten. Refer to Appendix C for recommended torque.
d. Grease threads of dust cap (if any) and install snug.
e. Install left crank onto left side of spindle with arm pointing opposite direction of right side arm.
f. Install bolt/nut and tighten (figure 7.12).
g. Grease threads of dust cap (if any) and install.

External Bearing Crankset Systems

External bearing crankset systems integrate the bearings, cranks, and spindle (figure 7.13). Examples are Shimano® Hollowtech II, FSA® MegaExo, Race Face X-type, Truvativ® Giga X Pipe, SRAM® (Red, Force, and Rival), and Campangolo® Ultra Torque. These systems tend to be proprietary and do not necessarily share interchangeable component parts.

External bearing crank set system from Race Face®

The bearings may sit outside the face of the bottom bracket shell (figure 7.14). These systems use non-serviceable cartridge bearings, and the entire bearing assembly is replaced when it wears out.

Externally mounted bottom bracket bearings

ParkTool

The spindle of the external bearing system crank is a permanent part of either the left or right crank depending upon manufacturer. The other arm slides onto splines of the spindle, and is then secured. Crank installation and removal procedures vary between manufacturers.

There may be some service of the bearing for the external bearings of these systems. If the external cap can be safely pried free, the seal can then be lifted up and out with a bearing pick or a very small-tipped screwdriver (figure 7.15). The bearings may be cleaned if necessary and fresh grease added. Re-install seal and cap.

FIGURE: 7.15

Carefully lift and remove seal to access bearings for cleaning

Bearing Cup Installation

External bearing crank systems use threaded cups that press against the shell face. It is important that the shell surfaces are machined square to the threads and one another. Misaligned shell faces can cause the bearing cups to twist out of alignment as they seat and secure to the frame. A misaligned shell face may show up when a crank spindle appears to not be centering in one bearing after being installed through the opposite bearing. Another indication of poor shell face alignment is if the bearings do not seem to spin evenly or if the bearings wear out prematurely.

The triple crankset bearing cups of Shimano®, Race Face®, and FSA® are designed to be spaced 75.5mm apart. The cranksets are supplied with three spacers of 2.5mm. The crankset can be fitted to bikes with a 68mm or 73mm bottom bracket shell width. If the bike uses a front derailleur with a built-in mounting bracket ("E-type"), it is counted as a spacer. Any chain guide mount is also counted toward the width total. See Table 7.1 for arrangement of spacers.

TABLE: 7.1	External Bearing Crankset System Spacer Arrangement		
BOTTOM BRACKET SHELL WIDTH	LEFT SIDE OF BIKE	FRONT DERAILLEUR OR CHAIN-GUIDE	RIGHT SIDE OF BIKE
68mm	One 2.5mm spacer	Clamp-on front derailleur Two 2.5mm spacers	Two 2.5mm spacers
68mm	One 2.5mm spacer	E-type front derailleur	One 2.5mm spacer plus E-type bracket
73mm	No spacers	Clamp-on front derailleur	One 2.5mm spacer
73mm	No spacers	E-type front derailleur	E-type bracket

The Truvativ® Giga X Pipe Stylo uses spacers under the bearings. For the single speed or triple crankset, use one spacer per side with a 68mm shell, and no spacers for the 73mm shell.

The external bearing system design for double chainring cranksets (road) from Shimano®, FSA®, and Truvativ® are made for 68mm bottom bracket shells. No extra spacers are required or used for these systems. Bearings simply install into the shell.

The bearing cups from Shimano®, Campagnolo®, FSA®, Truvativ® , SRAM, and Race Face® all use the Park Tool BBT-9 or BBT-19 Bottom Bracket Tool. The cups have 16 notches that are engaged by the tool. The BBT-9 is a hand tool. The BBT-19 allows use of a torque wrench.

The procedure for external bearing installation:

   a. Prepare threads of shell with grease, anti-seize, or a mild thread locker.

   b. If applicable to the brand, install correct number of spacers as described above on cup marked with "R" (drive side). Install dust seal on cup. Thread the drive side cup counter-clockwise into right side of bike. Tighten fully, approximately 305 to 435 inch pounds. Using the BBT-9, apply approximately 45 to 60 pounds of effort on the handle (figure 7.16).

   c. Install correct spacers as needed on cup marked "L" (non-drive side). Thread cup clockwise into left side (non-drive) of bike and tighten fully as before. Cups are ready for crank installation.

Tighten bearings using Park Tool
BBT-9 Bottom Bracket Tool

Install crank with spindle through both bearings

There is no bearing adjustment during bearing installation. Cranks are pushed slightly against the bearing for a light pre-load as part of crank installation for all models. Campagnolo® Ultra Torque cups contain no bearings. Bearings are installed on spindle.

Crank Installation and Removal of Compression Slotted Arm Cranks: Shimano® and FSA®

The Shimano® Hollowtech II and FSA® MegaExo may both use a left crank with a compression slot that is secured by two pinch bolts. These systems do not use a conventional crank puller. A threaded cap is used to bring the arm against the bearings. The cap acts as a bearing adjustment only and does not hold the arm in place.

The procedure for Shimano® Hollowtech II and FSA® MegaExo crank installation:

a. Grease spindle surface and install drive side crank and spindle from the right side through both bearings (figure 7.17).

b. Place drive side crank in the 6 o'clock position. Hold left side arm in 12 o'clock position and press arm onto spindle using hand pressure.

c. Grease threads of crank cap and secure gently. Cap pushes arm to bearing. Recommended torque is only a very light 4 inch pounds. Crank should not push into bearing with force. Over tightening will cause bearings to drag and wear. FSA® MegaExo cranksets use an 8mm hex wrench for cap. Shimano Hollowetch II uses the star fitting of the Park Tool BBT-9 or equivalent tool.

d. Grease threads of arm pinch bolts and secure. Switch between bolts repeatedly to ensure both are fully tight.

The procedure for Shimano® Hollowtech II and FSA MegaExo removal:

a. Loosen fully any pinch bolts on left side crank (figure 7.18).

b. Remove the left side crank cap counter-clockwise. Shimano® cranks use the star fitting on the Park Tool BBT-9 or equivalent tool. Cap is fitted with an eight-point socket fitting (figure 7.19). FSA® crank caps use an 8mm hex wrench.

c. Pull arm off spindle by hand. In some cases it may require light tapping with a soft mallet to remove arm if spindle/arm interface is dirty or sticky.

d. Pull drive side arm to the right. This removes spindle from bearings and the bike. It may be necessary to use a mallet to tap the spindle.

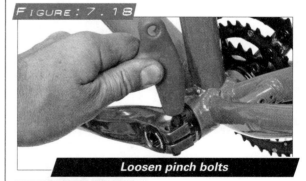

Loosen pinch bolts

BBT-9 tool is used to remove crank cap

ParkTool™

Installation and Removal of Shimano® Ocatalink External Bearing Crank

Shimano® produces a version of XTR and Dura-Ace carbon Hollowtech II cranks that use an Octalink spindle fitting at the left arm. An adjustable ring is installed against the inboard face of the left crank to adjust the bearing system.

The procedure for Shimano® Octalink external bearing crank installation:

a. Grease spindle surface and install drive side crank and spindle from the right side through both bearings.
b. Check the bearing adjusting nut is fully threaded against left crank (figure 7.20).
c. Grease splines of spindle end. Align splines of left arm to splines of axle. Install arm on axle.
d. Grease threads of crank bolt, install, and secure fully.
e. Install threaded crank cap using Shimano pin tool TL-FC35 (figure 7.21). Thread is left hand; turn counter-clockwise to install.

Loosen nut and turn clockwise against crank

Install crank cap with TL-FC35

Bearing adjustment is made after arm is mounted and fully secured. The adjusting nut turns against the bearing face to remove play and to stop the arms from moving side to side. It is only necessary to snug the ring against the bearing face. Do not turn the ring with excessive force. The nut can also be turned by hand (figure 7.22) or with Shimano TL-FC17. Secure adjusting nut binder bolt.

Turn nut to adjust lateral play in cranks

Crank removal requires a tool from Shimano, the TL-FR35. The left arm does not utilize the one-key release system and does not use the traditional crank puller.

The procedure for Shimano® Octalink external bearing crank removal:

a. Use the TL-FC-35 to remove the threaded crank cap ring clockwise. Cap ring acts to protect thread, and it does not retain bolt or secure arm.
b. Do not remove the crank bolt after removing the crank cap. Thread the TL-FC35 into the arm hand tight by turning counter-clockwise.
c. Use 8mm hex wrench and turn crank bolt counter-clockwise. Crank bolt will back against the TL-FC35 and pull the arm off the spindle (figure 7.23). Remove the TL-FC35 from the arm by turning it clockwise after arm is fully removed.

Turn bolt counter-clockwise with TL-FC35 installed in arm

Installation and Removal of Race Face® X-type Cranks

The spindle of the Race Face® X-type crankset is fitted permanently to the left arm. There is no crank end cap for bearing adjustment. Instead, the crank uses elastomer spacers that will preload the bearings when the arm is tightened. The alignment of the front rings to the rear sprockets, called "chainline", is manipulated with two spindle spacers, and each is 1mm thick. Using one spacer on the left and right side of the spindle will place the middle ring of the crankset 49mm from the center plane of the bike. Using only one spacer against the left arm will move the ring inward one millimeter for a chainline of 48mm (figure 7.24). Using two spaces on the right side will result in a 50mm chainline.

FIGURE: 7.24

Moveable chainline spacer installed next to left crank

The procedure for Race Face® X-type crank installation:

a. Grease spindle surface.
b. Install left crank with spindle through left side of bike after installing appropriate chainline washers. The fit of the spindle may be snug and some mild force may be necessary. Use a soft mallet with care. Guide the spindle through the right cup and install any needed chainline washers. Grease internal threads of spindle and grease spindle splines. Spline system of right arm is unique to the X-type and will not interchange with other ISIS Drive® types.
c. Align right arm 180-degrees from left arm and begin to turn bolt clockwise using an 8mm hex wrench. Secure bolt to a torque of 360 to 600 inch-pounds. Bolt will come to a "hard stop" as the arm fully presses to spindle.

The Race Face® X-type right side crank has a special one-key release system. The retaining cap uses a left-hand thread and is secured to the arm with a 10mm hex wrench. It is not necessary to remove the one-key system in order to remove the arm.

The procedure for Race Face® X-type crank removal:

a. Loosen counter-clockwise right side crank bolt with 8mm hex wrench. The one-key release system will remove arm from spindle.
b. Remove any spacers from spindle.
c. Pull left crank with spindle toward left. Use a soft mallet only if necessary to remove crank and spindle from bike.

Installation and Removal of Truvativ® Giga X Pipe and SRAM Cranksets

The spindle of the Truvativ® Giga X Pipe and SRAM crankset is permanently fixed to the drive side (right side) arm. The drive side cup has a rubber lip that compresses as the arms are pressed. As the left arm is tightened onto the spindle, it compresses into the lip to apply pressure to the bearings.

The procedure for crank installation:

a. Grease the splines and surface of the spindle.
b. Insert right side crank and spindle through the right side cup.
c. Install left arm and tighten to a torque of 420 to 480 inch-pounds (figure 7.25).

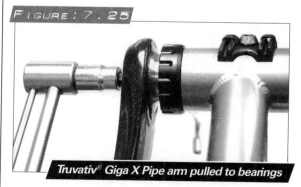

FIGURE: 7.25

Truvativ® Giga X Pipe arm pulled to bearings

The procedure for crank removal:
  a. Loosen the crank bolt on the left arm. The one-key release system pulls the arm from the spindle.
  b. Pull the right arm and spindle from the bearing cups. If necessary, use a soft mallet with care to remove the crank and spindle from the bike.

Campagnolo and Fulcrum: Ultra-Torque Crank

Ultra Torque left and right cranks are fitted with one-half of the spindle system. The end of spindle end is machined in a gear shape to mate with the opposite arm. The bearing is pressed tight to the arm spindle. The threaded cups act as a retainer for the bearings on the cranks.

Bearing removal and replacement for the Ultra Torque system requires special tooling and is not a recommend procedure for the home mechanic.

The procedure for Ultra-Torque crank removal:
  a. Use needle nose pliers to remove the bearing-retaining clip from the right side cup (figure 7.26).
  b. Use a long 10mm hex to loosen and remove the crank bolt from the center of the spindle (figure 7.27).
  c. Pull each arm from the bottom bracket.
  d. Remove the wavy washer from left cup.

FIGURE: 7.26

Remove bearing-retaining clip from cup

FIGURE: 7.27

Remove crank bolt with 10mm hex key

The bearing adjustment is by pressure from the "wavy washer" in the left side cup. This washer is used to account for variations in frame shell widths. For the common "English" or BSC shell, the acceptable width is from 67.2 to 68.8mm. For Italian-threaded bottom brackets, it is 69.2mm to 70.8mm.

The procedure for Ultra-Torque crank installation:
  a. Install wavy washer into left cup or place on left arm.
  b. Install right arm through right cup. Align left arm and install through left cup (figure 7.28).
  c. Apply grease or anti-seize to threads of crank bolt and install through right side axle center.
  d. Secure bolt fully. Recommended minimum torque is 370 inch pounds (42 Nm).
  e. Install bearing retaining clip to right cup.

FIGURE: 7.28

Install arm and wavy washer into left side cup

Non-Threaded Crankset- BB30 and BB90

There are also new bottom bracket and crank systems that are becoming available from some manufacturers. Service procedures and options will vary with design and make.

The BB30 system uses a non-threaded bottom bracket of approximately 42mm inside diameter. Cartridge bearings are pressed in place. The crank spindle is 30mm diameter and is fitted through the bearings (figure 7.29).

BB30 bottom bracket crank and compatible shell

The BB90 standard is a similar concept but uses a smaller bearing outside diameter and a 24mm inside diameter. The two systems do not interchange. Service is similar for both. Bearings are driven out from the inside, and then new bearings are pressed in the frame.

Bottom Bracket Bearing System

The cranks are attached to a spindle or axle, which is supported by the bottom bracket bearings. These bearings see a lot of load and wear from riding. Bottom bracket bearings are supported by the bottom bracket shell and are usually the lowest point of the bicycle. Any water that gets inside the frame tends to drain to the bottom bracket shell.

The bearing systems on bikes typically use ball bearings. Round ball bearings are trapped between two bearing surfaces. The bearing surfaces and balls are greased to minimize wear. These systems are shielded from dirt by covers and seals. Excessive exposure to the elements will increase wear on the bearing surfaces and shorten bearing life.

Bearing surfaces are made from hardened steel or, in some cases, from ceramic material. The surfaces are cut typically by grinding. Even the highest quality bearing surfaces will have slight microscopic grinding marks. Better quality bearing surfaces are ground smoother and will have less friction and resistance to turning. Ball bearings roll on curved bearing surfaces. Bearings will have some friction as they rotate. This is normal and does not affect the ride. Generally, the lighter load a bearing is expected to experience, the "smoother" the feel. Bearings experiencing more stress and load will seem to have more drag. For example, a bearing for a rear derailleur pulley, which is designed for lower loads, will seem to have less spinning resistance compared to a bottom bracket bearing, which experiences more load.

The two basic ball bearing systems are the cartridge bearing systems and the adjustable bearing systems. Neither system is inherently better for use on a bicycle. The adjustable-type systems can be overhauled, re-greased, and then adjusted. The cartridge-type systems rely on replacement of the cartridge bearing rather than cleaning and greasing.

Cartridge bearings use either an industrial or rolling element bearing. Ball bearings are trapped between inner and outer rotating races (figure 7.30). There should be no play between the inner and outer races of the cartridge. With use, play will develop between these two races and the entire cartridge unit will require replacement.

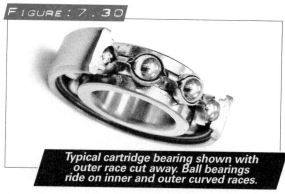

Typical cartridge bearing shown with outer race cut away. Ball bearings ride on inner and outer curved races.

A bottom bracket spindle must be compatible with the crank. The square-spindles and square cranks while appearing very similar are generally not interchangeable between brands. Consult the manufacturer. Additionally, there are different spindle lengths available. Spindle length is measured end to end. The longer the right side of the bottom bracket spindle, the farther the chainrings will sit from the frame. There are limits to where the cranks can be placed, as described in Chapter Nine, Derailleur Systems, Chainline, page 126.

Round spindle standards include the Shimano® Octalink V1 and Octalink V2 systems, ISIS Drive®, and the external bearing systems. The various external bearing crankset systems vary on interchangeability between manufacturers.

The common threading for bottom brackets is the ISO standard (International Thread Standard). This is also called the BSC (British Standard Cycle) or "English" threading, which is a thread size of 1.37 inches x 24 tpi. The left side (non-drive side) thread is a right-hand direction thread, which removes counter-clockwise and tightens clockwise. The right side (drive side) thread is a left-hand direction thread. It removes clockwise and tightens counter-clockwise.

There are some exceptions to the ISO bottom bracket threading. Bikes made in Italy may have both drive and non-drive right hand thread, which are both removed counter-clockwise. The thread sizing is 36mm x 24 tpi. This bottom bracket is too large to fit into an ISO sized frame. The ISO bottom bracket will simply slide into the larger "Italian" threading with no thread engagement. The Italian thread is often designated with "36 x 24" markings on the flange of the bottom bracket bearing. Additionally, French-made bikes prior to 1985 may have a 35mm x 1mm threading with left and right cups being right hand thread.

The bottom bracket must also be compatible with the shell width. There are now several possible standards. Shell width is measured from face to face of the shell in millimeters. Some bottom bracket models will work on more than one shell width. In Table 7.2, only the 68mm and the 73mm are currently common widths.

TABLE: 7.2 Bottom Bracket Shell Widths	
SHELL WIDTH- FACE TO FACE IN MILLIMETERS	TYPICAL USES
68mm	Many road and MTB bikes, both cross country and downhill.
70mm	Road bikes with the 36mm x 24tpi "Italian" threading.
73mm	Many MTB bikes, both cross country and downhill.
83mm	Downhill and freeride bikes.
100mm	Downhill, freeride and oversized tire bikes.

If a bottom bracket bearing seems to install with excessive force, the shell threads may require tapping (figure 7.31). A professional mechanic will be able to diagnose and repair this problem.

Another machining issue is called "facing" (figure 7.32). The left and right shell faces should be machined or faced so they are parallel to one another. The shell can become deformed during welding or even simply from being made less than precise. If the shell faces are deformed,

left and right side bearings may not be properly aligned to one another.

FIGURE: 7.31

Tapping the internal threads of a bottom bracket

FIGURE: 7.32

Facing the shell surface

As a rule, if the bearings use the shell face as a reference for the bearing race alignment, facing is important. If the bearings do not use the shell face for bearing race alignment, facing is not needed. There are cartridge-type bottom bracket bearings where the bottom bracket housing contains a non-removable and non-adjustable bearing. The bearing adjustment is made at the component factory and does not rely on the shell faces for bearing surface referencing. Unless the shell faces are extremely deformed, facing will not be required.

Bottom Bracket Tool Selection

Bottom brackets are designed with tool fittings to allow installation and removal. Do not attempt to "fake" the tool by unusual service techniques, such as with a punch and hammer. Table 7.3 outlines the common bottom bracket fittings and the Park Tool choice. The list of brands and models is not exhaustive because new models are brought to market often. Inspect the lockring or cups of the bottom bracket and check the Table 7.3.

Tools which interface

TABLE: 7.3 Bottom Bracket Tool Selection

BRAND / MODEL EXAMPLES	BOTTOM BRACKET FITTING	APPROPRIATE PARK TOOL PRODUCT	TOOL & NUMBER OF SPLINES OR NOTCHES IN BOTTOM BRACKET FITTING
Many Shimano® cartridge types, also Race Face®, FSA®			Park Tool BBT-22 20 splines
Bontrager®, Truvativ®			Park Tool BBT-18 8 notches
External bearing systems for Shimano® Hollowtech II, Campagnolo®, Race Face®, FSA®, Truvativ®		 	Park Tool BBT-9 16 notches / Park Tool BBT-19 16 notches
Campagnolo® Veloce, Mirage, Xenon		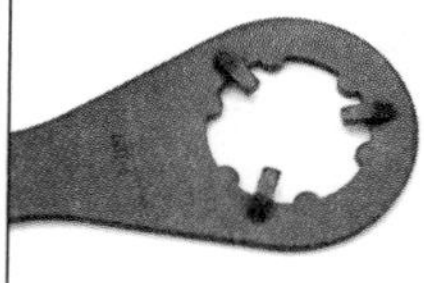	Park Tool BBT-4 6 notches
Campagnolo® Record, Chorus, Centaur			Park Tool BBT-5 12 splines
Adjustable type Shimano® Dura-Ace bottom brackets (BB-7700)			Park Tool BBT-7 6 notches
Lockring of various brands of adjustable bottom brackets		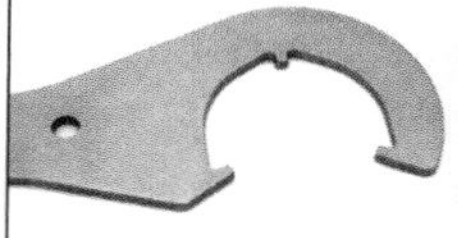	Park Tool HCW-5 3 or 6 notches (lockring on cup)
Adjustable bottom bracket, right side cup. Two wrench flats		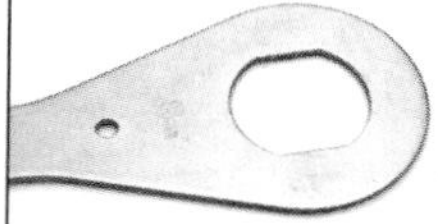	Park Tool HCW-4 2 flats at 36mm
Various adjustable bottom bracket left side cups			Park Tool SPA-1 2, 4, 6 or 8 holes of 3mm diameter

Park Tool

Cartridge Bottom Brackets

Cartridge bottom brackets use common industrial bearing designs, similar to bearings found in pumps, electrical motors, etc. These bearings are intended to be disposable. Generally, the bearings are used until they wear out, and then they are replaced.

For most brands of bottom brackets, the entire bottom bracket unit is replaced, including the spindle. To determine if the bottom bracket is worn out or has developed play, drop the chain off the chainrings to the inside. Grab both cranks firmly at the ends but do not hold the pedals. Push laterally with one hand and pull laterally with the other hand to force the arms side to side. If a knocking is felt, remove cranks and double check tightness of bearing locking cups or rings and check play again. If the cups are adequately tight and knocking continues, the bearings are worn, and the bottom bracket should be replaced. Next, spin the cranks while holding the frame (figure 7.33). Worn bearings will grind, and this can be felt through the frame as a vibration. If in doubt, compare the feeling of an old bottom bracket to that of one of a new bike.

FIGURE: 7.33
Spin cranks to feel for grinding of a worn bottom bracket bearing

Cartridge Bottom Bracket Removal and Installation
The procedure for cartridge bottom bracket removal:
  a. Remove both cranks.
  b. Insert bottom bracket cartridge tool fully into or onto fittings of non-drive cup (left side). Hold tool firmly in place while turning counter-clockwise to remove on ISO/BSC threaded bikes.
  c. Insert tool fully into or onto fitting of drive side (right side) cup. Remove by turning clockwise on ISO/BSC threaded bikes.

If the bottom bracket is difficult to remove, it can be useful to clamp the tool to the cup. If the spindle is hollow, use a quick release lever to hold the tool firmly in place (figure 7.34). If the spindle is not hollow, use a long bolt of the same thread as the crank bolt. The teeth of the cups may be shallow, and this technique can prevent the tool from slipping.

FIGURE: 7.34
Use skewer to secure tool to cup fittings

It is common for cartridge bottom brackets to be marked "Left" and "Right." These markings refer to side of bike, not thread direction (figure 7.35). The drive side of the bike is the "right" side, and the non-drive side is the "left" side. For the common ISO/BCS threading, the "right" side will have left hand threading, and the "left" side will have right hand threading.

FIGURE: 7.35
Bottom bracket marking indicating side of bike

There are two critical issues regarding thread preparation for the bottom bracket. First, the threads need lubrication to pull up fully tight. Second, the threads should be protected from corrosion. Grease will help for both issues, but anti-seize compounds are far more durable and are better at preventing corrosion (figure 7.36). Anti-seize is especially recommended for titanium frames.

Lubricating threads of the bottom bracket

Another thread option is to use a service removable thread-locker. Place a bead of the thread locker around the first three or four threads on both lockrings. The thread-lock will form a seal against water. Use of a thread locker is especially recommended for Italian-threaded bottom brackets, which tend to loosen during use.

Plastic lockrings or cups need only grease on the threads. Do not use thread-locker compounds on plastic as they may cause the plastic to become brittle.

When threading a bottom bracket into the frame, begin turning by hand to feel and avoid cross threading. Look at opposite side of the bottom bracket shell, and keep the spindle centered in the shell. If spindle appears off-center in the shell, it may be cross-threaded (figure 7.37).

If spindle appears off-center in the shell, bottom bracket may be cross-threaded

The procedure for cartridge bottom bracket installation:

    a. Prepare the threads of the bottom bracket with grease, anti-seize, or thread locker.

    b. Look on body of cartridge for "L" and "R" marking. The "L" goes to the left side of bike, and the "R" goes to the right (drive train) side. For most bikes, right side ("R") has a left-hand thread. Thread the drive train side by turning counter-clockwise. If bottom bracket has a plastic threaded side and a metal threaded side, install the metal threaded side first.

    c. Once threads are correctly aligned, thread body fully into bottom bracket shell using bottom bracket tool.

    d. Install locking cup or ring into other side of shell and tighten both sides to manufacturer's torque (figure 7.38). See Appendix B for torque specifications.

Use a torque wrench to secure and lock bottom bracket in place

Adjustable Bottom Brackets

Adjustable bottom brackets include some square-spindle bottom brackets and the Shimano® Dura-Ace 7700 bottom bracket. These bottom brackets may be dismantled and cleaned (figure 7.39). Adjustable-type bearing systems are sometimes referred to as "cup and cone" systems. A convex and a concave bearing race oppose one another, trapping the ball bearings between them. If the adjustment is too tight, there will be too much pressure on the bearing surfaces. The system will "bind" and quickly wear out. If the adjustment is too loose, there will be movement or "play" between the parts. This causes a knocking in the bearing surfaces, and the surfaces will wear out prematurely.

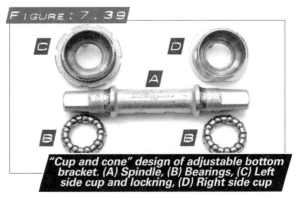

"Cup and cone" design of adjustable bottom bracket. (A) Spindle, (B) Bearings, (C) Left side cup and lockring, (D) Right side cup

ParkTool

For adjustable bearing systems, the bearing surfaces move on threaded parts. It is normal for threaded parts to have play between the internal and external threads. For example, a bearing cup will wiggle in the shell thread until the lockring is tightened down against the frame. Play in the thread is removed when a locking nut or ring is tightened. When checking bearing adjustments, the lockring must be tight. Play felt after the ring is tight will come from the bearing adjustment, not from thread movement.

The goal for adjustable-type bearings is to have the bearings rotate as freely as possible without any knocking or play. When beginning a bearing adjustment, start with it loose and then proceed to tighten the adjustment in small increments until the play disappears. This ensures the adjustment is as loose as possible but is without play. In most cases, try to make small changes in increments of $1/32$ of a complete rotation.

Adjustable Bottom Bracket Removal

When dismantling components, it is a good idea to take written notes of the parts orientation. For a bottom bracket spindle, one side of the spindle may be longer than the other side. Note which side was longer or shorter, and reassemble in the same orientation.

If the bottom bracket is being overhauled, it is optional to remove the fixed side (right side) cup. Removal makes inspection and cleaning easier. The cup may remain in the frame. It will simply slow the service.

The procedure for adjustable bottom bracket disassembly:
  a. Remove cranks.
  b. Using a lockring spanner, loosen and remove left side lockring.
  c. Use a pin spanner or appropriate tool and remove adjustable cup (left side) (figure 7.40).
  d. Remove bearings and spindle. Note and record if right side or left side of spindle seems longer.
  e. Remove any dust sleeve from inside the bottom bracket shell.
  f. Remove bearings from right side cup (inside shell).

  g. Fixed cups (right side) are commonly left hand threaded. If removing for service, use a fixed cup spanner and remove clockwise (for the common BSC threading).
  h. Clean all parts in solvent and dry.

FIGURE: 7.40
Remove adjustable cup (left side), lockring & bearings

After cleaning and drying all parts, inspect for wear and damage. View cups and spindle races for pitting and damage. There will likely be a smooth line worn on both cup and spindle. There should not be holes or gouges in either. Use a ballpoint pen to trace the bearing path (figure 7.41). Roughness and wear will be felt as the ball of the pen passes over worn areas. This roughness will get worse with use. It does not "smooth out" or "break-in" with time.

FIGURE: 7.41
Trace bearing surface to feel for roughness

If the ball bearings have a shiny silver color and are smooth, they can be re-used. If the bearings appear discolored, they should be replaced. The ball bearings are generally the last part of the system to wear out. If the bearings are worn, it is likely that the cups and races are also worn.

Adjustable Bottom Bracket Installation

Thread preparation is critical in bottom brackets. Use either grease or anti-seize for cups. Fixed cups (right-side) may also use mild thread-lockers rather than lubrication. The common bearing size for square-spindle adjustable bottom brackets is ¼ inch.

The procedure for adjustable bottom bracket installation:

a. Prepare threads using grease or anti-seize compound. Right side (drive side) cup may use a thread locker as an option.
b. If removed, install fixed cup (right side). Even if fixed cup was not removed, check for cup tightness. For ISO/English threading, turn counter-clockwise. Secure to a minimum of 360 inch-pounds.
c. Heavily grease bearing cages. Press grease into cage and between bearings.
d. Refer to notes from disassembly and place bearing retainer on fixed cup side (right side) of spindle. Place the open side of cage against the cone-shape of the spindle. Install spindle through shell and into fixed cup.
e. Install any dust sleeve.
f. Grease second bearing cage and install into adjustable cup (left side). Place the open side of the cage towards cone-shape of the spindle.
g. Thread adjustable cup (left side) into place.
h. Install but do not tighten lockring onto adjustable cup.

Adjustable Bottom Bracket Adjustment

Rotating bearings should be adjusted to be as loose a possible but without play or knocking. To ensure you are making adjustments in small increments, use a piece of tape as a reference. Use about two inches of masking tape and make pen marks on one edge every ⅛" (3mm). Stick the tape on the left side of the bottom bracket shell so the marks face outward. These will be reference marks when adjusting the bearings and represent the small increments used when turning the adjustable cup (figure 7.42).

Use a sticker for reference marks when adjusting bearings

If bottom bracket bearing surfaces are worn out, it will not be possible to have a smooth adjustment when play disappears. Worn bottom bracket parts will need to be replaced.

The adjustment procedure below assumes the fixed cup (right side) is fully secure. If the bottom bracket was not disassembled, it is still important to test that it is secure. Remove cranks and loosen left side cup by turning counter-clockwise ½ turn. Hold spanner firmly to right side cup and check its security by tightening counter-clockwise. If cup seems tight, trust that it is tight.

The procedure for adjusting bottom bracket bearings:

a. Re-install right crank only and tighten fully. Arm will be used as a lever to check for play in adjustment.
b. Gently tighten adjustable cup (left side) clockwise. Turn it just to the point you can feel it bump into the ball bearings.
c. Use marker and make a line on the cup face. Have a look at the reference tape and note which mark aligns with cup reference mark. It is also possible to use a mark already on the cup, such as the first letter of the manufacturer if the cup is stamped.
d. Hold the adjustable cup firmly with the correct spanner. Using the lockring spanner, tighten the lockring fully. Locking typically requires 300-360 pounds/inch.
e. Check for knocking in the spindle. Grab end of right crank and push left to right. Repeat this as you rotate the crank all the way around.
f. If there is no play, adjustment may be too tight. Loosen lockring and loosen cup slightly to create play. Secure lockring and check for play.

ParkTool

g. If there is knocking (play), make note of which reference tape mark aligns with the cup mark. Loosen the lockring counter-clockwise. Move the adjustable cup clockwise one mark at the reference tape. Secure the lockring and check for play.

h. Repeat tightening one mark at a time until play disappears, checking for play with the right crank in different positions of rotation. When play is not felt at any rotation, adjustment is finished.

i. Use solvent to remove pen mark from cup or frame.

j. Install left side crank.

Chainrings

Chainrings are toothed sprockets attached to the cranks. Cranks may be designed to accept one, two, or three chainrings. Some models of cranks are designed so the rings are replaceable. The old ring is unbolted and removed, and a new ring is installed. Different rings may also be fitted if the rider desires a different gear ratio. There are models of cranks that use chainrings permanently mounted to the arm, and the entire crankset must be replaced if the rings wear out or are damaged.

The part of the crank that attaches to the chainrings is called the "spider." The spider may have three, four, five, or six mounting arms. The chainring mounting holes must match the spider mounting holes in order to fit. As the chainrings turn, the mounting bolts trace a circle. This circle is called the "bolt circle diameter," abbreviated as BCD. New chainrings must match both the number of mounting holes and the bolt circle diameter (figure 7.43).

Bolt circle diameter of a five-arm crankset

If there are four or six arms on the crank, measure the bolt circle diameter using opposing chainring bolts. It is easier to measure edge-to-edge on the bolt, rather than center-to-center.

It is difficult to directly measure the BCD of five-arm spiders. Measure one "cord," which

is one side of the five-sided pentagon created by the bolts (figure 7.44). Measure from bolt to adjacent bolt. Multiply this figure by 1.70 (the mathematical constant for pentagons) to get the diameter, which is the BCD.

Measure pentagon cord by measuring bolt-to-bolt

Table 7.3 below lists the bolt-to-bolt (cord) measurements for the common BCD five bolt chainrings as well as the common BCD's for the four arm cranks.

TABLE: 7.3	Bolt Circle Diameter
BOLT CIRCLE DIAMETER (BCD)	CORD MEASUREMENT (FIVE SPIDER ARMS ONLY)
Four Arm Spider Cranks	
58	N/A
64	N/A
104	N/A
112	N/A
146	N/A
Five Arm Spider Cranks	
56	32.9
58	34.1
74	43.5
94	55.3
110	64.6
118	69.4
130	76.4
135	79.4

Chainring Replacement

Replaceable chainrings are held to the crank by special fine thread fasteners called chainring bolts. The bolt may use a Torx® T30 or a 5mm hex wrench. The nut is made with only a slot to hold. Use a chainring nut wrench, such as the Park Tool CNW-2, to hold the chainring nut while the bolt is turned. Chainring bolt threads should be lubricated or treated with a mild thread locker before installing and tightening.

Before removing the old chainrings, pay special attention to how they are oriented on the cranks, because there is a left and right side of the ring. Additionally, some chainrings may have specially shaped teeth and shifting ramps to assist shifting. These features require correct alignment on the crank for them to work. Inspect chainrings before removal and make a note on special ramps or markings (figure 7.45).

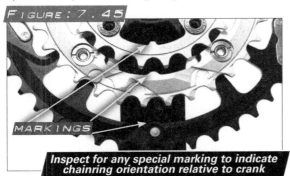

FIGURE: 7.45

MARKINGS

Inspect for any special marking to indicate chainring orientation relative to crank

Chainring Wear & Damage

The chain meshes with the chainring as it turns. The leading or forward part of the chainring tooth takes the load as the bike is ridden. With use, the tooth wears down, and eventually develops a hooked or "sharktooth" shape. The chainring teeth may also wear thin. Shifting performance will suffer and the chain may skip on the chainring when pressure is applied to the pedals. Compare old suspect rings to new ones of the same type (figure 7.46).

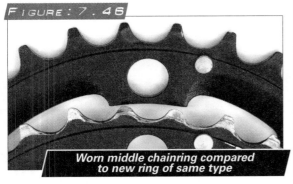

FIGURE: 7.46

Worn middle chainring compared to new ring of same type

If a tooth is bent, it may cause shifting problems. It may be possible to pry it back in line. Use a small adjustable wrench and close the jaws on the bent tooth. Bend the tooth back slowly while checking often so as not to over correct. Severely bent teeth may break off, but, even if the tooth breaks, the ring may still be useable. Ride the bike after the repair and shift back and forth testing the result. If shifting is

adequate, the ring is useable.

A bent tooth on the largest ring can be directly grabbed for alignment. Bent teeth on the middle or smallest rings are difficult to access with a tool. The bent tooth will typically have been bent inward, towards the bottom bracket. It must be bent back to the outside (away from the bottom bracket). The outer ring usually prevents any tool from working on the tooth. It is possible to remove the ring with the bent tooth for alignment.

Begin by spinning the rings without the chain in place. Inspect which tooth appears bent and mark the tooth on the ring. Remove the ring from the spider. Find the bent tooth. Use a small adjustable wrench to straighten the tooth. Do not grab on the ring itself, just the tooth. Hold the ring firmly below the wrench and bend the tooth slightly back. Compare bent tooth to the other teeth (figure 7.47). It may be necessary to remount the ring and try shifting. If shifting is poor, then remove and repeat the repair.

FIGURE: 7.47

Sight along the chainring to find any bent teeth

Chainrings may appear to wobble from side to side as the cranks turn. There may be some slight alignment problems with the chainrings or with the mounting arm. If the wobble is minor, it may even be improved by moving the drive side crank to a different spindle orientation. If the movement is enough to affect derailleur setting, it is sometimes possible to bend rings to improve run-out.

The ring may also become bent from impacts, such as a chain getting jammed between the frame and the ring or even from very stressful riding loads. Some emergency repair by rebending is possible, but the ring will never be perfect. Four-spider rings are especially susceptible to bending under hard use. It is best to replace bent rings rather than repair them.

ParkTool

CHAPTER 8

Chains

The chain connects the front chainring(s) to the rear sprocket(s). Chains are made of repeating pairs of outer and inner plates are held together by rivets (figure 8.1). A roller separates the pair of inner plates. The rivet is pressed tightly through the outer plates and pivots freely on the inner plates and roller.

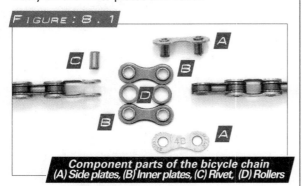

FIGURE: 8.1

Component parts of the bicycle chain
(A) Side plates, (B) Inner plates, (C) Rivet, (D) Rollers

Chains pass through the frame to form a closed loop. Some chains use either a special connection rivet or a "master link" to close the loop. Master links are specially made outer plates that mate together to hold the chain closed. Older-style chains use any of the original plate rivets themselves to join the chain.

Drive train manufacturers design the derailleurs, rear sprockets, shifters, and chain to work together as a system. Chains vary in side plate design and width. These differences cause variations in shifting performance between brands and models. Chains should be selected to be brand-compatible with the particular shifting system of the bicycle. Contact chain manufacturers for details on compatibility.

Chain specification is designated by width of the roller and by the width measured across the rivet. There are two roller widths commonly used on bicycles: 3/32-inch, used on derailleur bicycles, and 1/8-inch, used on some one-speed bikes.

Chain width across the rivets varies correspondingly with the number of rear sprockets. Bicycles with ten sprockets on the rear hub use chains approximately 6mm wide. Nine sprocket bikes may use chains 6.5 to 7mm. Six, seven, and eight-speed systems use a chain approximately 7mm wide. A narrower chain can generally be used on sprockets designed for wider chains. A wider chain, however, cannot be used on sprocket sets designed for narrow chains. One speed chains measure approximately 9mm, and are not designed for shifting on multi-speed cogs.

Chain Sizing for Derailleur Bikes

A chain that is too long or too short may cause shifting and riding problems. A chain that is too long will sag between derailleur and chainrings when the bike is in the smallest rear sprocket and smallest front chainring (figure 8.2). The chain may have low tension in this position, but it should not droop or sag onto the chainstay.

FIGURE: 8.2

Chain sag in the smallest front to smallest rear sprocket position

Another symptom of a long chain is the chain contacts itself as it passes by the upper derailleur pulley when the bike is in the smallest rear sprocket and smallest front chainring (figure 8.3).

FIGURE: 8.3

Chain contact indicating chain is too long

Conversely, a chain may be too short. Shift to the largest chainring and second largest rear sprocket to diagnose a short chain. Chain tension will be tighter in this position. Inspect chain for a double bend ("S" bend) as it passes through the pulley wheels (figure 8.4). Shift slowly and carefully to largest rear sprocket. If chain appears to jam, it is too short. Even if the chain does shift but loses the double bend at the pulley wheels, it is too short (figure 8.5). In extreme cases, trying to shift to the large rear sprocket and largest front chainring combination may damage the derailleur and or the derailleur hanger.

Double bends at pulley wheels indicate adequate chain length

Double bends are lost with chain only one link too short

The rear derailleur cage takes up chain slack as the chain is moved between the various front and rear gear combinations. Some bicycles are fitted with sprocket combinations and derailleur models that do not allow the derailleur to take up the chain slack in every gear combination. The sprocket selections exceed the capacity of the derailleur.

If the derailleur capacity does not match or exceed the sprocket range on the bike, the chain length will appear either too long in the smallest sprocket to smallest chainring combination, or too short in the largest sprocket to largest chainring combination. This is also the case when a "short cage" derailleur is used on a bike with a wide gear range. When using a derailleur that does not meet the gearing capacity, it will be necessary to avoid certain gear combinations that cause problems in pedaling or shifting. For more discussion of derailleur capacity, see Derailleur Capacity & Maximum Sprocket Size in Chapter 9, Derailleur Systems.

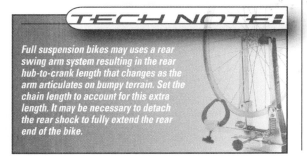

TECH NOTE!

Full suspension bikes may uses a rear swing arm system resulting in the rear hub-to-crank length that changes as the arm articulates on bumpy terrain. Set the chain length to account for this extra length. It may be necessary to detach the rear shock to fully extend the rear end of the bike.

New chains are packaged longer than needed for most bicycles. New chains almost always have to be "cut" (a link separated or removed) to fit each bike. To remove a chain, a link also must be separated or cut. To install and size a new chain, a chain tool is required.

Chain tools are made up of a driving pin and a cradle to hold the chain-roller (figure 8.6). Some models have two chain support cradles. The primary cradle supports the chain for pressing the chain rivet in and out. The tight link cradle is only for fixing a tight link. The Park Tool CT-4 Professional Chain Tool uses a pocket to hold the chain rather then a cradle system.

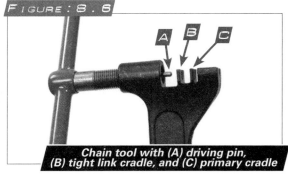

Chain tool with (A) driving pin, (B) tight link cradle, and (C) primary cradle

The chain is sized to the particular bike and gear combination. Removal of the old chain is part of discussion of Shimano®, Campagnolo®, SRAM®, master-link, and re-useable rivet chains in the sections that follow.

The procedure for sizing derailleur chain:

a. With no chain is place, use shift levers to position the front derailleur over the largest chainring and the rear derailleur on the smallest sprocket.

b. Thread the new chain through the front derailleur, but do not thread the chain through the rear derailleur. This is for sizing the chain only and not for routing and joining the chain. Simply wrap the chain around the largest front chainring and around the largest rear sprocket.

c. Pull the chain tight and note the closest rivet where the two ends could be joined (figure 8.7). Keep in mind a chain can only be joined by mating inner and outer plates. If the selected inner and outer sections will not meet, round up and move to the next closest pair that would be possible to join.

d. From the closest rivet where it could be joined, count over an additional two rivets (figure 8.8). This is adding one-inch to the length to the shortest length from step "d".

e. Cut the chain at this point. Cutting the chain too long will be easier to rectify than cutting it too short. Cut the end with inner plates. See below for the procedures for cutting specific brands of chains.

FIGURE : 8 . 7

Wrap chain around largest front and rear sprockets

FIGURE : 8 . 8

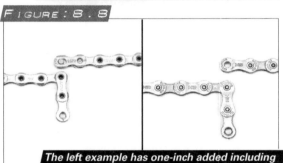

The left example has one-inch added including master link. The right example uses special connecting rivet and also has one-inch added.

If a new chain is being installed and the old chain is the correct length, the new chain may be shortened to match before installation. Remove the old chain and lay it on a flat surface with the plates aligned vertically. Pull the chain straight. Lay the new chain next to the old chain in the same fashion with inner plates of both chains at one end. The new chain may not exactly match rivet to rivet toward the end of the chains. Push the links of the old worn chain back to match up with pins of the new chain. Locate the matching end rivet on the new chain with the rivet on the old chain. You must also account for any master link used. Cut at this point.

Shimano® Chain With Connecting Rivet

Shimano® chains use a special connecting rivet to install new or to remove and re-install. This connecting rivet has special flaring that is guided in by a long, tapered pilot (figure 8.9). The pilot

is snapped off after rivet is fully installed. Only Shimano® brand chains should use the Shimano® connecting rivet. The 7- and 8-speed chains use a black connecting rivet. The narrower 9-speed chain uses a silver-colored connecting rivet. The Shimano® CN-7800 chain for 10-speeds uses a silver colored rivet with an extra-machined line for identification on the pilot. The Shimano® CN-7801 or CN-6600 chain for 10-speed sprockets uses a connecting rivet with three machined identification lines. The 10-speed chain rivets are not interchangeable.

FIGURE : 8 . 9

A   B   C   D

Special connecting rivets from Shimano®
(A) Rivet for 7 or 8 speed chains
(B) Rivet for 9-speed chains
(C) Rivet for CN-7800 10-speed chains
(D) Rivet for CN-7801/CN-6600 10-speed chains

The procedure for removing the Shimano® chain:

a. Select a chain rivet identical to adjacent rivets. Do not select a previously installed connecting rivet or a rivet immediately adjacent to a connecting rivet.

b. Place the roller of the chain fully in the primary cradle of the chain tool.

c. Turn the chain tool pin until it contacts the chain rivet and stop. Inspect that the chain tool pin is centered on rivet.

d. Turn handle and drive rivet from chain plates (figure 8.10). If tool will not fully drive the rivet from the chain, the special connecting rivet will be used to drive out the original rivet when joining the chain.

e. Back out chain tool pin and lift chain out of cradle.

f. Remove chain from bicycle.

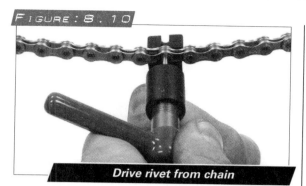

Drive rivet from chain

The design of the Shimano® chain requires that the special connecting rivet lead the outer chain plates as it engages the sprockets (figure 8.11). When installing the Shimano® chain, insert the connecting rivet into the left rivet of an outer plate when viewing the chain between the lower derailleur pulley and lower section of front chain wheel.

Connecting rivet correctly pressed into leading side of outer plates

The procedure for installing the Shimano® chain:

  a. Lubricate connecting rivet.

  b. Install correct Shimano® connecting rivet into chain outer plate. The tapered end enters the side plate first. The connecting rivet will protrude toward mechanic and will be driven toward the bike.

  c. Unthread chain tool pin into tool body to make room for special connecting chain rivet in cradle of tool.

  d. Place chain roller with rivet into primary cradle of chain tool.

  e. Drive connecting rivet into chain (figure 8.12). The connecting rivet will drive out the original rivet if it was left in chain. Continue to drive chain tool pin until it is almost adjacent to outer side plate.

  f. Remove the chain from the tool and inspect the rivet. The non-tapered end of connecting rivet should protrude same as any neighboring rivet. Press further with the chain tool pin if necessary.

  g. Break off pilot of connecting rivet. Use groove of CT-3 or CT-5 Chain Tool body, or hole in body of CT-4, and twist pilot sideways (figure 8.13). Pliers can also be used to break pilot. Inspect rivet again and press further if necessary. Rivet should be centered between outer plates.

  h. Inspect for tight links and repair as necessary. See page 100, Tight Link Repair. Rivet should be centered between outer plates.

Drive new connecting rivet into chain

Break off pilot after connecting rivet is pressed

After installing a replacement chain rivet, the rivet is left in the chain and never again removed to separate the chain. Re-using the same rivet hole wears plate holes and may weaken the chain or cause it to snap during a ride. Use other original rivets for future chain cutting.

Campagnolo® 10-speed Chain

Campagnolo® 10-speed chains use a special system called the HD-Link for joining chains. A new chain will be joined with only one special rivet. If a chain is removed from a bike, however, it must be joined with the HD-Link, which consists of a short section of links and two special piloted rivets. The HD-Link is 7 links of the chain. There are outer plates at each end (figure 8.14). These ends must attach to the inner plate section of the chain. It is necessary to shorten the chain by as many links as the section that is installed with the HD-Link.

Campagnolo® HD-link and
the two piloted rivets

The procedure for installing the Campagnolo® chain:

a. Remove old chain. Cut at section of chain opposite any special rivets. Pull chain from bike.

b. If re-installing the original chain, shorten chain to amount equal to HD-Link. Remove 7 links from side with outer plates. Each end of the chain must have inner plates to connect to the outer plates of the HD-link.

c. Lubricate HD-Link pilots and rivets.

d. The rivet uses a removable pilot. Engage rivet into pilot and engage both in the chain plate facing inward, which is the plate facing the spokes. The pilot is then pushing outward and away from the spokes. The chain tool handle should be toward the spokes, and the tool pin should drive toward the mechanic and away from the bike's mid plane (figure 8.15).

e. When driving the rivet, it is especially important to press downward with the thumb on top of the chain to keep it fully engaged in the tool. The Park Tool CT-4 uses a pocket to hold chain in place (figure 8.16).

f. After the rivet is fully pressed, remove the pilot by pulling outward. Inspect rivet for centering between outer plates.

g. Repeat process for second rivet and pilot as necessary.

Push the Campagnolo connecting
rivet from inside the bike outward

Park Tool CT-4 with special
chain holding pocket

Chain With "Master-link"

Several chain manufacturers offer a "master-link" to join the chain, which allows the end of the chain to be joined without a connecting rivet. Be sure to read the manufacturer's specific directions. Typically, the bicycle chain ends must have inner plates on each end before joining. Neither chain end has an outer plate with a rivet. The master link comes as two outer plates joined by an inner rivet, which snap together. Install one piece through the inside face of the chain and install second piece through the outside of the other chain end (figure 8.17). Engage the two pieces so link rivet mates to link plate hole. Pull chain to lock the link. To fully lock chain, move link to top section between rear sprockets and front chainrings. Hold wheel and press on pedals to lock link. Inspect link to ensure that it is fully engaged.

Common derailleur chain master link

Some brands of master links are re-useable, while others must be replaced after each removal. Use a chain tool on the rivet of a non-removable master link and push it through the outer plate. This will destroy the link. Install a new master link when installing the chain.

For re-useable master links, drop the chain off the front rings to relax tension. Squeeze the outer plates together. Push one plate forward and one plate backward. This will disengage the two outer plates. Pull plates sideways and remove the master link pieces from the chain (figure 8.18).

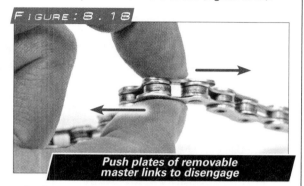

FIGURE: 8.18

Push plates of removable master links to disengage

Chain With Reusable Rivets

There are some brands and models of chains that are serviced by pressing out a rivet partially, then re-pressing the same rivet to join the chain. Generally, these tend to be only older style for the wider chains for 5-, 6-, or 7- cog rear sprocket sets, or for two-sprocket bikes. Check the manufacturer's literature when in doubt.

The procedure for removing chain with re-useable rivets:

    a. Place a roller of the chain fully in the primary cradle of the chain tool.

    b. Drive chain tool pin until it contacts chain rivet.

    c. For most brand chain tools, turn handle 5 complete turns (4 complete turns for the Park Tool CT-3). Use care not to drive out chain rivet.

    d. Back out the chain tool pin and lift chain out of cradle.

    e. Grab chain on either side of protruding rivet. Flex chain toward the protruding chain rivet and pull on chain to separate.

    f. Remove from bicycle by pulling on rivet end of chain.

The procedure for installing chains with re-useable rivets:

    a. Re-install chain on bike with protruding rivet facing toward mechanic.

    b. Open empty outer plates slightly and insert inner plates. Push inner plates until hole aligns with chain rivet.

    c. Back the chain tool pin into tool body to make room for chain rivet.

    d. Place roller into primary cradle with chain rivet facing chain tool pin.

    e. Drive chain rivet back into chain. Take care to center rivet exactly between both outer plates. If more chain rivet appears on one side of outer plate than other, push rivet until it is evenly spaced (figure 8.19).

    f. Inspect for tight links and repair as necessary. See page 100 Tight Link Repair.

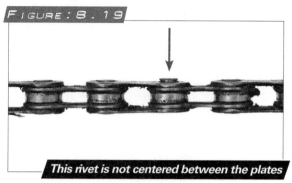

FIGURE: 8.19

This rivet is not centered between the plates

New Chain Installation on Derailleur Bikes

It is necessary to route the correctly sized or cut chain through the front derailleur, rear derailleur, and frame before it is joined. It may be useful to have another derailleur bike on hand as an example of chain routing when attempting this procedure. The process described here will ensure that the left outer plate on the lower section of chain will receive the Shimano® connecting rivet (if a connecting rivet is used).

The procedure for installing a sized chain:

    a. Shift derailleur to smallest front and rear sprockets.

    b. Beginning at crankset, feed the end of chain with inner plates between the cages of the front derailleur and back to the top of the rear sprockets (figure 8.20).

    c. Guide chain over the top and then behind smallest rear sprocket.

    d. Pass chain in front of top derailleur pulley and then in a straight line to the backside of the lower pulley. Be sure chain stays inside built-in guides on the cage (figure 8.21).

    e. Pull chain end toward chainrings.

    f. Join chain according to type or model of chain described in section on Chain Cutting. If tension makes joining chain difficult, drop chain off chainring and onto bottom bracket.

    g. Test chain for tight link and repair as necessary. See page 100, Tight Link Repair.

Feed chain from front to back

Route chain through rear derailleur

Tight Link Repair

A tight link occurs when a chain does not pass smoothly through the bends of the rear derailleur. The inner plates and outer plates do not pivot freely around the rivet and feel "tight" when the chain bends. This may be from a lack of lubrication at the offending link or the result of improper chain installation. If the two outer chain plates are pushed tightly against the inner chain plates, the link will tend to hop and skip at the derailleur. If the pressure on the inner plates can be removed, the tight link can be fixed.

Some chain tools have a tight link repair system built into the tool. Some very narrow chains may not fit the tight link cradle. Repair these narrow chains by flexing by hand as described below.

To locate a tight link, put the chain in the smallest rear sprocket in back and on the middle ring of a triple crankset or the smallest ring of a double crankset. This relieves tension on the chain and allows problem links to show up. Back pedal slowly and watch chain as it passes through the two pulley wheels of the rear derailleur. Look for a popping or jumping of the chain or movement in the derailleur arm. Keep backpedaling slowly. Tight links should show up as they pass by the bends of the lower pulley wheel (figure 8.22).

Watch for jumping or hopping of chain while backpedaling

Isolate the tight link and move it to the lower section of chain between chainring and rear sprockets. Engage tight rivet in tight link cradle. Turn chain tool handle until the pin just touches rivet of tight link and note the position of the handle (figure 8.23). Turn handle only ⅛ turn clockwise. Remove chain tool and feel tight link. Repeat as necessary, pushing rivet from other side of chain. Inspect chain rivet. Rivet must be centered in chain plates.

Press as little as necessary to spread outer plates of tight link

It is also possible to repair tight links without the tight link cradle system. This method requires physically stressing and flexing the chain laterally. Use care not to bend and deform the plates by using too much force. To avoid damaging your chain, practice on a section of scrap chain. Use care when handling a dirty chain. If this is a problem, use a rag over the chain.

Locate the tight link as described above. Grab either side of chain with your hands, and place both thumbs at the tight rivet. Pull outward with your hands, while pressing inward with your thumbs to flex the tight link (figure 8.24). Reverse pressure to flex chain the opposite direction. Press inward with your hands while pressing outward with the index fingers centered on tight rivet. Test link to see if it moves freely and repeat if necessary.

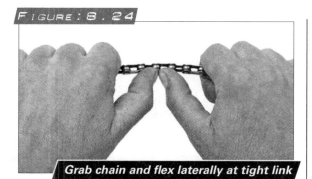
Grab chain and flex laterally at tight link

Chain sizing and tension adjustment: two-sprocket bicycles

Two-sprocket bicycles or "single speeds" are bikes with a single sprocket at the cranks and a single sprocket at the rear wheel. Two-sprocket bikes include most of the internally-geared hub bikes, one-speed bikes (such a coaster brake bikes), BMX/Freestyle, and track bikes. These bikes require a shorter chain than derailleur-equipped bicycles.

Typically, two-sprocket bicycles use horizontal dropouts. This allows chain tension to be adjusted by moving the rear sprocket forward or backwards relative to the front sprocket. Dropouts may be either forward or backwards facing (figure 8.25).

Horizontal dropout on a one-speed bicycle

Chain length for bikes without a chain tension device is ideally set to allow the hub axle to sit approximately half-way in the dropouts. Similar to derailleur chains, the length is changed in increments of 1-inch.

The procedure for determining two-sprocket chain length:

a. Install rear wheel in the bike. For horizontal dropouts, place the axle all the way forward in the dropout slot. With forward facing dropouts, secure the axle nut so they are fully engaged on dropouts but as much forward as possible.

b. Wrap the chain around the front and rear sprockets. The front sprocket can be used to help hold the end of the chain while determining chain length.

c. Place the chain end on the front ring so the chain end will be on the ring about the 2 or 3 o'clock position (figure 8.26). Engage any master link to account for the extra length when determining chain length.

d. Pull the chain snug and find the closest rivet on the lower section that would connect to end coming from the upper section. The outer plate must attach to an inner plate.

e. If the appropriate inner and outer plates of the chain ends are short of meeting, add two rivets (1- inch) to the chain length. If appropriate chain ends meet with no chain slack, add one inch to chain length. The chain must have enough slack in this position to allow it to be lifted from front ring.

f. Make note of the appropriate rivet to use in shorting the chain.

g. Remove the rear wheel and shorten the chain accordingly.

h. With chain correctly routed through frame, join ends of chain.

i. Install wheel and confirm chain length and chain tension are acceptable.

Use front ring to help hold chain end

Chain Tension- Two sprocket Bikes without tension idler device

Chain tension on two-sprocket bikes should be set tight enough so that it does not come off during use and operates smoothly when pedaled. Bikes without a chain tension idler arm are adjusted by moving the rear hub forward or backward in the dropouts.

The procedure for adjusting two-sprocket chain tension:

a. Install the rear wheel with chain over both rear and front sprockets.

b. Pull back on wheel and align wheel centered in frame. Secure axle nuts or quick release.

c. Check tension on chain. Push the chain downward and upward in the middle. There should be approximately a total of one inch (25mm) movement of the chain up and down between the front and rear sprockets (figure 8.27).

d. To change the tension, loosen the axle nuts and move the wheel forward or back slightly. Inspect that rear wheel is centered in frame and resecure axle nuts.

e. Turn pedals and check for any tight and loose positions as the crank arms turn. It is not uncommon for sprockets to be out of round. This will result in the chain being tighter in some points of its rotation. After setting chain tension, pedal the bike in a repair stand and check the tension all the way through the crank rotation. If necessary, readjust so there is only one-quarter inch (6mm) movement at the tightest point.

f. Test for a loose adjustment. Pedal and push sideways on the chain at a point in between the front and rear sprockets. The chain will make a rattling sound, but it should not derail. If the chain comes off, increase tension by moving the wheel further back.

g. If the bike uses a coaster brake or a band brake, secure the brake arm to the bike.

Pull up and down at middle of chain to test tension

Chain Tension Using Idler Chain Tension Device

If the bicycle uses a vertical dropout, it is typically necessary to use an idler wheel as a tension device. Vertical dropouts do not permit the adjustments necessary to set chain tension. A chain tensioner is fitted to the derailleur mount, and provides a single pulley wheel that will tension the chain (figure 8.28). A common rear derailleur may also be used as a tensioner idler simply by setting the limit screw so the upper pulley is aligned with the single cog.

Vertical dropout with a chain tension device

The chain tension idler arm is similar to the cage of a derailleur. A spring gives tension to the idler pulley, which will take up chain slack. To determine chain length, wrap the chain over front and rear sprockets, and around the pulley. Pull chain tightly to determine shortest possible length and then add 1 inches (2 links) of extra chain. Select link and cut chain accordingly.

Chain Tension: Eccentric Bottom Brackets on Tandem and Single Speeds

The eccentric bottom bracket design allows the crank and rings to move forward or backward to adjust chain tension. It is found on the front part of tandems and some single-speed bikes. Eccentric bottom brackets use an oversized shell that houses the bottom bracket bearing unit (figure 8.29). The axle is offset to the center of the shell. When the eccentric is rotated around in the frame shell, the crankset will get farther away, and then closer to the rear axle. The eccentric is rotated until there is correct chain tension and then locked in position.

Eccentric bottom bracket with setscrew binders

There are several systems of locking the eccentric. The frame shell may be split and held secure with a pinch-bolt, similar to stems or seat tube clamping systems. Other designs use a wedge-bolt system, similar to wedge-type quill stems. The bolt tightens and the wedge jams inside the frame shell to hold the eccentric. Another option uses setscrew fittings welded into the shell.

To set chain tension with eccentric systems begin by loosening the binder on the bottom bracket shell. There will commonly be pinholes for a pin spanner such as the Park Tool SPA-1. Rotate the eccentric in the shell and note changes in chain tension. Tension increases when crank is rotated forward. Set tension so there is approximately ½" (12mm) play in chain when pulled up and down between front and rear sprockets.

Tandem bicycles connect the front rider ("captain") to the person behind ("stoker") by a single loop of chain. The chain is engaged on the front ring and rear ring such that front and rear cranks are synchronized.

To install a front tandem chain, loosen eccentric and rotate bottom bracket so spindle is rotated toward the back. Begin with both left side cranks pointing directly down at the 6 o'clock position. It can help to remove the right side cranks, which allows the left side arms to point downward from their weight.

Pull the connecting chain taut above the front and rear rings. Use care not to move cranks and lay chain onto rings. Joint chain at lower section of chain. Chain length is set in one-inch increments. Only inner and outer sections of chain may be joined. Pull chain snug to determine which link to cut. Cut the next link one inch longer if necessary. Set chain tension with eccentric as described above.

Chain Wear and Damage

The chain is a critical part of bicycle performance and safety. Chain will tend to fail when under load, which is the worst possible time. The common cause of chain failure is the result of a rivet being pulled from an outer plate (figure 8.30). This is typically the result of a poorly installed chain. Inspect chains often. Sight the chain from above and look at each rivet for centering in the side plates. If a rivet sticks out of one plate more than the other links, the suspect link may fail. Use the chain tool to correct this problem. Also inspect the side plates for spreading. If a chain becomes jammed during an over shift, it may stress the plates, pulling them apart. Inspect for twists and wear at the rollers (figures 8.31 and 8.32).

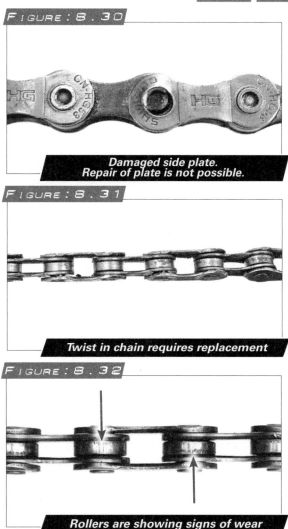

FIGURE: 8.30

Damaged side plate. Repair of plate is not possible.

FIGURE: 8.31

Twist in chain requires replacement

FIGURE: 8.32

Rollers are showing signs of wear

As the chain is used, wear develops at the rivet and inner plates where it pivots (figure 8.33). This wear or "play" is at each link. The cumulative effect of wear in many links is that the chain appears to "stretch." However, chain plates do not literally stretch and get longer; the wear is in the joint and rivet. Reversing the chain or flipping the chain around will not add to chain life, as the rivets will still have the same amount of wear.

FIGURE: 8.33

WORN

NEW

Worn rivet on left compared to new rivet on right

Bicycle sprocket teeth are cut to fit chains with one-half inch between each rivet, but not even brand new bicycle chains measure exactly one-half inch between rivets. A small amount of play must be included for new chains to bend. As the chain is ridden and it wears, play at each link gets greater, and the distance between each rivet increases. Eventually, the chain rollers will no longer sit fully down in the sprocket teeth. The rollers will begin to ride up the shoulder of the sprocket teeth. The chain will then skip over the teeth, especially when extra force is applied to the pedals. Although chain-manufacturers vary, most recommend 9- and 10-speed chains be replaced when the chain reaches approximately 0.75 of 1% wear from the nominal ½ inch pitch. This wear can be measured with chain measuring tools such as the Park Tool CC-2 or CC-3 Chain Wear Indicators (figure 8.34). Replacing worn chains will help to get more life out the rear sprockets, which tend to more expensive.

FIGURE: 8.34

The Park Tool CC-3 Chain Checker wear indicator fitting in chain, showing the need for chain replacement

As the bike is ridden, the entire drive train will wear. Generally, it is most economical to replace the cheapest item first in order to extend the overall life of the drive train. The cheapest component of the chainrings, chain, and rear sprockets is the chain, and it also suffers the most wear. Chains and sprockets often wear out together. If a new chain skips over worn rear sprockets or front sprockets, then the sprockets must also be replaced.

Chain Cleaning

There are more moving parts in the chain than any other part on the bike. Dirt and grit in the chain will wear on the rivets. Cleaning will add life to the chain and improve performance. Before cleaning the chain, brush clean the derailleur pulley wheels. It may be necessary to scrape the sides with a screwdriver if extremely dirty. Scrape rear sprockets with gear comb, such as the Park Tool GSC-1, or the blade of a thin screwdriver. Also wipe the chainrings if they are extremely dirty before cleaning the chain.

Chain cleaning tools, such as the Park Tool CM-5 Cyclone Chain Scrubber, make cleaning the chain easier. Generally, these systems are boxes that hold solvent and brushes. Passing through the brushes and solvent cleans the chain. Follow manufacturer's directions for use. Expect some spray of dirt and solvent when using any chain cleaner. Using a diluted soap solution for a second scrub will also help the cleaning process. To protect the floor, place newspaper or a drop cloth under the bike. Used as part of a regular cleaning schedule, these systems can add to the life of the chain (figure 8.35).

FIGURE: 8.35

A chain cleaning system speeds chain cleaning

Chains can also be removed and cleaned off the bike. Use a sink, pan, or large can. Remove the chain, grab by one end, and fold once in the middle. Lay the chain on a flat surface and coil the chain with loose ends in middle. Place chain in the pan and cover with solvent. Allow it to soak for some time. Use rubber gloves to protect the hands and work with adequate ventilation. Use a stiff bristle brush and scrub the plates on both sides of the chain. Unfold the chain and scrub downward on rollers and between side plates. Flip chain and scrub other side the same way. Rinse chain in solvent. Remove it from solvent and allow solvent to drip off as much as possible. Wipe with rag and allow to completely dry before lubricating. If available, use compressed air to blow-dry the chain, especially between rollers. Wear safety glasses when using compressed air to blow dry the chain.

Dispose of old solvent properly. Contact your local hazardous waste disposal site, state, or county agency.

Chain Lubrication

Chain rivets and link pivots require lubrication. The chain rivet and the narrower pair of chain plates rotate when traveling around a sprocket. Lubrication is required only at the rivet, not all over the outer plates. A drip applicator helps avoid applying too much lubrication, which can attract dirt. Proper lubrication will take time and patience. While lubricating, inspect the chain rollers and rivets.

It is best, of course, to begin with a clean chain. In any case, wipe chain off with a rag. Inspect chain for a master link or connecting rivet to act as a reference. Apply a drop of lubricant on each roller and at each side plate at the rivet (figure 8.36). Lubricate each rivet between rear sprockets and front chainring. Turn pedals backwards to advance to the next section of unlubricated chain. Lubricate this section and again advance chain. Continue until each rivet is lubricated once. Avoid over-lubricating the chain.

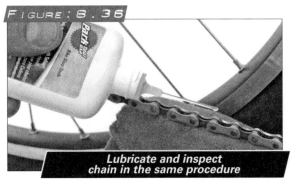

FIGURE: 8.36

Lubricate and inspect chain in the same procedure

After lubricating, turn pedals repeatedly to allow lubricant to work into pivots. Wipe outside of chain with a rag to remove excess lubricant. Repeat when chain appears dry.

CHAPTER 9

Derailleur System

Derailleur bicycles have several sprockets on the rear hub and may have multiple chainrings on the front cranks. By using different combinations, the cyclist will find low gear ratios for going uphill and high gear ratios for going downhill. The derailleur pushes or "derails" the chain to move it from one sprocket to another. The derailleur system consists of the shift levers, cable housing, derailleur cable, and the derailleurs. The entire system requires occasional maintenance, adjustment, and parts replacement.

Some manufacturers use reference numbers on shift levers. These are arbitrary numbers and do not represent gear ratio order. For example, the number "6" showing on a lever does not mean the sixth gear out of the total number of ratios available. There is no agreement between manufacturers on these reference numbers, and they will not be used here. This chapter will use the terms "inner" and "outer" sprockets, as well as "smallest" and "largest" sprocket.

Cable System

The connection between the shift lever and the derailleur is the cable system. The cable system consists of the inner derailleur cable and outer derailleur housing. The housing is the casing that routes the derailleur cable from the shift lever to the frame and then eventually to the derailleur. Motion of the derailleur cable causes the derailleur to move. Dirty, rusty, or worn derailleur cables and housing will not consistently and effectively transfer the shift lever motion to the derailleur.

Derailleur cable systems generally use "compressionless" derailleur housing. Compressionless housing is stiffer than brake housing and offers better shifting performance. The derailleur cable runs inside a plastic liner, which is surrounded by support wires that run longitudinally with the cable (figure 9.1). Compressionless housing is available in a 4mm or 5mm outside diameter. There is no effective difference between the two, but the mandatory housing end caps must match the housing diameter.

FIGURE: 9.1

Compressionless derailleur housing with outer plastic cover cut away showing support wires inside

"Braided" or "woven" housing may be used for both brake and derailleur housing (figure 9.2). The outer support wires are woven in a mesh around the liner.

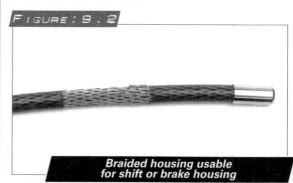

FIGURE: 9.2

Braided housing usable for shift or brake housing

A third option is the "articulated housing," which uses small metal segments strung together like beads over a liner (figure 9.3). The articulated housing can be effective when tight bends in the housing are required. There is very little flex with the articulated housing.

FIGURE: 9.3

Articulated housing on a rear derailleur

Compressionless and woven derailleur housing should be cut with proper bicycle cable cutters. The cutting jaws surround the cut and shear the multiple strands of compressionless housing, woven housing, brake cable, and derailleur cable. With a firm hold near the cutting area, hold housing squarely with the cutting jaws and squeeze the handle (figure 9.4). Cutting may slightly deform the housing end. Use the reforming jaws section of the Park Tool CN-10 Professional Cable and Housing Cutter and gently re-shape the housing (figure 9.5). If the housing liner is pinched closed, open the liner with a sharp pointed object, such as a seal pick or safety pin.

FIGURE: 9.4

Hold compressionless housing square to jaws of cable cutter

FIGURE: 9.5

Re-shape compressionless housing after cutting

Derailleur cables are typically 1.1mm to 1.2mm in diameter with a small cylindrical head on one end about 4mm (5/32") in diameter (figure 9.6). The cable head will sit in a socket or carrier in the shift lever. The lever moves the carrier or socket, which pulls on the cable. High quality derailleur cables have a smooth outer finish to reduce drag in the derailleur housing. Some brands of derailleur cable are coated to help reduce drag and friction. A derailleur cable should never be used as a brake cable.

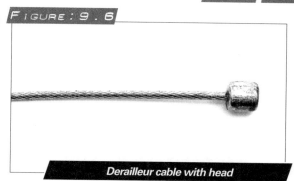

FIGURE: 9.6

Derailleur cable with head

If the derailleur cable is partially cut anywhere between the lever and the cable pinch bolt, it should be replaced. Even the failure of a single strand of cable will eventually lead to a cable break (figure 9.7).

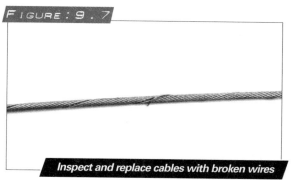

FIGURE: 9.7

Inspect and replace cables with broken wires

Cable Housing Lengths

Acceptable derailleur housing lengths will help ensure that the bike shifts well. Generally, derailleur housing should be as short as possible, yet still approach the derailleur housing stops in the frame, adjusting barrel, shift lever, and derailleur in a straight line. If the housing is too long and forces the cable to pass through excessive housing, it will add friction.

If the housing is too short and creates kinks even in the end caps, it will also mean excessive friction. Short housing will also bend or twist the end cap as it sits in the barrel adjuster (figure 9.8). Properly-sized housing will enter the derailleur in a straight line and will not bend the end cap (figure 9.9).

ParkTool

FIGURE: 9.8

Housing does not enter the barrel adjuster in a straight line, indicating housing is too short

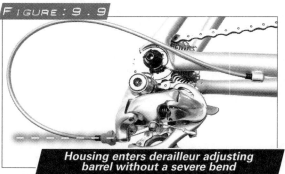

FIGURE: 9.9

Housing enters derailleur adjusting barrel without a severe bend

On some bicycles, the front housing loops from the shift levers to the frame may be purposely switched from left to right sides. The left shifter housing is passed to the right side stop and vice versa. This is called "crossing-over" (figure 9.10). The derailleur cable must then cross back over in order to arrive at the corresponding derailleur. Crossing-over may in some cases reduce bends in the housing by creating a straighter line for the housing. This can also help eliminate housing rub on the frame. Crossing-over, however, will not work well on all bikes. If the cable rubs on a frame tube, such as the down tube, or if there are severe bends resulting in other parts of the system, do not cross over. It is both common and acceptable for the derailleur cables to lightly touch when crossing back.

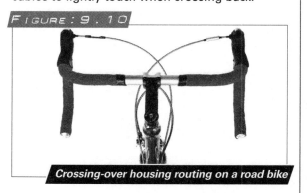

FIGURE: 9.10

Crossing-over housing routing on a road bike

Cable Lubrication

Dirty and rusty cable systems will not move easily and shifting will be difficult. The derailleur cables can often be wiped clean and re-lubricated without taking them off the bike. Shift the rear derailleur to the sprocket with the tightest derailleur cable tension. Stop pedaling the bike and release derailleur cable tension by shifting the lever as if shifting to the other extreme sprocket. Do not pedal. Push the derailleur body to further release tension for extra slack on the derailleur cable. Pull housing ends from guides and stops (figure 9.11). Wipe derailleur cable clean and apply light lubricant. If wiping does not remove rust, derailleur cable should be replaced. Push derailleur again to release tension in order to get housing back into the stops. Pedal the bike to shift the derailleur. Double check that housing is fully back into all stops.

FIGURE: 9.11

Remove housing from stop to clean and lubricate cable

Some bicycle designs route the housing internally through the frame tubing (figure 9.12). Better bike designs use an inner guide to route the derailleur cable and/or housing in and out of the frame. If there is no guide inside, it can be difficult to get the housing through. Feed the housing through one end and then use a stiff wire, such as a spoke, to help catch and guide the housing out the frame hole at the other end. To replace housing that is already in place, feed a derailleur cable into the back end of the housing and out the front. Pull the housing from the frame while leaving the derailleur cable in place to act as a guide when installing the new piece. Feed the derailleur cable into the new housing and push the new housing along the cable into the frame.

Internally routed housing

Shimano® trigger shifter with outboard cable installation

Shift Levers

The derailleur cable head will sit in a socket or carrier in the shift lever. The shift lever moves the carrier or socket and pulls the cable. Indexing shift levers use "clicks" or stops at pre-determined positions. Some bicycles use a "friction" system where the lever has no pre-set stops. Cyclist must listen and feel when the derailleur has reached correct alignment under the appropriate sprocket to avoid ticking noises and rubbing of the chain.

Some models of front derailleur shifters allow for "half" clicks and allow the front derailleur to be "trimmed." This slight movement of the cage is used to prevent rubbing when the chain moves left to right on the rear sprocket combinations.

Flat Bar Shifters

Flat bar trigger shifters mount adjacent to the grips. Shimano® produces "dual control" brake/shifter combination sets. If the lever is integrated with the brake, alignment preference should be given to the brake lever. Set levers at approximately a 45-degree downward slope from horizontal using the mounting bolt. Some models of shifters also include a separate lateral positioning option.

Shimano® has numerous models and generations of trigger-type shifters. There are two common cable installation methods. Inspect outboard for a screw head. Shift the lever so the cable is in the most relaxed position with no tension. Remove the screw. Detach cable from derailleur and push the cable head out of the lever (figure 9.13). Install new cable and install screw.

Another Shimano® trigger shifter derailleur cable installation system involves removing shrouding. Shift to the most relaxed derailleur cable position and detach cable from derailleur. Inspect for small screws and pivots on shifter. Remove screw(s) and remove or pivot cover. The cable end is fitted to a cable end carrier. It may require a small screwdriver to lift carrier and install cable end (figure 9.14).

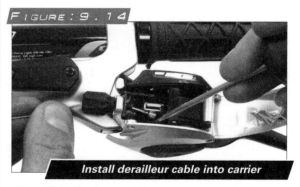
Install derailleur cable into carrier

The SRAM® trigger shifters can use a plastic access screw. Shift to the most relaxed derailleur cable position and detach cable from derailleur. Remove screw and push cable out. For installation, make sure small lever has been pushed to return cable carrier to the most relaxed position. Feed cable through hole and out barrel adjuster. It can be difficult to find hole for cable, and it can be helpful to use a flashlight shined through barrel adjuster (figure 9.15). Look for light source and feed cable accordingly.

ParkTool

Feed cable through shifter aiming for the light

The SRAM® X.0 shifters use a cover plate over the cable carrier. Remove the T-nut counter-clockwise top of the carbon plate. Use fingers if possible, or needle nose pliers, but only if necessary. Cable end is under shifter return spring. Use a small-tipped screwdriver or seal pick to carefully lift cable end while pushing on cable (figure 9.16).

Carefully remove cable from shifter

Installation is basically the reverse process. It can help to give a bend to the end of the cable to help feed it through cable carrier. Removing barrel adjuster provides a large hole for cable to pass. Pull cable into place and check the spring was not displaced. Re-install barrel adjuster and re-install cover plate finger tight.

Twist-Grip Shifters

Twist-grip shifters mount to flat or upright handlebars. The levers can be rotated around the handlebars. Levers mount to the handlebar between the brake levers and the grips. Check that shifters do not interfere with brake levers when brake levers are squeezed fully closed. Rotate shifter body so housing follows a smooth line to the frame stop. Look for a setscrew that locks the lever to the handlebars (figure 9.17).

SRAM® Twist-grip shifter and location of setscrew

There have been different generations of twist-grip shift levers, and installation of the derailleur cable can vary. A common style has an access hole with a plastic or rubber cover. Shift the lever to the most relaxed derailleur cable position and remove the cover. Detach the derailleur cable from the derailleur and then push the derailleur cable toward the lever. Some models may have a small setscrew over the derailleur cable end. Use a hex wrench to remove this screw. Other models use a small clip to hold the derailleur cable end. Use a small screwdriver to pry back the clip and then push the cable to remove it from the lever (figure 9.18).

Use screwdriver to access cable

Above-The-Bar Shifters

The above-the-bar shifters are designed for upright handlebars. Placement should be close to the grip, and the body of the shifter should point downward at a slight angle (figure 9.19).

The cut end of derailleur cable is simply fed through a hole in the shift lever and then through the housing to the derailleur.

Above-the-bar shift lever

Drop Bar Integral Brake & Gear Shifters

Shimano®, SRAM® and Campagnolo® drop bar levers combine shifting and braking into the same lever system. Brake lever placement will determine how the shift levers are aligned (figure 9.20).

Align brake levers relative to handlebar drop

The derailleur cable end attaches to the shift lever by fitting through a small socket. The cable anchor pivot is sometimes difficult to see. Begin by shifting the smaller lever repeatedly. This places the socket in the most relaxed cable tension position.

For Shimano® shifters, feed the cut end of the cable through the socket and pull it fully through until the head engages inside the socket (figure 9.21).

Feed derailleur cable into the socket at top of lever

For Campagnolo® Ergo levers, begin by shifting the smaller lever repeatedly. Pull the rubber lever hood back to expose the cable anchor. Feed derailleur cable upward through anchor and out the top of the lever (figure 9.22). Housing and end cap enter lever from the top and run underneath the handlebar tape.

For Campagnolo® Ergo shifters, look under rubber hood when installing new derailleur cable

For SRAM® levers, the cables install from the inside face of the lever body. Pull cover back on lower portion of lever to expose wire access hole. The wire must make a relatively quick 90-degree turn from horizontal to vertical. It can be useful to give the cable a slight curve (figure 9.23). It is best to use new shift wires or wires that have been soldered. Freshly cut wires may have difficulty making the bend. Secure the housing to the bar with tape.

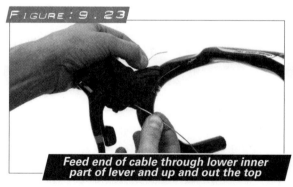

Feed end of cable through lower inner part of lever and up and out the top

Down Tube Shifters

The shifters may be mounted on the down tube for some road bikes (figure 9.24). The frame will have a fitting for the levers, and there is no positioning adjustment for these levers.

FIGURE: 9.24

Typical down tube shifters

The cut end of derailleur cable is fed through a hole in the lever and down below the bottom bracket to the appropriate derailleur.

Bar End Shifters

Bar end shifters are fitted into the ends of drop style handlebars or to the end of "aero" handlebars (figure 9.25). These levers secure inside the ends of the bars in place of end caps. The derailleur housing is then routed along the handlebar underneath the bar tape. The derailleur cable is fed through a hole in the lever and through the housing.

FIGURE: 9.25

Bar end shifter in aero handle extensions

Front Derailleur

The front derailleur shoves the chain off one chainring and onto another. The derailleur uses a cage that surrounds the chain, and the cable pulls the derailleur cage along with the chain. A spring in the derailleur returns the cage when the derailleur cable is relaxed. A properly adjusted front derailleur should shift the chain between the front chainrings but will not throw the chain off the chainrings. The basic adjustments for the front derailleur are the height, rotation, limit screw settings, and derailleur cable tension (index setting).

The common front derailleur secures to the seat tube with a clamp that is sized for the seat tube diameter. Clamp sizes are available in 28.6mm, 31.8mm, and 35mm diameters. Some clamp models are designed to use shims that will accommodate all of the common size tubes.

The Shimano® "E-plate" front derailleur models do not have height or rotation adjustments. These models mount on a plate, and both height and rotation settings are pre-set.

Another front derailleur mounting system is commonly referred to as a "braze-on." A bracket is mounted to the seat tube and allows limited height and rotational settings.

Derailleur design will vary with the crankset type used. The common mountain bike triple crankset has a wide spread of chainring sizes and uses a cage with a relatively wide inner plate. This derailleur is called a "deep cage." Road bikes tend to have two front chainrings and do not require a wide plate. This is called a "shallow cage" derailleur (figure 9.26). Consult a professional mechanic for the correct design for your bike.

FIGURE: 9.26

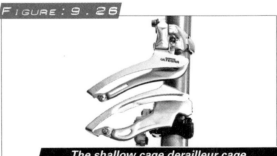

The shallow cage derailleur cage on top and the deep cage below

The front derailleur cage is moved by a parallelogram. This linkage system allows the cage to move parallel to the chainring as it moves laterally. There are two basic linkage designs: the "top swing" and the "bottom swing." The top swing and bottom swing derailleurs differ in placement of the parallelogram in relation to the derailleur clamp.

The "top swing" attaches with the parallelogram swinging above the clamp (figures 9.24 and 9.25). The "top swing" derailleur clamp will end up lower on the seat tube as compared to a bottom swing derailleur. Some bike frames will only allow the mounting of a top swing derailleur because of a water bottle fitting or suspension fittings on the seat tube.

The bottom swing derailleur is designed so the parallelogram attaches and swings below the clamp (figures 9.27 and 9.29). The clamp will end up higher on the seat tube as compared to a "top swing" derailleur.

The derailleur cable pulls the linkage of the front derailleur. The cable may come up from the bottom bracket. These models are described as bottom pull, as it is pulled from the bottom (figures 9.27 and 9.28). If the cable comes down the seat tube, it is referred to as a top pull (figures 9.29 and 9.30).

FIGURE: 9.30

Top pull-top swing

FIGURE: 9.27

Bottom pull-bottom swing

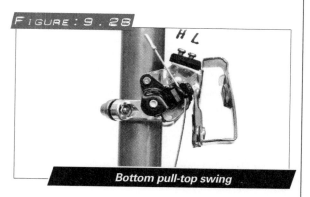

FIGURE: 9.28

Bottom pull-top swing

FIGURE: 9.29

Top pull-bottom swing

Derailleur Cable Attachment

The derailleur cable attaches to the front derailleur at the pinch bolt mechanism. Unthread the bolt and look for a groove in either the plate or derailleur arm. The derailleur cable will lay in this depression or notch (figure 9.31). Inspect the pinch bolt mechanism and keep the cable aligned with the groove. There may also be a tab system. The tab is used to prevent the washer from rotating. The derailleur cable is not usually routed around the tab.

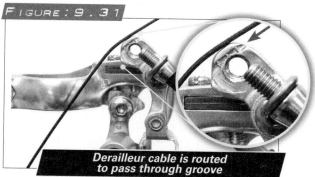

FIGURE: 9.31

Derailleur cable is routed to pass through groove

While the bolt is loose, lubricate the threads. Pull the derailleur cable snug and secure the bolt. The typical torque for the pinch bolt is approximately 35 inch pounds. The derailleur cable will be flattened where it is pinched.

Height Adjustment

If the derailleur cage is too far above the large chainring, it will shift poorly. If the derailleur is too low, it may scrape against the chainrings and jam the chain when shifting. The proper height can be set with or without attaching the derailleur cable.

ParkTool

The procedure for setting front derailleur height:

a. Pull front derailleur cage plate until it is directly over outer chainring teeth. Use either the cable or pull directly on the cage.

b. The gap between the teeth of the outer chainring, and the lower edge of the outer cage plate should be 1-2mm or about the thickness of a U.S. penny. Using the penny as a feeler gauge, fit it between the chainring teeth and the cage plate. It should just fit (figure 9.32).

c. To lower cage, release derailleur cable tension completely by shifting to the innermost chainring. Any cable tension will pull the derailleur downward and make height even more difficult to set.

d. Note angle of outer cage plate relative to the chainring. It should be parallel to the chain.

e. Front derailleur clamps typically leave a mark on the frame, which is useful as a reference when changing height. Loosen the derailleur clamp bolt, change derailleur height, and return the cage to its original rotation relative to the chainring. Tighten clamp bolt. Move the outer cage plate over outer chainring and check height again.

f. Repeat process until cage plate height is 1-2mm above outer chainring. For triple chainring bikes, inspect that the inner derailleur cage plate is not striking the middle ring. It may be necessary to raise the derailleur slightly.

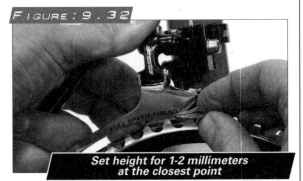

Set height for 1-2 millimeters at the closest point

If the derailleur cannot be set to an acceptable height, it may be incompatible with the front chainring sizing. Additionally, the frame may not permit an ideal setting, or there may be a chain guard the prevents a lower setting (figure 9.34).

FIGURE: 9.33

A lower setting is not possible with this chain guard

Height Adjustment

The front derailleur cage should be parallel to the chain. The chain angle moves, however, when the rear derailleur is shifted left and right. Use the outermost (smallest) rear sprocket when checking the cage rotation. If the derailleur cage is rotated too far from this position, it will shift poorly or rub on the chain. Rotation of the braze-on mount or clamp mount derailleurs can be changed. There is no rotation option for the E-plate mounted derailleurs. The derailleur cable should be attached while inspecting rotation.

The procedure for setting front derailleur rotation:

a. Shift chain to outermost chainring and outermost rear sprocket.

b. Sight chain from directly above chainrings. Consider the chain as representing a straight line. Compare this line to the outer derailleur cage plate. Outer cage plate and chain should be parallel (figure 9.34). Keeping the cage and chain parallel will minimize the risk of the chain jumping off the outermost chainring. If the cage is not parallel, there will be a relatively large gap at either the back or the front end of the cage. Then the derailleur may overshift the chain past the chainring (figures 9.35 and 9.36).

c. If the derailleur cage must be rotated, note direction of desired rotation.

d. Release derailleur cable tension by shifting to the innermost chainring.

e. Many clamps leave a slight marking on the frame. Use a pencil to make two reference marks on the frame, one for height and a second, vertical mark, to reference rotation. Use the marks to avoid inadvertently changing height.

f. Loosen clamp bolt and slightly rotate in correct direction. Use care not to change height. Tighten clamp bolt.
g. Shift to outer chainring and observe rotation alignment.
h. Repeat adjustment if necessary.

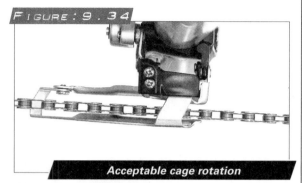

FIGURE: 9.34

Acceptable cage rotation

FIGURE: 9.35

Misaligned cage, rotated too much clockwise. Notice end of cage is inward, toward the bike mid plane.

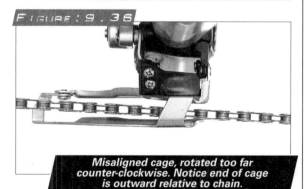

FIGURE: 9.36

Misaligned cage, rotated too far counter-clockwise. Notice end of cage is outward relative to chain.

Although the above procedure usually creates the best alignment, there are situations where the back end of the cage is best rotated inward or outward. For example, after properly setting the limit screws, a derailleur may seem slow when shifting inward and may benefit from having the cage rotated slightly clockwise. This moves the back end of the cage closer to the chain if viewed from above and can more effectively push the chain inward to the next sprocket. Double check all limit screw settings after any changes to rotation.

Limit Screw Adjustment

Limit screws stop the inward and outward travel of the front derailleur cage by striking pieces of the moving linkage system. Limit screws are marked "L" and "H" (figure 9.37). The L-limit screw will stop the inward motion of the derailleur toward the smallest chainring or "low" front gear, and the H-limit screw will stop the outward motion of the derailleur toward the largest chainring or "high" front gear. The L-limit screw also keeps the chain from falling off the smallest ring on to the bottom bracket. Similarly, the H-limit screw keeps the chain from falling off the outside of the largest sprocket. Set the limit screws before setting index shifting with cable tension. The screws use a nylock fitting to prevent them from moving after adjustment. If the screws seem to move too easily, remove the screw and apply a mild thread locker. Do not lubricate these screws.

FIGURE: 9.37

Location of limit screws

L-limit screw

Although the limit screws stop the derailleur, it is the derailleur cable and derailleur spring that make the derailleur move. If the derailleur cable has too much tension, the derailleur will not rest on the L-limit screw stop. If the derailleur cable tension were to change, for example, from the cable system setting and stretching, the derailleur inner limit would also change and possibly cause the chain to fall off the chainrings.

The procedure for adjusting the L-limit screw:

a. Shift chain to innermost rear sprocket and innermost front chainring. Inspect derailleur for mark indicating "L" screw.
b. Check derailleur cable tension. It should be fairly loose at this time. If derailleur cable is taut, turn barrel adjuster clockwise into lever. The barrel adjuster is typically located where the cable

housing enters the shift lever. If barrel adjuster is already fully turned into the housing, loosen the derailleur cable pinch bolt, slacken the derailleur cable and retighten the bolt.

c. Sight the gap between the chain and inner cage plate. Only a small gap should be visible, 1/16" or 1mm, or about the thickness of a U.S. dime (figure 9.38).

d. Pedal bike slowly and continue to sight gap. Set clearance at narrowest or tightest point in the chainring rotation. Adjust L-limit screw so there is a small gap between the inner cage and chain. Pedal the bike and check that chain is not rubbing cage while chainrings and chain turn.

  1. If there is no gap and chain is rubbing cage, loosen L-limit screw 1/8 turn (counter-clockwise). Inspect for gap again and repeat until slight gap appears.

  2. If the gap appears larger than 1mm at its widest point, tighten the L-limit screw, in small increments until the gap closes.

e. Test the shift by shifting chain to next chainring. Then shift back to the innermost chainring. If chain shifts quickly to the smallest ring, limit screw setting is adequate. The shift outward away from the smallest ring is not determined by the L-screw. Do not be concerned, as any H-limit corrections will be made shortly.

f. If the shift to the smallest ring from the next ring is slow (requires more than one pedal revolution to initiate shift), turn L-limit screw counter-clockwise 1/8 turn and repeat test. Repeat 1/8 turn increments until shifting is adequate. The gap will open wider than the 1mm target but will still be as small as possible with adequate shifting.

g. If chain is shifting beyond the inner chainring and falls off the chainring, the gap may be too large or cage alignment may be off. Tighten L-limit screw 1/8 turn and check shift again. If chain ends up rubbing inner cage of derailleur yet still drops off inner chainring when shifting, other problems such as chainline or derailleur rotation exist.

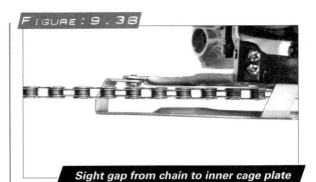

FIGURE: 9.38

Sight gap from chain to inner cage plate

H-limit screw

The H-limit screw stops the outward travel of the front derailleur. When viewing the H-limit screw adjustment, make sure there is enough tension on the derailleur cable by either keeping extra pressure on the lever or by pulling the exposed derailleur cable taut by hand. Use a rag to protect your hand if pulling on the derailleur cable. If pulling the cable is not an option, maintain pressure on the shift lever to ensure the derailleur is pressing against the H-limit screw.

The procedure for adjusting the H-limit screw:

a. Shift to outermost sprocket in rear and outermost front chainring. Inspect derailleur for mark indicating H-limit screw.

b. Pull derailleur cable with a hand on the cable itself to increase tension to ensure derailleur is against H-limit screw (figure 9.39). Alternatively, maintain pressure on shift lever.

c. Check gap between chain and outer cage plate. Only a small gap should be visible, about 1/16" or 1mm. Pedal bike slowly and continue to sight gap. Set clearance at tightest point in chainring rotation (figure 9.40).

d. If chain is rubbing cage, loosen H-limit screw 1/8 turn and pull on derailleur cable. Check gap again.

e. If chain is not rubbing, tighten H-limit screw repeatedly until chain does rub cage then loosen H-limit screw 1/8 turn and check again.

f. Test shift to the large chainring. Shift derailleur from small or middle chainring to largest chainring using hand pressure on derailleur cable rather than shift lever. If shifting is slow, loosen H-limit screw 1/8 turn and repeat test. If chain shifts over the outside of the large chainring and onto the crank, the outer-limit is set too loose. Tighten H-limit screw and test shift again.

g. If chain ends up rubbing outer cage of derailleur yet still drops off outer chainring when shifting, other problems such as chainline or derailleur rotation exist.

FIGURE: 9.39

Pull derailleur cable tight to force derailleur cage to limit screw

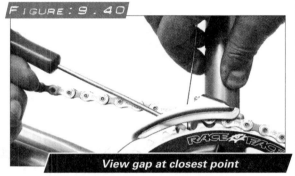

FIGURE: 9.40

View gap at closest point

Index Adjustment- three chainring bikes

The front derailleur system may have an index setting. If the shift lever has three distinctive stops or clicks, it is indexing. If the front shift lever is a friction type without any clicks, there is no index setting. If the front shift lever has multiple clicks, such as some twist grip style shifters, it is shifted similar to friction levers. Set indexing only after completing limit screw setting.

The procedure for adjusting the index shifting on three chainring cranksets:

a. Shift chain to middle chainring in the front and innermost rear sprocket.

b. View gap between inner cage plate and chain. Gap should be as small as possible without rubbing chain. To reduce gap, increase derailleur cable tension by turning barrel adjuster counter-clockwise. Check gap again.

c. If chain is rubbing cage, turn barrel adjuster clockwise.

d. If barrel adjuster is all the way in or out and no adjustment is possible, reset derailleur cable tension. Shift

to innermost chainring and loosen derailleur cable pinch bolt. Pull derailleur cable with a fourth-hand tool and tighten pinch bolt. Repeat adjustment procedure of derailleur cable tension from "a".

e. Test shift front derailleur to all three front chainrings.

Index Adjustment Two Chainring Bikes

If the shift lever has distinctive stops or clicks, it is indexing. If the front shift lever is friction without any clicks, there is no index setting. Set the indexing only after checking and setting the limit screws. If there is rubbing of the cage it will be the result of derailleur cable tension. Loosening limit screws will not move the cage.

The procedure for adjusting index shifting on two chainring cranksets:

a. Shift chain to outer chainring in the front and outermost rear sprocket.

b. View gap between outer cage plate and chain.

c. If outer cage plate clears the chain, index setting is adequate.

d. If plate is rubbing chain, increase derailleur cable tension by turning adjusting barrel counter-clockwise and check again.

e. If barrel adjuster is all the way in or out and no adjustment is possible, reset derailleur cable tension. Shift to innermost chainring and loosen derailleur cable pinch bolt. Pull the derailleur cable with a fourth hand tool and tighten pinch bolt. Begin adjustment of derailleur cable tension as in step "a."

f. Test shift front derailleur between front chainrings.

Front Derailleur Performance

There are limits to the performance of the front derailleur. There may be certain gear combinations that simply do not work well or cause problems. For example, when the bike is used with the smallest front chainring and the smallest rear sprocket, the chain may rub against an adjacent chainring or the derailleur. This is called "cross-chaining." As a simple rule, if a gear combination causes a rubbing problem, avoid that gear (figure 9.41). If there is no rubbing, the gear is usable.

FIGURE: 9.41

Rubbing chain-to-ring contact. No derailleur adjustment will prevent this.

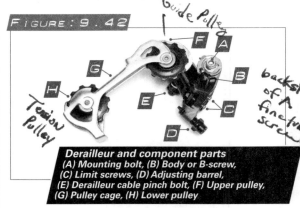

FIGURE: 9.42

Guide Pulley

F A

G

B   backs of A fine tun screw

H

E   C

Tension Pulley

D

Derailleur and component parts
(A) Mounting bolt, (B) Body or B-screw,
(C) Limit screws, (D) Adjusting barrel,
(E) Derailleur cable pinch bolt, (F) Upper pulley,
(G) Pulley cage, (H) Lower pulley

Another chain rub problem can occur when pedaling in the largest front chainring and the smallest rear sprocket. Very hard pedaling will flex the frame slightly with each stroke, which may cause a chain to rub on the largest sprocket even for properly adjusted bikes. Loosening the H-limit screw and then tightening the index setting cable tension will move the front cage out more. This may stop the rubbing, but it may also cause the chain to shift over the largest chainring and come off. If all aspects of front derailleur adjustments are correct on this bike, the rider is simply exceeding the engineering and design capabilities of the machine. Front derailleur performance issues are related to chainline.

Rear Derailleur   *Purpose is:*

Rear derailleurs push or (1) "derail" the chain from one rear sprocket and move it to another. The upper derailleur pulley is also referred to as the "G-pulley" or guide pulley. The G-pulley guides the chain to the sprocket and, when moved, pushes the chain to the next sprocket. The derailleur body is fitted with a spring that is pulled tightly or released by the derailleur cable. Pulling the derailleur cable moves the derailleur cage and guide pulley in one direction and tightens the spring. Relaxing derailleur cable (2) tension allows the spring to move the body and pulley in the opposite direction. The useful terms in the derailleur are outlined next (figure 9.42).

The rear derailleur attaches to the frame at a fitting called the derailleur hanger. The hanger has a tab that acts as a stop for derailleur rotation (figure 9.43). Derailleur mounting bolts use a 10mm x 1mm thread. Grease the bolt before installing. When installing the derailleur, use care that any stop screw or plate on the derailleur clears the hanger tab. Hold the derailleur clockwise from its "normal" position while engaging the thread. The torque for the mounting bolt is modest or about 70 inches/lb for most makes. Test that the derailleur is freely pivoting on the hanger.

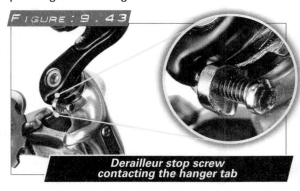

FIGURE: 9.43

Derailleur stop screw contacting the hanger tab

Derailleur Capacity & Maximum Sprocket Size

The rear derailleur is usually selected to be compatible with sprocket sizing used on the bicycle. Derailleurs are made with specifications as to the "maximum sprocket size" and the "total capacity." The maximum sprocket size is the largest rear sprocket the derailleur will accept. For example, a bike with a 32-tooth rear sprocket should use a rear derailleur with a maximum sprocket size of at least 32.

The total derailleur capacity refers to the derailleur's ability to take up chain slack as the derailleur shifts between different gear combinations. The capacity requirements of

the bicycle are determined by the sprocket sizes. The difference between the smallest and largest chainring sizes is added to the difference between the smallest and largest sprockets of the rear sprockets. For example, if a bike has a front crankset with 22-32-46 tooth chainrings, the spread between the front extremes is 24 teeth. If the rear sprocket sizing is 13-14-15-17-19-21-23-26-30 teeth, the spread is 17 teeth. The total capacity requirements are then 17 plus 24, or a total of 41. A derailleur rated for a total capacity of 41 or greater would take up the slack for any gear combination. However, it does not mean that every gear combination will work well, only that the derailleur will take up the slack.

Derailleurs are available that do not take up chain slack in every gear combination. In the example above, if the bicycle is fitted with a derailleur with a rated capacity of 33, the derailleur will not be able to take up the slack in all gear combinations. The chain will hang slack when it is on the inner front chainring and in the 13, 14, 15, 17 or 19 rear sprockets. If the chain were shortened to accommodate these gear combinations, it would be too short when the bike is in the 46 tooth front chainring and the several of the larger sprockets in the back. When sizing a chain with a derailleur violating the total capacity needs of the bike, it is best to use the sizing method in Chapter 8, Chains. This will allow shifting to largest rear and front sprockets, but the chain will hang slack is some small front chainring and small rear sprocket combinations. It will be necessary to avoid those gear combinations that cause problems in pedaling or shifting or to replace the derailleur with a model of greater total capacity.

Check with derailleur manufacturer for specifications on maximum sprocket size and total capacity. As a general rule, total capacity increases as the derailleur cage gets longer, and the distance between pulley wheels increases. Short cage derailleurs, those with approximately 50mm between pulley wheels, will have a capacity of about 29 teeth. Medium cage derailleurs (approximately 73mm) will have a capacity of approximately 33 teeth. Long cage derailleurs (approximately 85mm) will have a capacity of approximately 45 teeth.

Derailleur Cable Attachment

The derailleur cable attaches to the rear derailleur at the pinch bolt mechanism. The derailleur cable is flattened by a plate and bolt (figure 9.44). Unthread the bolt and look for a groove in either the plate or derailleur arm. The derailleur cable will lay in this depression or notch. Inspect the groove and keep the derailleur cable in line with it. There may also be a tab system. The tab is used to prevent the washer from rotating. The derailleur cable is not usually routed around the tab.

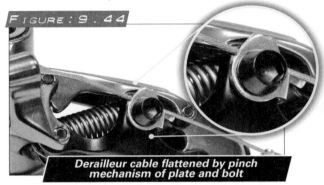

FIGURE : 9 . 44

Derailleur cable flattened by pinch mechanism of plate and bolt

While the bolt is loose, take the opportunity to lubricate the threads. Pull the derailleur cable snug and secure the bolt. The typical torque for the pinch bolt is approximately 35-inch pounds. Again, the derailleur cable will be flattened where it is pinched.

Limit Screw Adjustment

Derailleur pulleys are limited in both inward and outward motions by using the derailleur limit screws. Limit screws will strike and stop the derailleur linkage as it articulates through its motions. The limit screws are usually marked "H" and "L." The H-limit screw controls the outermost limit of the derailleur, and the L-limit screw controls the innermost limit. The location of limit screws on the derailleur body may vary between manufacturers. Always look for the "H" and "L" marked adjacent to the screws. For some models you may need to inspect the linkage and determine which screw is the H-screw or L-screw (figure 9.45).

ParkTool

FIGURE: 9.45

This limit screw will stop the linkage as it moves outward, making it the H-limit screw

Properly set, the derailleur will shift to both the extreme outward sprocket (the smallest in size) and the extreme innermost sprocket (the largest in size). The limit screws do not control the derailleur on the sprockets between the two extremes. The sprockets between the extremes are set using the barrel adjuster and tension on the derailleur cable during indexing adjustments.

Using the shift lever to adjust limit screws can cause confusion and problems because it tends to focus attention on the derailleur cable tension (indexing) rather than limit screw settings. Instead of using the shift lever, pull the derailleur cable with one hand to simulate shift lever action (figure 9.46). This will help eliminate confusion between indexing problems and limit screw problems. Before adjusting the limit screws, practice shifting with this method. If it is not possible to pull the cable by hand, maintain pressure on the lever to ensure the derailleur is pressed to the limit screw.

FIGURE: 9.46

Pull derailleur cable by hand to isolate limit screw performance

Turning the limit screws adjusts the travel limit of the pulleys. Tightening the screw restricts the travel but loosening allows more travel. The purpose of the following procedure is to find the tightest H-limit screw setting that will allow a good shift to the outermost sprocket and the tightest L-screw setting that will allow a good shift to the innermost sprocket.

It is normal for a chain to make some noise during a shift. The shift may appear subjectively "noisy," "loud," or "rough." Factors like the type of chain or sprocket, the wear on each, and the amount and type of lubrication will affect the noise a chain makes during shifting. The limit screws typically can do nothing to affect the noise during the shift between sprockets.

H-Limit Screw

When adjusting the H-limit screw, pay special attention to the outward shift from the second smallest sprocket to the outermost sprocket. Also notice how the chain rides on the outermost sprocket. Do not be concerned, however, with how the chain rides when it is held on the second sprocket. That is a function of derailleur cable tension, not limit screw settings. Do not become confused between issues of derailleur cable tension and limit screw setting. Cable tension controls indexing, but limit screws control the two extreme cogs. Again, when possible, simply pull the derailleur cable by hand rather than using the shift lever.

The procedure for adjusting the H-limit screw:

   a. Shift chain to outermost (largest) chainring. Shift chain to outermost rear sprocket (smallest sprocket).

   b. Check tension on rear derailleur cable. If derailleur cable appears to have any tension, it may interfere with the H-limit screw setting. Turn adjusting-barrel clockwise to eliminate derailleur cable tension.

   c. Pedal bike at a quick cadence, approximately 60 rpm or more. Pull derailleur cable to shift derailleur one sprocket inward. Adjust pull on derailleur cable until chain rides quietly on second sprocket. Release derailleur cable quickly to shift back to outermost sprocket and note shift.

   d. If the shift outward seems acceptable, tighten H-limit screw ¼ turn clockwise and repeat shift. Even if the shift appears acceptable, continue tightening H-limit screw by ¼ turn increments and checking shift until the shifting becomes slow or hesitant to the outer sprocket. The goal is to find the point at which the limit screw is too tight, then back it off until it is just right. Another symptom of a too tight H-limit screw is when the chain is on the smallest sprocket but makes a rattle from rubbing the second sprocket inward. View this last symptom by looking under the rear sprockets where the chain meets the sprockets. The inner plate of the chain will rub against the next sprocket inward, making the noise.

e. When symptoms of a too tight H-limit screw appear, loosen H-limit screw ¼ turn and check shift again. Repeat process of shifting and correcting by ¼ turn increments. When too tight symptoms disappear, H-limit screw is at tightest acceptable setting. The H-limit screw setting is done.

L-limit Screw

The L-limit screw stops the derailleur from moving inward (toward the spokes). The limit screw does not make the derailleur move, pulling the derailleur cable makes the derailleur move. The L-screw allows the pulley wheels to shift the chain to the innermost sprocket, but not off the sprocket into the spokes. When adjusting the L-screw, be concerned with the inward shift from the second-to-innermost sprocket to the innermost sprocket. Additionally, notice how the chain rides on the innermost sprocket.

The procedure for adjusting the L-limit screw:

a. Shift bike to middle chainring of three chainring bikes or smaller chainring of double chainring bikes.

b. Pedal bike at a normal riding cadence, approximately 60 rpm or more.

c. Pull rear derailleur cable by hand to shift derailleur inward from second to innermost sprocket to the innermost sprocket.

d. If shifting seems adequate, tighten L-limit screw ¼ turn and repeat shift. Continue to tighten L-screw until symptoms of an overly tight screw appear. The goal is to find the point at which the limit screw is too tight, then back it off until it is just right. The symptoms are an unshiftable chain or even a hesitant chain while pulling on the derailleur cable. Also, listen for a loud chain rattle when the chain is riding on innermost sprocket.

e. When symptoms of a too tight L-screw appear, loosen L-screw ¼ turn and check shift again. Repeat the process of shifting and correct each time with

¼ turn. When too tight symptoms disappear, the L-screw is at tightest acceptable setting and limit screw setting is done.

B-Screw Adjustment

After setting the L-screw, check the "B-screw" for an adequate setting. The B-screw controls the derailleur body angle, hence the name, B-screw. Adjust the distance between pulley and sprocket when the chain is on the smallest sprocket in front and on the largest sprocket in back. This places the upper pulley and largest rear sprocket at their closest point.

Shimano®, SRAM® and Campagnolo® locate some B-screws behind the derailleur's upper mounting bolt (figure 9.47).

FIGURE: 9.47

B-screw location

If the indexing is already set, shift to the innermost sprocket. Otherwise, pull the rear derailleur cable and shift to the innermost (largest) rear sprocket. Hold tension and view the upper pulley relative to the largest sprocket. If the pulley is rubbing against the sprocket, tighten the B-screw to increase upper pivot spring tension, which pulls the pulley back and away from the sprocket. If there is a gap between the upper pulley and sprocket, loosen the screw. Back pedal to double check for rubbing. If the upper pulley rubs against the sprocket, it will wear out.

Campagnolo® model derailleurs may have a tension adjustment at the pulley cage and not at the upper pivot. The screw is basically a "rack and pinion" system. The cage spring plate rotates to increase or decrease tension of the cage. The tension of the upper pivot and lower cage pivot springs oppose one another. In this system, the upper spring tension is fixed (figure 9.48). Increasing cage tension (turning screw clockwise) in the cage will bring the upper pulley closer to the sprocket. Decreasing cage tension (turning screw counter-clockwise) will increase the distance between upper pulley and sprocket.

B-screw location for Campagnolo®

SRAM® derailleurs do not use a spring in the upper mounting bolt. A screw behind the upper mounting bolt adjusts the distance from the upper pulley to the largest sprocket. This concept is also used by the Shimano® Shadow derailleur. Adjust so there is approximately a 6mm (¼ inch) gap between from the pulley and sprocket. Use a 6mm hex wrench to estimate this gap (figure 9.49). Tighten the B-screw to pull body back, and that will increase the distance between sprocket and pulley. Loosen the screw to decrease gap size.

Upper pulley to largest rear sprocket setting for SRAM® and Shimano® Shadow derailleurs

Index Adjustment

The indexing procedure here assumes that there are no unusual problems such as bent derailleurs, bent derailleur hangers, or excess derailleur cable friction from dirt in the housing. Additionally, manufacturers design shift levers and drive train components to work within their system. Mixing brands of components within the drive train may result in less than optimal shifting. Problems resulting from mixing different designs are referred to as incompatibility problems.

The rear indexing is adjusted by changing the derailleur cable tension. For conventional derailleurs (other than Shimano® Rapid Rise), increasing derailleur cable tension moves the rear derailleur inward or toward the spokes. Decreasing derailleur cable tension allows the

derailleur to move outward. The derailleur cable tension will not stop the derailleur at its extreme limits. The H-limit screw stops the derailleur at its outermost setting, and the L-limit screw stops the derailleur at its innermost setting.

Modern indexing shift levers use "dwell," which is a hesitation between movements in the lever. These hesitations are timed to match the movements of the derailleur and the spacing in the rear sprockets. The design of some derailleur and shift lever brands requires more of a push (or twist) of the lever to complete the shift. The amount of extra push or twist is not consistent between manufacturers and each rider must learn the particular attributes of his or her system. In other words, an index lever may, in some cases, need to be "finessed" to shift properly.

Changes to derailleur cable tension are made at the adjusting barrel. Adjusting barrels may be located either at the rear derailleur, the shift lever or both. The goal of adjusting the indexing is to find the tightest derailleur cable tension setting that will allow good shifting to the gears normally used. This setting will allow the longest lasting indexing adjustment as the system wears and the cable system stretches with use. To find the tightest derailleur cable setting, begin by purposely making the setting too tight and then relax tension slightly.

There are two basic symptoms for a "too tight" derailleur cable: a rattling noise from the chain rubbing against the next sprocket inward or a slow or hesitant outward shift. These are symptoms for conventional rear derailleurs that sit outward when derailleur cable tension is released.

Noise from the chain riding on the sprocket is a useful symptom for setting indexing tension. There is, for any given bike, a "base level" of noise from the chain as it passes over the sprocket teeth. To demonstrate the "base level" noise, shift the bike to the second sprocket by pulling the derailleur cable. Continue to pedal and move the derailleur cable slightly to hear changes in the level of noise. The quietest level of noise may be considered the base or normal level for that bike. When the derailleur jockey wheel is out of alignment, the chain may make excessive noise.

The procedure for adjusting the rear index setting:

    a. Set limit screws, if not already done.

    b. Shift chain to outermost rear sprocket (smallest). Shift chain to outermost (largest) chainring in front.

c. Test initial derailleur cable tension. Pedal a normal cadence and shift rear derailleur with one click on lever. Use care to only move lever one position. If derailleur moves one sprocket, tension is adequate. Proceed to "e" below.

d. If derailleur fails to shift one sprocket, derailleur cable may be too slack. Return lever to relaxed derailleur cable position. Turn barrel adjuster fully into derailleur body (or shift lever) then turn counter-clockwise two turns to allow for index adjustments. Loosen derailleur cable pinch bolt and gently pull on derailleur cable with fourth hand tool or pliers to remove slack (figure 9.50). Tighten derailleur cable pinch bolt. Attempt shift again. If derailleur will not shift one sprocket after removing slack, return lever back to outermost sprocket position and increase derailleur cable tension by turning barrel adjuster counter-clockwise ¼ turn and attempt shift again.

e. Once derailleur and lever are on second sprocket, pedal the cranks and increase derailleur cable tension by continuing to turn adjusting barrel counter-clockwise until a definite rattling is heard. Rattle is from the chain scraping against the next sprocket (figure 9.51).

f. Once a too-tight rattle is achieved, turn barrel adjuster ¼ turn clockwise to release derailleur cable tension and pedal again. Listen and look for signs of scraping or rattling. Continue turning barrel adjuster ¼ turn clockwise at a time until rattle disappears.

g. Shift derailleur one sprocket inward at a time, listening for signs of rattle, indicating a too tight derailleur cable (figure 9.51). Turn adjusting barrel ¼ turn clockwise to eliminate rattle. Continue shifting inward one sprocket at a time. Adjust only if rattling is heard and seen. Note: Do not attempt to shift to largest rear sprocket while the chain is in the largest front sprocket. This gear is normally not used and adjusting tension to this shift may compromise other commonly used gears.

h. Shift to innermost (smallest) chainring and check shifting again. If no rattling is present, index adjustment is done.

Pull excessive slack from cable

Look for rattle under rear sprockets

Shimano "Rapid Rise™" Derailleur—Indexing Adjustment

Shimano "Rapid Rise™" derailleurs use a return spring that puts the derailleur under the innermost rear sprocket when the derailleur cable tension is released. This is also called "low normal". A loose derailleur cable will cause the chain to rub against the next sprocket inward.

The procedure for adjusting the indexing on Rapid Rise™ derailleurs:

a. Mount the bike in a repair stand.

b. Set limit screws.

c. Shift chain to the innermost rear sprocket and the middle chainring of a threechainring bike (or the smaller chainring of a double chainring bike.).

d. Pedal and shift lever one position. If chain will not shift, release lever and increase derailleur cable tension.

e. When the chain is on the second to largest sprocket, pedal and turn barrel adjuster clockwise to relax derailleur cable tension until chain be to rattle against next sprocket inward.

f. Turn barrel adjuster counter-clockwise ¼ turn until chain runs smoothly on second sprocket.

g. Shift up (outward) one sprocket at a time, trying each gear. Turn barrel adjuster ¼ turn counter-clockwise if too loose derailleur cable symptoms occur in other gears.

h. Shift to all other normal gear combinations and test adjustment. Make corrections as necessary in ¼ turn adjustments.

Chainline

Chainline is the relation of the front and rear sprockets to the center plane of the bicycle (figure 9.52). The bike center plane is an imaginary plane running from front to rear through the middle of the bike. As an example, a front crankset and/or front derailleur might be designed to have a chainline of 50mm. The front derailleur would then work best when the middle of the chainrings are 50mm from the bike centerline.

FIGURE: 9.52

Chainline in relationship to the bike mid plane.
(A) Distance from middle of front chainrings to mid plane
(B) Distance from middle of rear sprockets to mid plane

Chainline can also refer to the relative position of the front and rear sprockets to each other without regard to the bike centerline. This is called "effective chainline." Effective chainline is simply the difference between "A" and "B," but distance "A" is not always designed to be equal to "B." For example, for most three chainring bikes, the middle of nine rear sprockets will be approximately 45mm from the bicycle mid plane or distance "B." The manufacturer's specified chainline of triple cranksets ranges from 47 to 50mm, distance "A." In this case, the front chainrings are not designed to align directly with the middle of the rear sprockets.

Drive train manufacturers do not generally consider all gear combinations to be usable. For example, a "27-speed" bike has three chainrings in front and 9 sprockets in the rear for a total of 27 gears. There are likely to be several gear combinations that are exact or very close duplicates. It is also likely that the chain will rub the side of the middle chainring when the chain is on the smallest sprocket in front and possibly 2 or 3 of the smallest sprockets in back. This is simply the limitation of the design. If the front crankset were moved outward until there was

no rubbing in these combinations, there would likely be other shifting problems in other gear combinations, such as the largest chainring and several of the inner rear sprockets.

Sprocket combinations that should be avoided are termed "cross chaining." Drive train manufacturers vary on exactly which combinations should not be used. Generally, it is assumed that the smallest front chainring and smallest rear sprocket will not be used, nor will the largest rear sprocket in combination with the largest front chainring. As a practical matter, each bike may be different as to which exact gear combinations is unusable.

Here's a rule of thumb. If the bicycle shifts well, the chainline should be considered adequate, but chainline adjustment may be needed if:

- Chain jumps off large chainring when front derailleur is correctly adjusted for height, rotation, and limit screw settings.
- Chain rides off lower derailleur pulley teeth when derailleur or hanger is not bent.
- Chain rattles on inner faces of front chainrings in what should be usable gears.
- Chain derails off inner chainring when front derailleur is correctly adjusted for height, rotation, and limit screw settings.
- Front derailleur cannot be adjusted to stop over shifts while still allowing good shifting.

Moving the front chainrings can make changes to chainline. By using different bottom bracket spindle widths, the chainrings can be moved inward or outward. Shorter spindles move the chainrings inward, and longer spindles move the chainrings outward. On some models, a thin spacer can be placed under the right side cup of the bottom bracket to move the chainrings outward. There are limits to this, however, because it results in less thread engagement for the right side cup. There are limits to moving a derailleur inward, toward the bike mid plane. The chainrings may end up rubbing the frame. Additionally, the front derailleur may not work well with the front chainrings too close to the frame.

Chainline manipulation with the rear sprockets is generally more limited. The freehub mechanism cannot be moved laterally on the hub shell. If the hub uses a threaded axle, spacers may sometimes be moved under the cone locknut to shift the rear sprocket positions. If spacers are moved from the right side to the left side, double-check that the chain will not strike the frame when on the smallest rear cog. It is important not to change

the fit on the hub into the frame. Any change of axle spacing will also change the centering of the wheel rim over the hub. Double-check and correct dish if the spacers were manipulated.

The bicycle is designed for forward pedaling. There are times, such preventing the inside pedal from striking a tight corner, when a cyclist may want to pedal backwards. When pedaling forward, the chain is guided to the rear sprocket by the upper derailleur pulley, which is very close to the sprockets. When a cyclist backpedals, the chain is guided to the rear sprocket by the front chainrings, which will be some distance away. The chain may disengage or become jammed when it is backpedaled because the front chainrings cannot keep the chain guided straight to the sprocket. Disengagement is likely to be worse in gear combinations where the chainline is offset the greatest. It may be possible to minimize back pedaling problems by changing chainline, but, again, this may result in other problems.

Derailleur Hanger Alignment & Repair

The rear derailleur is mounted to the bike at the derailleur hanger. The hanger should be aligned parallel to the rear sprockets. A bent or misaligned derailleur hanger will result in poor shifting performance (figure 9.53). The derailleur hanger can become bent when the bike is crashed, bumped with force, or if something, such as a stick, becomes caught in the derailleur when riding. A misaligned hanger may also just be a manufacturer defect.

FIGURE: 9.53

A bent hanger from impacts to rear derailleur

Many hangers can be bent, aligned, rebent, and realigned again. This is because there is very little stress from riding the bike or shifting gears. As a rule of thumb, if a hanger survives a repair by bending, it will survive the riding.

To check alignment and repair the derailleur hanger, use a derailleur hanger alignment gauge, such as the Park Tool DAG-1 Derailleur Alignment Gauge. The tool extends the plane of the hanger and compares it to the rim. If the hanger is aligned to the rim, it will also be aligned to the rear sprockets.

Bolt-on or replaceable hangers may be aligned (figure 9.54). However, these types of hangers can be difficult to fix if the clamping design of the hanger to the frame is inadequate. Replaceable hangers may move in the frame mount, which changes the alignment of the hanger and derailleur. Before checking alignment on replaceable hangers, double-check the security of hanger to frame bolts or screws.

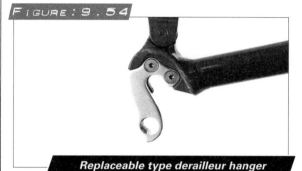

FIGURE: 9.54

Replaceable type derailleur hanger

The procedure for derailleur hanger alignment:

a. Mount the bike in a repair stand. Level the bike, as it would appear on flat ground.

b. Check that the rear wheel is mounted straight in the frame.

c. Remove rear derailleur from hanger. Derailleur may hang from housing.

d. Install DAG-1 into hanger and tighten handle. If the DAG-1 does not thread easily into the derailleur hanger, chase and clean the threads using a tap as necessary. Do not use the DAG-1 threads as a "chaser" of bad derailleur hanger threads.

e. Rotate the arm toward the left side of the rim at the nine o'clock position. Rotate the tire valve to the same position. Use the valve on the rim as a constant reference point when checking the hanger (figure 9.55). By checking the same point on the rim, wheel trueness or dish will not affect alignment.

f. Loosen the sliding gauge knob and move the sliding gauge to contact the rim, then secure the knob.

g. Push gauge bracket toward hub before rotating arm. This prevents gauge from being forced against rim.

h. Rotate DAG-1 and rim valve 180 degrees to the three o'clock position. Slide indicator toward rim to same point near valve.

i. There are three possible results:

Condition 1: The gauge barely touches the rim or has a small gap less then 4mm. In this case, the hanger is aligned horizontally.

Condition 2: The pointer is away from the rim some distance. The hanger is misaligned (figure 9.56). If the distance is greater then 4mm, the hanger will need re-alignment. Use a 4mm hex wrench to gauge the gap.

Condition 3: The pointer strikes inside the rim, which indicates a misaligned hanger (figure 9.57). It is easier to determine the error by seeing the gap between the rim and gauge. Reset tool to rim contact at the 9 o'clock position and rotate back to the 3 o'clock position. There will be a gap between the rim and the gauge.

j. Bend the derailleur hanger a small amount using the DAG-1 tool. Then re-check both sides. Reset gauge and remeasure gap. Generally, it is best to bend with the DAG-1 arm next to the chainstay (figure 9.58). This allows you to use the stay for leverage and to control the amount of bending either inward or out.

k. Repeat bending and checking until the gap is less than 4mm. A 4mm gap at the rim means the hanger is off less than a millimeter at the sprockets, where the derailleur actually shifts. Use a 4mm hex wrench as a "go-no go" gauge.

l. When the horizontal positions are aligned, move on to check the 6 o'clock and 12 o'clock position. Set gauge to the 6 o'clock position, and then check at the 12 o'clock position.

m. Rotate DAG-1 and rim valve 180 degrees If the gap exceeds the 4mm tolerance, bend accordingly in small increments, rechecking and resetting the gauge (figure 9.59). When the gap is less than 4mm, keep the same setting and check at the 9 o'clock position. When three points that are 90-degrees apart are within 4mm, hanger is aligned.

n. Remove the tool and re-install the derailleur.

o. Check settings on both limit screws and check index settings.

FIGURE: 9.55

Set DAG-1 to reference rim at the nine o'clock position

FIGURE: 9.56

Gauge indicating misaligned hanger

FIGURE: 9.57

Reset gauge if it falls inside rim

FIGURE: 9.58

Use the frame to control bending of the hanger

FIGURE: 9.59

Use a 4mm gauge to check the tolerance

FIGURE: 9.61

*Unworn pulley wheel on left
and extremely worn pulley on right*

The threads of the derailleur hanger are commonly 10mm x 1mm. If the derailleur installs with difficulty, the threads of the hanger should be tapped. As a test of thread acceptability, fully tighten the derailleur. If the derailleur bolt does not strip, the hanger is usable. If the threads strip and fail, it is possible for a professional mechanic to install a coil thread or a t-nut repair system (figure 9.60). These repairs work well when properly done and allow the bike to be used as normal.

FIGURE: 9.60

T-nut thread repair of a stripped hanger

Derailleur Wear and Service

Both derailleurs will eventually wear out with use. Play and excess movement develop at the pivots. Grab the lower cage of a rear derailleur and pull left to right to test play. It may help to compare the play in the old derailleur to new models. Replace the derailleur when the cage at the lower pulley has more then a ¼-inch (6mm) movement.

Chain travels over the pulleys and pulley teeth, which causes wear. Worn pulley wheels will not engage well with the chain (figure 9.61). The pulley wheels usually can be replaced.

The rear derailleur can be brushed off and lightly scrubbed with soap or solvent. Use care not to get solvent in the upper and lower pivots. A solvent in the cage pivots will ruin the grease inside. It is also possible to disassemble, clean, and re-assemble some rear derailleurs. Overhaul of the rear derailleur is not discussed in this book.

The front derailleur can be flushed with degreaser, dried, and relubricated at the spring and all pivot points with a light lubricant. The pivots of the cage will eventually develop play and slop with enough use. Grab the back end of the derailleur and pull from side to side. Compare the old derailleur to the movement on a new derailleur. The cage may also be gouged or damaged from dragging on a chain. Front derailleurs typically have no replaceable parts and, when the derailleur wears out, should just be replaced.

Troubleshooting Derailleur Systems

Poor or inconsistent shifting can be the result of several problems or combinations of problems. It is often necessary to check each part of the shifting system to find the problem and solve it (Table 9.1 Troubleshooting Table).

TABLE: 9.1   *Troubleshooting Table*

SHIFTING OR RIDING SYMPTOM	POTENTIAL PROBLEM	POTENTIAL SOLUTION
Chain skips in all gear combinations	Poor indexing adjustment	Re-adjust indexing
Shifting is slow or hesitant for either inward and outward shifts	Friction in the cable system	Lubricate and/or replace cable and housing
Shifting is slow or hesitant on inward shifts	Poor indexing adjustment with cable tension too loose (Rapid Rise® likely too tight)	Increase cable tension. Rapid Rise® decrease cable tension
Shifting is slow or hesitant on outward shifts	Poor indexing adjustment with cable tension too tight (Rapid Rise® likely too loose)	Decrease cable tension. Rapid Rise® increase cable tension.
Chain skips under pressure in only 1, 2 or 3 rear sprockets	Sprockets and chain may be worn out	Inspect and replace sprockets and chain
Chain shifts off of largest front chainring	Front H-limit screw too loose, or rotation of cage is off	Inspect and correct cage rotation as necessary. Check H-limit screw setting.
Chain shifts off of smallest front chainring	Front L-limit screw too loose, or rotation of cage is off.	Inspect and correct cage rotation as necessary. Check L-limit screw setting.
Chain shifts slow or not at all to largest front chainring	Front derailleur cable tension too loose, H-limit screw too tight, and/or rotation of cage is off.	Check front index setting. Check derailleur rotation and H-limit screw setting.
Chain shifts slow or not at all to smallest front chainring	Front derailleur cable tension too tight, and/or L-limit screw too tight, and/or rotation of cage is off	Check front index setting. Check derailleur rotation and L-limit screw setting.
Chain shifts well to largest front chainring but outer cage rubs after shift is completed	Front derailleur cable tension too loose	Increase front derailleur cable tension
Chain skips under load at front chainrings	Front chainrings worn	Replace chainrings

CHAPTER 10

Internal Gear Systems

The internally-geared hub allows for different gear ratio selection without a derailleur system. These hubs contain a series of gears called "planetary gears" that act as a transmission.

A center gear, called the sun gear, is fixed to the axle and engages the outer gears known as the "planets." All planets are engaged into the "planet carrier" that drives the hub shell. The planet gears engage or disengage the sun gear for a particular gear ratio. The internally-geared hubs use a special keyed washer and axles with flats that prevents the axle from rotating in the dropout (figure 10.1). Wheel installation, cable attachment, and gear adjustment are reviewed here. Internal hub service is best left to professional mechanics.

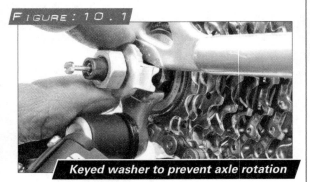

Keyed washer to prevent axle rotation

Internally geared hubs use one of the middle gears as the "neutral" or 100% of the front ring-to-rear cog ratio. This gear will act as if the bike were a single speed. Gears on either side of this neutral gear will either reduce it by some amount or increase it. For example, the first gear of the DualDrive® hub reduces the gear to 73% of the middle position, and third gear increases it to 136% of the middle position.

SRAM DUALDRIVE®

The SRAM DualDrive® hub offers three internal gear choices. The hub is also fitted with a freehub and cassette that is shifted by a derailleur. The internal hub gears can be viewed as a replacement of the three front chainring choices.

The internal hub gears are shifted through a small rod on the right side of the axle. The shift lever attaches to the click-box, which pulls the shifting rod and moves the planetary gears inside the hub. The wheel can be removed to service the tire and tube, and the cable can be replaced.

The procedure for wheel removal:
  a. Shift internal shift lever toward lowest gear range (to the left). Shift the external derailleur to smallest rear cog on derailleur.
  b. Push button on click-box downward to release box from shifting rod. Pull click-box off of right side axle (figure 10.2).
  c. Loosen left and right axle nuts. Shifting rod may remain in right side but use care not to bend or damage rod.
  d. Remove wheel from bike.

Remove click box to access axle nuts

The procedure to install wheel:
  a. Install wheel in frame and align. Use care to position special alignment washer in frame dropout.
  b. Secure axle nuts fully.
  c. If shifting rod was removed, re-install and gently secure with screwdriver.
  d. Push button downward on click-box and install box on axle by pushing box against axle nut.
  e. Push click-box button upward from below to engage lever arm on to shifting rod. Test by pulling gently on click-box away from hub.

The rear derailleur is adjusted as any other derailleur system. See Chapter 9, Derailleur Systems, for rear derailleur adjustments.

The internal gears of the DualDrive® are adjusted by changes in cable tension from the shift lever. To adjust the three internal gears, shift lever to the middle position. Inspect inside the window of the click-box for the lever with a yellow mark. Use barrel adjusters to change cable tension and move yellow mark to adjustment mark on window of click box (figure 10.3). Test adjustment by shifting to all three possible positions.

Adjust cable tension until yellow mark aligns between marks

The DualDrive system has two cables at the shift lever. One wire shifts the derailleur. A second cable shifts the rod at the click-box. The derailleur cable installs under a ring-cover, which is held by a screw. Disconnect cable from rear derailleur and remove screw on ring cover at lever (figure 10.4). Pull cover outward to expose cable end and push out old shift cable. Lubricate new cable and install through hole left by old cable. Push cover to lever and install screw and secure.

Cable access of the SRAM double control lever

The procedure for internal shift cable installation:

a. Remove click-box as describe in wheel removal above.

b. Remove back-end of click-box. Hold main body of box and push downward on corner end of click-box (figure 10.5).

c. Loosen cable pinch bolt inside click-box and pull cable from click-box.

d. At shift lever, remove cover over internal shift cable (figure 10.6).

e. Push old cable from lever. Lubricate install new cable and route though lever and housing back to click-box. Thread barrel adjuster fully into click-box.

f. Thread cable into pinch bolt mechanism. Push click-box to housing end cap, while pulling back on lever. Secure pinch bolt (figure 10.7).

g. Cut cable end very short (1-2mm) to allow end cap installation. Cable end must not interfere with click-box end cap.

h. Push click-box button downward and install rear click-box on axle. Push upwards on button. Shift the lever to middle position.

i. Adjust gears as described in Gear Adjustment above.

j. Install rear cover of click-box.

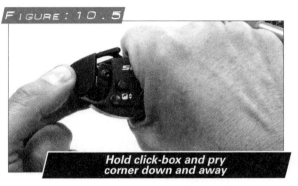

Hold click-box and pry corner down and away

Remove and install cable at shift lever

Pull cable snug and secure pinch bolt

SRAM® I-Motion 9

The I-Motion 9 hub offers nine different gears. The sixth position is considered "neutral." Gears above it increase in ratio, and gears below it are reduced. It is necessary to detach the shift cable when removing the wheel. Internal hub service should be left to professional mechanics.

The procedure to remove rear wheel:
a. Turn shifter to 1st gear.
b. Slide quick-disconnect sleeve on connecting tube and slide it away from hub.
c. Pull connecting tube down and away from hub fitting (figure 10.8).
d. Loosen axle nuts. Remove coaster arm locking bolt if applicable.
e. Remove wheel.

FIGURE: 10.8

Remove connecting tube

The procedure to install wheel:
a. Install washers with serrations toward frame. Washer lugs must fit into dropouts to prevent axle rotation.
b. Tighten drive side then non-drive. Check and correct chain tension as necessary.
c. Install and secure coaster arm locking bolt if applicable.
d. Move shifter to first gear.
e. Open quick disconnect sleeve and connect catch to shifting stud at hub.

The procedure to adjust gears:
a. Shift bike to 6th gear.
b. View window at right side of hub for red and yellow marks.
c. Use barrel adjuster a connecting tube and adjust cable tension until yellow marker on moving indicator aligns with red marker of hub (figure 10.9).
d. Test gears by shifting through gear range.

FIGURE: 10.9

Align marks are hub to adjust gears

The procedure to change cable:
a. Shift to first gear.
b. Remove quick-disconnect sleeve from hub.
c. To remove old cable, pull at connecting tube away from housing and cut cable.
d. Remove adjusting barrel from connecting tube.
e. Remove coil spring and remaining shift wire and connection nipple from connecting tube. Loosen setscrew in connection nipple and remove old cable.
f. Using a small-tipped screwdriver, remove cable cap from shift lever. You may need the screwdriver to also help pull the head of the cable out. Push cable while engaging cable end with tip of screwdriver (figure 10.10).
g. Install new cable through shift lever. It can be helpful to slightly bend end of new wire to feed it through bend in lever.
h. Route new cable through housing. Ensure all end caps are fully pressed onto housing.
i. With shift lever in 1st gear and housing fully seated, cut cable a distance of 105mm (4 ⅛") past the housing end cap.
j. Install adjusting barrel and coil spring over wire.
k. Carefully compress coil spring over cable and install connection nipple onto end of cable. Secure setscrew to hold cable (figure 10.11).
l. Install connection nipple and cable into connecting tube. Asymmetrical shape of nipple will fit tube in only one orientation. Nipple should be visible at end of tube with open end facing hub connection stud.
m. Thread barrel adjuster fully on to connecting tube.
n. Install quick-disconnect sleeve to hub and adjust hub gears as described above.

Remove cable from shifter

Secure shift wire setscrew

Shimano Inter-7 or Inter-8 Hub

The Inter-7 or Inter-8 hubs use a "cassette joint" on the right side to actuate the gears. When installing wheel, it may be easier to work with the bike upside down. This allows the use of two hands to manipulate parts.

The procedure for wheel removal:

a. Shift lever to 1st gear on the indicator.
b. Remove housing for housing stop at hub cassette joint. Pull at housing end and disengage from housing stop (figure 10.12).
c. Detach cable anchor from cassette joint. Rotate anchor and lift it from hook in joint.
d. Loosen axle nuts and remove wheel.

Release cable from housing stop to detach anchor from cassette joint

The cassette joint consists of three pieces and is held to the hub by a lockring. The cassette joint may stay together for wheel service. Turning the lockring lever counter-clockwise releases the joint. To install the joint, align a series of yellow dots on the assembly. Turn lockring clockwise 45-degrees to lock cassette joint (figure 10.13).

Cassette joint of Inter hub system

The hub axle uses special keyed washers to prevent the axle from rotating in the dropouts under load. Align the cable-housing stop of the cassette joint so it points toward the shift cable. For hub models with coaster or band brakes, secure left side braking arm to frame. Install wheel and adjust chain tension as on a single speed system.

The common shifter for the Inter hub systems is the Revo® shifter. To install a new shift cable, remove the cover screw and lift cover from lever body. Turn shifter to gear 7 or 8, whichever allows better access to cable end. Push on exposed cable adjacent to barrel adjuster to gain cable slack. Use a small-tipped screw driver to remove cable end from lever (figure 10.14). Install new cable first through barrel adjuster and then route cable back into cable end anchor. Install cover and cover screw and shift lever to 1st gear.

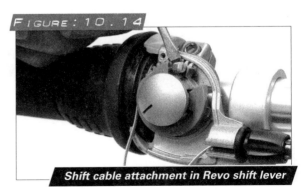
Shift cable attachment in Revo shift lever

ParkTool

Align shifting adjustment marks at joint

Route shift cable through housing to rear hub. A pinch bolt mechanism is used to attach cable anchor to cassette joint. Pull firmly on cable to ensure it is seated in the housing stops. Back out barrel adjuster approximately 2 turns from full engagement to allow adjustment. Secure pinch mechanism so there is a distance of approximately 100 millimeters from the end cap to center of bolt (figure 10.15). Secure nut; cable will flatten at pinch mechanism.

Measure approximately 100mm between end cap and center of pinch bolt

Gears are adjusted by alignment marks on the cassette joint. The marks are visible both from above and below the bike.

The procedure for gear adjustment:

a. If not already done, engage cable anchor bolt to cassette joint (figure 10.16).
b. For Inter-7 and Inter-8 hubs and shifters, shift to the 4th gear position.
c. Use barrel adjust to change cable tension and align red marks on cassette joint (figure 10.17). Shift all gears after adjustment.

Engage pinch bolt into cassette joint

CHAPTER 11

Caliper Disc Brake System

D isc brake systems use a caliper mounted near the dropouts of the frame or fork ends and a rotor (disc) mounted to the hub. The brake pads are housed in the caliper and are forced into the rotor, which slows the bike by converting speed into energy of heat. Disc brakes can be effective in wet weather where mud, dirt, and water are a concern in braking. The system can generate significant heat from slowing the wheel and bike. Allow rotor and caliper to cool before servicing. The rotors are made of machined steel, and the edges can be sharp. Always use care when working with or around disc brakes.

Caliper Types

Disc brake systems can be either mechanical or hydraulic. Mechanical systems use calipers that are cable actuated, similar to rim caliper brakes, with brake housing and an inner brake pulled by a brake lever (figure 11.1).

FIGURE: 11.1

Mechanical disc brake with brake wire

Hydraulic caliper systems use pistons and sealed tubing to push brake fluid from the lever to the caliper (figure 11.2). The brake relies on the entire system being sealed when the lever is pulled.

FIGURE: 11.2

Hydraulic disc brake

Disc brake calipers mount to fittings on the bicycle frame and fork. There are two standards. The International Standard (IS) uses two mounting tabs with holes spaced 51mm apart (figure 11.3). The caliper mounting bolts are positioned perpendicular to the rotor.

FIGURE: 11.3

IS disc caliper mounting system on rear seat stay

Another mounting system is the post mount (figure 11.4). Caliper mounting bolts of the post mount are parallel with the rotor. Mounting holes are spaced 74mm apart. Brake calipers designed for the post mount system can be fitted with adapters to work with the International Standard.

FIGURE: 11.4

Post Mount system on a fork

Brake pads for both mechanical and hydraulic systems are available in various compounds. Generally, a softer organic or resin material will tend to squeal less, which can be an issue in some systems. These will also offer the user more modulation or the ability to brake lightly. These types of pads, however, will also wear more quickly. The harder sintered or semi-metallic pads will last longer, especially in wet and muddy conditions (figure 11.5), but they may be noisier.

FIGURE: 1 1 . 5

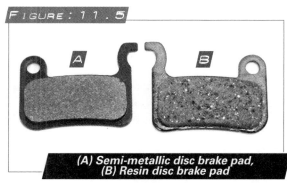

**(A) Semi-metallic disc brake pad,
(B) Resin disc brake pad**

The brake pads should be kept clean of fluids and grease. Contaminated pads should be replaced. A light sanding with very fine emery cloth can help to clean marginal pads. Use isopropyl alcohol or similar solvent when cleaning rotor surface of dirt or film. Do not use a solvent or cleaner that contains oils or leaves an oily residue.

Brake pads wear thin with use. Most manufacturers list specifications for minimum pad thickness. Pads should never be worn down to where the metal holder is showing or contacting the rotor. It is common for new disc pads and rotor to require "burnishing" or breaking in. This may take several uses of the brake under loads. The heat of burnishing helps remove solvents and any residue from the pads and rotors.

Rotors

The rotor or disc of the disc brake system secures to a disc-specific hub. The common system uses six bolts. Use a mild thread locker on the threads and secure the bolts. Many brands use rotor bolts requiring the use of a Torx T-25 wrench (figure 11.6). A Torx fitting is a special star shaped socket head bolt. Secure rotor bolts to manufacturer's torque specifications.

FIGURE: 1 1 . 6

Secure bolts using Torx driver

The rotor diameter may vary between models and brands. Rotor diameter sizes are available as 140mm, 145mm, 152mm, 160mm, 185mm, and 203mm. The brake caliper and rotor diameter must be compatible. A larger rotor provides more leverage during braking, which results in a more powerful brake. While different brands of rotors may interchange with calipers, do not attempt to change the rotor diameter from the caliper and/or caliper adaptor bracket design.

Rotors may also be designed to mount to the hub with a splined fitting, which uses a lockring similar to a cassette lockring. Use the Park Tool BBT-9 for rings with 16 external notches. Use the Park Tool FR-5 for rings with 12 internal notches, sized like the cassette lockring (figure 11.7).

FIGURE: 1 1 . 7

**Shimano XTR lockring system
using the FR-5 lockring tool**

Rotors may become bent or warped with use and abuse. Some re-bending for alignment may be possible. The Park Tool DT-2 Rotor Truing Fork allows bending at the outer edge of the rotor (figure 11.8). It can be useful to number the rotor arms to better track the repair progress. Mount the bike in a repair stand and spin the wheel. Watch for a wobble at the caliper or hold the DT-2 at the caliper as a rub indicator. Stop the wheel and note the location and direction of the rub. Move the rotor out of the caliper and use the DT-2 or adjustable wrench to bend this area slightly. Spin the wheel and check the rotor. Repeat as necessary. If rotor true does not improve, replacement is the best option.

FIGURE : 11.8

Re-bending a warped rotor

Rotors will thin and wear with braking. If there is an obvious step at the braking surface, replace rotor (figure 11.9). Manufacturers also specify a minimum thickness for rotor replacement.

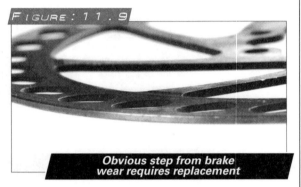

FIGURE : 11.9

Obvious step from brake wear requires replacement

Hydraulic Brake Levers

The hydraulic brake system use a piston at the hand lever called the "master cylinder." The lever is positioned on the handlebar similar to conventional or non-hydraulic levers. Set the angle for comfortable reach when the cyclist is in the saddle. The brake lever reach from bar to lever is adjusted behind the lever pivot. Turning the screw moves the lever relative to the handlebars (figure 11.10).

FIGURE : 11.10

Reach screw adjustment on the Shimano® brake lever

As the brake fluid heats, it expands. Hydraulic disc systems use a reservoir system that contains a bladder to allow for the expansion of the brake fluid. Some models use an "open system" while others use an enclosed bladder (figure 11.11). The master piston is sealed from the reservoir when the lever is pulled, but it opens to the reservoir when the lever is fully open.

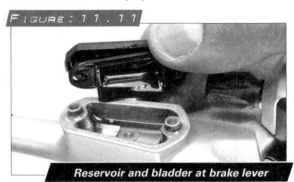

FIGURE : 11.11

Reservoir and bladder at brake lever

In all hydraulic systems, it is important that there is no air in the tubing or lines between the caliper and the lever piston. Air bubbles in the line will compress and cause the brake to feel soft when the lever is pulled with force.

Hydraulic Disc Calipers

The master piston at the lever pushes brake fluid through sealed brake tubing to another set of pistons at the caliper called the "slave cylinders". These pistons push the pads to the rotor. Because the hydraulic fluid does not compress or flex under stress, hydraulic systems are considered more efficient and higher performance than mechanical systems.

With use over time, brake fluid will become contaminated with dirt and moisture and should be replaced. It is critical to use the correct type of fluid for the specific brake. Some manufacturers specify mineral fluid, while others use an automotive brake fluid. The different types of brake fluid should never be mixed. Using the wrong fluid is likely to cause seals to fail and result in brake failure.

Automotive fluids are DOT (Department of Transportation) approved and are generally polyglycol fluids. The DOT fluids have different ratings, such as 3, 4 or 5. Contact the manufacturer for a specific recommendation. Automotive brake fluids are caustic and toxic. Work with care to avoid fluid contact with the outside of the lever or caliper, the bike, or your skin. When available, use protective gloves, such as ParkTool MG-1 Mechanic Gloves. During any work with hydraulic fluid, clean spills on the bike, caliper, or lever with a rag and isopropyl alcohol or soapy water. DOT hydraulic fluids can damage paint finish. Bleeding syringes for mineral fluid should not be used for automotive fluid or vice-versa.

Hydraulic systems should be inspected at all fittings and hose connections for leakage and seepage. Because most brakes use a reservoir at the lever, it is best not to store a bike upside down, or air may enter the brake lines. If the bike has been upside down, allow it to sit several minutes before use and test the levers by pulling with force.

When servicing hydraulic brakes, work in clean conditions. Use care to keep hydraulic pieces, such as the bladder, clean and away from dirt. The caliper pistons and seal will wear out with time and use and require replacement. Caliper piston overhauls should be performed by professional mechanics.

Hydraulic Brake Caliper Alignment

For some disc caliper systems, it can be difficult to view the caliper-to-rotor alignment because pads are inside caliper body and have tight tolerances to rotor. It can help to place white paper or equivalent behind the area you are viewing. Shine a flashlight on the paper to highlight pad and rotor (figure 11.12).

FIGURE: 11.12

Use a white background to help in viewing pad to rotor alignment

Inspect old pads when removed. If pads are worn unevenly, it may be a sign that the caliper is misaligned to the rotor (figure 11.13). Disc pads are designed to strike the rotor face flush. The caliper body may have a lateral adjustment and allow adjustment of the two edges of the pads. The other two edges of pad should also strike rotor flush. Depending upon the design of the caliper, the full alignment will rely on the square-machining of the caliper mounts to

the rotor. If no adjustment of caliper to rotor will stop rubbing and strike the rotor flush, the mounts may require machining. Consult a professional mechanic.

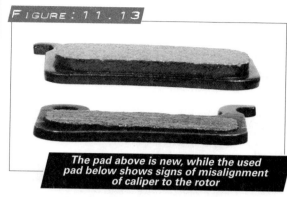

FIGURE: 11.13

The pad above is new, while the used pad below shows signs of misalignment of caliper to the rotor

The procedure for caliper alignment for post mount or IS mounted with adaptor bracket:

a. Fully loosen caliper-mounting bolts. This will allow the caliper to move sideways.

b. Depress the brake lever to secure pads against the rotor and maintain pressure. This will move the caliper so pads are aligned to the rotor. Inspect caliper and brake pad pistons. Push caliper left or right until pistons appear centered over rotor. Maintain pressure on the rotor and tighten the caliper mounting bolts (figure 11.14).

c. Release lever and inspect this initial pad alignment. Ideally, the pads should clear the rotor with no rubbing. In some cases, however, a light rubbing may occur and should not affect performance. Fine-tune the pad alignment by fully loosening one mounting bolt while keeping the other bolt snug. This will allow you to push the caliper while pivoting off the snug bolt.

FIGURE: 11.14

Align caliper and pads to rotor, then tighten caliper-mounting bolts

Disc brake calipers may be designed to bolt directly to the IS mounts. This design has no built-in lateral adjustment, and it is necessary to use thin washers and shims to adjust the caliper. A shimming washer can be placed between the frame or fork mount and the caliper body (figure 11.15). View pad to rotor alignment and then add or subtract washers as necessary. The upper and lower mounts may require different amounts of shimming.

FIGURE: 11.15

Add shim washers to move caliper and pads laterally

Shimano® Hydraulic Brakes

Shimano® brake systems use mineral fluid. Never use an automotive DOT brake fluid in a system requiring mineral fluid. Shimano® offers a special bleed kit that allows the brake to be bled from the caliper upward to the lever. The procedure below assumes this is not available and bleeds the brake from the lever down to the caliper, which is a slower and less efficient process but will achieve the same results.

Brake fluid can become dirty with use and may become contaminated with moisture. If the bike is used extensively, the fluid should be replaced once a year.

The procedure below outlines a complete fluid change and uses gravity to pull fluid through the system and out the caliper. It will be necessary to rig a waste collection bottle or bag at the caliper.

The procedure for fluid change and brake bleed:

a. Mount bike in repair stand and remove wheels.

b. Remove brake pads to avoid contamination by brake fluid.

c. Rotate bike as necessary until tubing has a continuous upward slope from the brake caliper to the reservoir (figure 11.16). Caliper may also be removed as necessary to achieve as much of a vertical line as possible from caliper to lever.

d. Install Shimano® caliper block #Y8CL18000 in place of pads. Block provides a stop to pistons when lever is operated. If this part is not available, substitute a clean 10mm hex wrench between pistons.

e. Attach bleed tubing to end of bleed nipple at caliper. Attach bleed bottle or bag to end of tubing to catch waste fluid (figure 11.17). (Note: it is useful to attached box end of wrench over bleed nipple. Then attach bleed hose. This holds wrench to nipple during process of bleed.)

f. Rotate brake lever on handlebar until top surface of reservoir is parallel with the ground.

g. Clean dirt from lever and wipe around reservoir tank cover. Unthread screws at reservoir tank cap. Remove reservoir cap and bladder.

h. Loosen bleed nipple at caliper body ⅛ to ¼ turn. Gravity will drain fluid from lever down through caliper and out to bleed nipple.

i. Maintain fluid height in reservoir as it drains out bleed nipple (figure 11.18). When clean fluid with no bubbles appears at bleed hose and reservoir is full, close bleed nipple. Air may remain trapped in caliper body. Encourage any air trapped in caliper or line to rise toward the reservoir by operating lever repeatedly while tapping caliper and line with a non-metallic lever.

j. Test lever by pulling. Piston should extend but be stopped by brake block. Lever will eventually become stiff and firm when pulled. If there is no resistance to lever, open bleed screw and continue to operate handle. This will pump more fluid into the system. Maintain fluid lever at reservoir.

k. When lever resistance stiffens, close bleed nipple. Hold lever closed and maintain pressure. Loosen bleed nipple to open system. Open and close system within one second, take notice if any of the expelled fluid contains an air bubble.

l. Release lever. Check reservoir tank and add fluid.

m. Operate lever repeatedly. If lever feels stiff with resistance at the end of its travel, line contains no air and is fully bled. If lever feels soft, repeat steps "j" through "m."

n. Check that reservoir tank is filled to top. Install reservoir bladder and cap. Expect some excess fluid to spill from lever. This is normal and ensures no air is below bladder. Tighten cap screws.

o. After bleeding, disconnect hose and bleed bottle or bag from bleed nipple. Clean the lever and caliper of any fluid.

p. Install brake shoes and wheel.

Rotate bike and lever for continuous upward slope

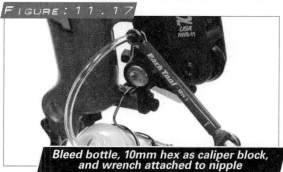

Bleed bottle, 10mm hex as caliper block, and wrench attached to nipple

Keep reservoir tank filled with fluid

If the brake lever appears soft, it is possible to bleed air without a full fluid change. Air must be purged and fluid level maintained in the reservoir.

The procedure for fluid change and brake bleed:

a. Proceed with steps "a" through "g" for fluid change and brake bleed above. Add fluid to reservoir if low, and operate lever.

b. Pull lever and check for resistance. If resistance is felt, hold lever closed. Open and close bleed nipple within one second.

c. Check fluid level and fill as needed. Repeat holding of lever while briefly opening and closing nipple.

d. If no resistance is felt at lever, the system contains a significant amount of air. Work lever repeatedly to work bubbles up and out of lever reservoir. Encourage any air trapped in caliper or line to rise toward the reservoir by operating lever repeatedly while tapping caliper and line with a non-metallic lever.

e. Check fluid level and fill as needed. Repeat holding of lever while briefly opening nipple.

f. When lever feels firm when pulled with force the system is bled.

e. Proceed with "n" through "p" in fluid change and brake bleed above.

Brake Pad Removal and Replacement

Brake pads wear thin with use. Most manufacturers list specifications for minimum pad thickness. For Shimano® pads, replace when pad material (not including pad holder) is less than 0.9mm thick.

As the pads wear, the pistons reposition closer to the rotor. It will be necessary to remove the rotor and push the pistons away from the center before installing new pads.

The procedure for Shimano® Hydraulic caliper pad replacement:

a. Mount bike in repair stand.

b. Remove wheel(s).

c. Rotate lever on handlebar until top surface of reservoir is parallel with the ground. Clean lever of dirt and wipe around reservoir cover.

d. Remove reservoir cover. This will allow excess fluid to spill from reservoir.

e. Remove pad fixing bolt clip and unscrew pad-fixing bolt (figure 11.19).

f. Remove pads by pushing them outward and away from hub axle. Note orientation of pad return spring between pads. This spring assists pad release from rotor during braking.

g. Wipe piston area clean. Use a clean rag and a mild solvent such as isopropyl alcohol to clean the piston faces and inside the caliper body.

h. Use a plastic lever, such as a tire lever, to push both pistons into the caliper body. Push near center of piston and avoid pushing edge of piston (figure 11.20). Excess fluid may spill from the reservoir during this process.

i. Place pad return spring between new pads (figure 11.21).

j. Install pads into caliper. Orient eyehole in pads and spring to align with pad-fixing bolt hole.

k. Install and secure pad-fixing bolt and any bolt clip.

l. Inspect fluid lever at reservoir and add fluid as needed. Replace bladder and reservoir cover. Secure screws and wipe any fluid off lever.

m. Install wheel and test brake by squeezing lever with force. If lever feels soft, system will require bleeding.

n. If pads drag or appear misaligned, align caliper to rotor.

FIGURE: 11.21

Pad return spring is placed between pads

Resetting Brake Pads

If the pads seem to rub on the rotor and re-alignment will not prevent this, the pistons may need to be reset. The procedure requires the use of a simple floating shim between pads in the caliper. Shimano® supplies this shim, part #Y8CL1200, with a new brake set. Alternatively, use a hard, flat material that is the thickness of the rotor. Park Tool cone wrenches, such as any of the Double-Ended Cone Wrench DCW, match the width of rotors and can substitute for the pad spacer.

FIGURE: 11.19

Remove bolt clip and unthread pad fixing bolt

The procedure for resetting pads:

a. Remove wheel(s) from bike.

b. Remove pad retention screw and remove pads. Use a clean rag and a mild solvent such as isopropyl alcohol to wipe clean the piston faces and inside the caliper body.

c. Use a plastic lever, such as a tire lever. Push each piston back into caliper body. Note whether the piston moves back out after being pushed back into caliper body. If a piston moves after being reset, there may be excess fluid in the system. Remove cover of reservoir. Allow excess fluid to spill out of the reservoir as the pistons are pushed into the caliper body. If the reservoir cap was removed, re-install it. Wipe fluid from lever.

d. Install pads, pad return spring, and pad retention screw.

e. Install floating shim (Shimano part #Y8CL1200) or a shim of equivalent thickness (figure 11.22).

f. Squeeze lever repeatedly. Pistons will automatically center to caliper body.

g. For bracket-mounted caliper bodies, loosen caliper-mounting bolts fully.

h. Install wheel. DO NOT squeeze the lever at this time.

i. Inspect pad alignment to rotor. Position caliper without squeezing lever. Caliper body should be positioned by centering the pads over rotor. Tighten caliper-mounting bolts and inspect.

FIGURE: 11.20

Push pistons back into caliper body

j. Squeeze lever and inspect pad alignment. Fine tune pad alignment as necessary.

FIGURE: 11.22

Install shim of equal thickness to rotor

Magura® Hydraulic Caliper Brakes

The Magura® hydraulic disc calipers use mineral oil in the hydraulic lines. Do not use DOT fluids or syringes that have pumped DOT fluid.

Brake pads should be changed when measured less than 2.5mm including pad holder. To change pads, remove wheel with rotor from frame. Do NOT squeeze lever when rotor is removed from caliper. Use a cone wrench or screwdriver to set pistons by pushing each one fully back into caliper. Remove pad-fitting screw. Pads sit on magnetic studs. Lift pads from caliper and install new pads. Install pad-fitting screw and secure. Install wheel and squeeze lever to bring pistons to rotor.

The Magura® caliper brakes bleed from the caliper upward to the lever. Two barbed fittings with tubing are required.

The procedure for bleeding caliper:

a. Mount bike in repair stand and rotate bike so tubing is vertical from the caliper to lever. If necessary, you may remove caliper from frame/fork.

b. Remove wheel.

c. Remove pads to avoid the chance of oil contamination (figure 11.23).

d. Set piston by using tire lever or cone wrench to push each piston fully back into caliper (figure 11.24).

e. Install a block inside caliper. Block should be approximately 10mm thick, such as a 10mm hex wrench. Hold block in place with a rubber band or tape as necessary.

f. Prepare injection syringe with mineral oil. Pull oil into syringe and hold syringe vertically to allow air to dissipate toward fitting. Tap syringe to encourage air to float upward.

g. Remove bleeding screw in caliper. Thread and secure barbed fitting of syringe.

h. Rotate lever so reservoir cover is level with ground. Wrap clean rags around lever to protect from drips or spillage.

i. Remove reservoir cover using T7 torx driver. Remove bladder from inside reservoir. Clean edge of reservoir and cover.

j. Push syringe until reservoir nearly overflows. Pull backward on syringe slowly and push forward again (figure 11.25).

k. Activate lever slowly and repeat pushing and pulling fluid. Inspect fluid exiting for any air bubbles. Push nearly entire contents of syringe into caliper but use care not to inject any air at the end of syringe stroke. While injecting, check and drain off fluid from reservoir (figure 11.26).

l. Check that reservoir is completely full and install bladder. Install reservoir cover and secure screws.

m. Remove syringe and barbed fitting from caliper.

n. Install bleed screw in caliper.

o. Wipe caliper and lever clean of fluid.

p. Remove block from caliper and install pads.

q. Install wheel and pull lever to move pads to rotor.

r. Lever should feel firm when pulled repeatedly with force. Repeat bleed as necessary.

FIGURE: 11.23

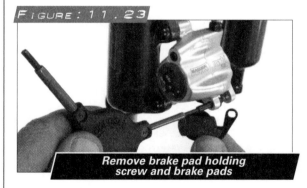

Remove brake pad holding screw and brake pads

FIGURE: 11.24

Push pistons into caliper

ParkTool

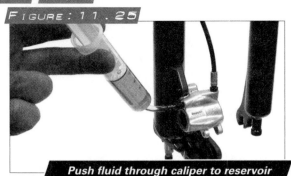

Push fluid through caliper to reservoir

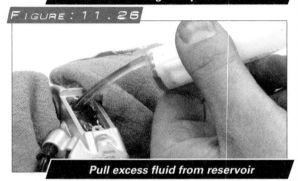

Pull excess fluid from reservoir

Hayes Hydraulic Caliper Brakes

The Hayes® hydraulic brake calipers are designed for Post Mount systems. Adaptor brackets are used to mount the caliper to IS mounts. Calipers are aligned as described in Hydraulic Caliper Alignment.

Brake Caliper Bleed

The Hayes® hydraulic brakes use only DOT 3 or DOT 4 brake fluid. Never use a mineral oil for this system. The brakes bleed from the caliper upward, and the excess fluid exits at the lever. The Hayes® bleed kit includes bleed fittings for the lever, small pieces of plastic tubing, and a squeeze bottle. The bottle permits fluid to be pushed into the system, and then to be sucked back out. This system of pressure then relief, helps to clear the system of air. A syringe can be substituted, but it is necessary to occasionally pull back on the plunger to flush the system of air. It is necessary to rig a bleed waste fluid collection bottle at the lever to catch the DOT fluid.

Procedure to bleed caliper:

a. Remove wheel. Rotate bike and/or brake levers as necessary so there is an upward flow from the caliper to the lever bleed screw.

b. Remove brake pads from caliper body. Grab post at end of caliper, push it way from the caliper body, and pull the pad from body.

c. Push each cylinder into the caliper body. NOTE: Use care not to break post in the center of each piston. Use a box end wrench and push the cylinder into the body (figure 11.27).

d. Inspect the lever for the bleed port screw. Loosen and rotate lever as necessary until screw or plug points upward to assist any bubbles to escape. The Hayes® 9 system uses a plastic plug. Remove plug carefully to not damage bladder. The bleed screw of the El Camino and Stocker models lever face upward and is the highest point in the system. Do not rotate these levers.

e. Remove bleed screw or plug from brake lever and insert bleed hose fitting. Arrange bleed hose and waste bottle to catch fluid. Use rags around lever to prevent fluid from getting on frame or other components. See possible bleed locations in figures 11.28, 11.29, and 11.30.

f. Locate bleed nipple on caliper body. Remove rubber cover from nipple. Attach tubing to end of bleed bottle. Fill bleed bottle with correct DOT brake fluid. Attach tubing to bleed nipple. Cut bleed hose short to maintain control of bottle or syringe. It can be helpful to use a small zip-tie to hold the tubing to the bottle.

g. Loosen bleed nipple ¼ turn. Squeeze bottle firmly for approximately five seconds to force fluid into caliper. Relax bottle to draw any air out of the caliper body. Continue to alternate between squeezing bottle for five seconds and releasing bottle until no air bubbles come out of caliper (figure 11.31). If using syringe, push fluid in, then draw back slightly to draw out any air of caliper.

h. When no more air bubbles appear in the bottle hose, continue to squeeze the bottle, and inspect the exit hole at the lever. Squeeze until the fluid appears clear with no bubbles. Close bleed nipple at caliper. Remove bottle or syringe and be careful not to drip fluid.

i. Repeat the setting of the pistons into caliper body to ensure excess fluid is expelled.

j. Install and secure the lever bleed-screw or plug. Return lever to normal position if it was rotated.

k. Immediately clean all parts with a rag and isopropyl alcohol. Install brake pads into caliper body.

I. Install wheel and rotor and test lever. The lever will feel loose for a few pumps until the pistons move toward the rotor. Lever should then feel firm when pulled with force. Inspect all fittings for leaks.

FIGURE: 11.27

Push piston into caliper body

FIGURE: 11.28

Bleed port location in front of Stocker lever

FIGURE: 11.29

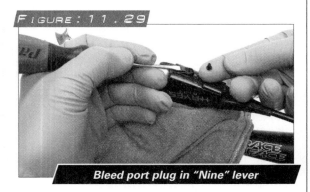

Bleed port plug in "Nine" lever

FIGURE: 11.30

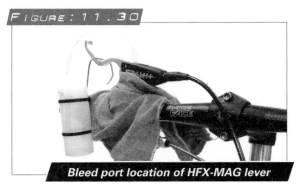

Bleed port location of HFX-MAG lever

FIGURE: 11.31

Squeeze and release pressure as fluid is pumped into caliper

Brake Pad Installation

Inspect caliper body for pad mounting type. If there are tabs at end of pads, use these to pull pad from body. If no tabs are present, inspect for and remove pad-holding screw.

Hayes® pads using tabs are held to the piston with a spring clip. To replace pads, remove wheel. Use tab on pad plate and pull pad toward center and pull outward from caliper body. Reset pistons before installing new pads. Use a box end wrench and carefully press each piston back into caliper body.

Pads are not symmetrical and are marked "inner" and "outer." Replace outer pad first, using tab to engage spring on to piston stud (figure 11.32). Install inner pad. Install wheel and squeeze lever repeatedly to bring pads to rotor.

FIGURE: 11.32

Hayes® piston with stud and brake pad with clip

Avid Hydraulic Caliper Brakes

Avid® provides brackets for IS mountings. The caliper will mount directly to post mounts. Avid® disc brakes use a ball-and-socket system for the caliper mounting bolts. This fixing system is similar to many brake pads on linear-pull caliper rim brakes (figure 11.33).

ParkTool

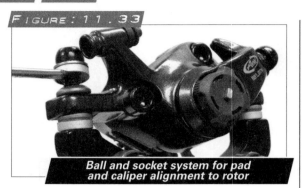
FIGURE: 11.33

Ball and socket system for pad and caliper alignment to rotor

FIGURE: 11.34

Push pad and piston back into caliper body

FIGURE: 11.35

Remove return spring from caliper

The procedure for caliper pad alignment:

  a. If the caliper is attached to a bracket, check that the bracket is fully secured to the frame or fork.
  b. Loosen caliper-mounting bolts so caliper is loose on bracket.
  c. Squeeze the lever to secure the pads to the rotor.
  d. Snug each caliper-mounting bolt. Alternatively tighten one bolt and then the other until both are fully secure.
  e. Release lever and spin rotor while inspecting alignment. Re-adjust as necessary.

The procedure for Avid® hydraulic caliper pad removal and replacement:

  a. Remove the wheel.
  b. Use a wide-tipped screwdriver or cone wrench, and insert it between pads. Twist the tool to push pads apart and to set pistons back into caliper body (figure 11.34).
  c. Squeeze tabs at end of pad together and pull pads outward and away from caliper. If pad return spring remains in caliper, push spring out from the top using hex wrench (figure 11.35).
  d. Place new pads over pad return spring. Spring should be sandwiched between new pads. Installation lever is set asymmetrically on pad. Align bridge of spring with caliper boss locators.
  e. Gently squeeze return spring and pads. Engage pads into caliper body. Pad installation lever orients away from brace bolts. Push return spring and pads into place. Pad locator will engage bosses in caliper boss.
  f. Install wheel and squeeze lever to move piston and pads back to rotor. Check pad alignment.

Avid® Brake Bleeding

The Avid® Juicy and Coda model hydraulic disc brake calipers use a DOT 4 or DOT 5.1 fluids. Do not use a mineral oil in this system. All models share the same concept and procedure for bleeding. The Avid brakes are bled from the caliper up to the lever. It's best to use the Avid® bleed kit with their hydraulic brakes. It includes two syringes with special threaded fittings, a bottle of DOT fluid, and a 8mm crow's foot in ⅜" drive. Store syringes with tubing clamps open. One syringe is used to push fluid, and the second is used to catch fluid at the lever.

Before beginning the bleeding procedure, prepare one of the two Avid® syringes. Open tubing clamp on the syringe and fill about one-half full with only DOT 5.1 or DOT 4 fluid. Clamp tubing clip shut. Hold syringe vertically and pull gently back on the plunger. This reduces pressure in the syringe and will cause any air bubbles to appear in the fluid (figure 11.36). Allow these to rise to the top and tap the side gently to help dislodge them. Unclamp tubing and push bubbles out the top. Close clamp and repeat process until fluid appears mostly clear on bubbles. Some very small bubbles will always be present and will not be a problem in the system.

FIGURE: 11.36

Prepare DOT fluid in syringe by purging air

The process for bleeding:

a. If present, set the volume of the caliper system with the adjusting knobs at the levers. Right-hand lever: turn knob completely counterclockwise, then back clockwise one turn. Left-hand lever: turn knob completely clockwise, then back counter-clockwise one turn.

b. Loosen bolts just enough to allow you to rotate the levers to different angles.

c. Rotate the bike and brake levers as necessary so there is an upward flow from the caliper to the lever bleed screw. Place a rag under and around the caliper to catch any drips. Wheels and rotors may stay in place.

d. Check that filled syringe is free of bubbles. At the caliper, remove bleed-port screw using a T10 Torx driver. Port screw is located in the center of the banjo bolt that attaches the hose to the caliper. Remove port screw and secure syringe and fitting. Leave syringe closed.

e. Rotate the brake lever so it is pointing down vertically. Use a toe strap or thick rubber band to close lever fully to bar or grip. This seals the master cylinder. (Note: if lever does not fully bottom against grip, check location of reach adjustment screw. Thread screw so it clears lever body if necessary.)

f. Remove lever bleed-port plug from using a T10 Torx wrench. Thread the empty syringe into the lever bleed port and secure (figure 11.37). Open clamp of syringe at lever. This syringe will accept the overflow from the caliper syringe during the bleeding process.

g. At the caliper, hold syringe with plunger upward and open tubing clip. Remove any air in the caliper body by first pulling back on plunger gently (figure 11.38). Draw back a small amount. Pulling back too far will drain reservoir and allow air to enter system. Tap on caliper body with plastic lever to assist

in dislodging any bubbles inside. Let any bubbles rise to the top of the syringe next to the plunger. Repeat pushing and pulling syringe until no bubbles appear to exit caliper. Close caliper syringe tubing clamp.

h. Remove strap or rubber from the brake lever to bleed hydraulic line. Keep both syringes vertical to keep bubbles from entering caliper body. Open caliper syringe tubing clamp and push down on the plunger until lever syringe is approximately ½ full of fluid (figure 11.39). Close clamp at caliper syringe.

i. Remove caliper syringe and replace with bleed port screw. Wipe any fluid that has dripped out.

j. Keep lever syringe vertical with clamp open. Gently pull back on syringe to draw out any air bubble from lever and reservoir. Slowly operate lever to free any air trapped in master cylinder (figure 11.40). Repeat pushing and pulling of syringe until no bubbles appear to exit lever.

k. Rotate lever level with ground with bleed port pointing upward.

l. Remove lever syringe. Carefully drip in one or two drops of fluid into opening of bleed port and install bleed port screw (figure 11.41). Wipe off any spilled fluid.

m. Rotate brake and shift levers back to riding position and secure.

n. Pull lever with force and inspect for any leaks.

o. Empty syringes into appropriate container and store syringes with clamps open.

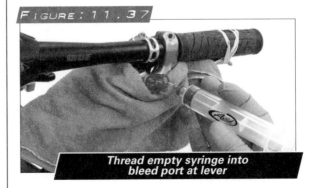

FIGURE: 11.37

Thread empty syringe into bleed port at lever

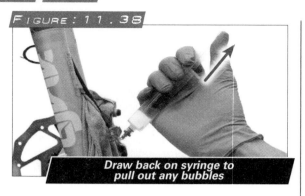
Draw back on syringe to
pull out any bubbles

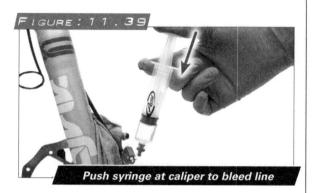
Push syringe at caliper to bleed line

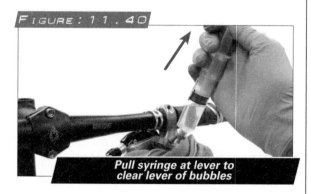
Pull syringe at lever to
clear lever of bubbles

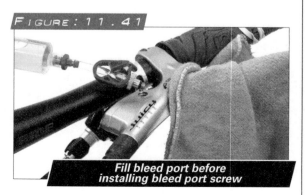
Fill bleed port before
installing bleed port screw

Mechanic Disc Calipers

Mechanical disc calipers use a cable that attaches to a lever arm. The arm is pulled which will push a piston with pad to the rotor. The common designs have one pad fixed (non-moving) and one pad moving with a piston. The moving pad is the outboard pad (away from the spokes), and it pushes the rotor to flex it inward to contact the non-moving inboard pad. Mechanical calipers typically operate with more tolerance between pads and rotor.

Brake Lever

Flat handlebar brake levers used with mechanical disc calipers are compatible with the linear-pull rim caliper brakes. The lever should be set for a comfortable reach and secured to the bar. The brake housing and brake wire are the same as with rim caliper brakes. Prepare housing and wires as with rim caliper brakes.

Disc calipers may be used with drop bar levers that are compatible for liner-pull rim caliper brake, also called "long travel." Mechanical pulley systems, such as the Travel Agent®, are available that allow the use of non-long travel levers, such as many road levers, with mechanical disc brakes.

Caliper Pad Alignment and Clearance

Most mechanical disc caliper share a common alignment procedure. The caliper body is mounted to either post mounts on the frame/fork or to an adapter bracket. On most mechanical calipers, only one pad moves to the rotor. The spinning rotor is flexed and is pushed over to strike a non-moving pad. The caliper body can be adjusted laterally over the rotor (figure 11.42).

Lateral adjustment mounts on caliper body

The procedure to align the common mechanical disc caliper:

a. Install cable and housing. Route inner wire to caliper. Pull slack from cable and secure cable pinch bolt. Cut cable end short enough so that is does not contact frame, caliper, or adaptor.

b. Loosen caliper mounting bolts.

c. Inspect caliper body for pad-adjusting screws that move pads in caliper body. There may be an adjusting screw or knob on inner or outer faces of body. However, some models have only one pad adjusting screw at the inner pad.

d. For caliper with both outer and inner pad adjusting screws/knobs: Turn outer pad adjustment clockwise one turn from being fully out. Turn inner pad adjusting screw in clockwise until pads lock against rotor. Secure each mounting bolt (figure 11.43). Loosen each adjustment screw/knob ¼-½ turn and check pad. Turn adjusting screw(s) in or out to adjust pad clearance for 0.2–0.4mm on each side of the rotor. This is approximately the thickness of the average business card.

e. For caliper with both outer and inner pad adjusting screws/knobs: Turn outer pad adjustment clockwise one turn from being fully out. Turn inner pad adjusting screw in clockwise until pads lock against rotor. Secure each mounting bolt. Loosen each adjustment screw/knob ¼-½ turn and check pad. Turn adjusting screw(s) in or out to adjust pad clearance for 0.2–0.4mm on each side of the rotor. This is approximately the thickness of the average business card.

f. Inspect pad alignment to rotor. Pads should appear parallel to rotor. To fine tune, loosen one bolt at a time to allow the caliper to move slightly to fine tune alignment (figure 11.44).

g. Test lever by pulling. Adjust feel by adjusting both pad adjustment screws in or out, if present. For models with only inner pad adjustment, use barrel adjuster on cable housing to move outer pad in or out.

FIGURE: 11.43

Position caliper and pads over rotor

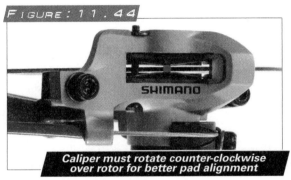

FIGURE: 11.44

Caliper must rotate counter-clockwise over rotor for better pad alignment

As pads wear with braking, use both pad-adjusting screws, if available, to move pad pistons closer to rotor. If both pads have an adjusting screw, tighten both sides. If only one adjusting screw is available, tighten that screw. However, use care when using the adjusting barrel or cable pinch bolt to account for pad wear. Caliper arm may bottom out on caliper body as it articulates, and prevent the pads from pressing on rotor.

Shimano Mechanical Disc Calipers

The Shimano® mechanical calipers align laterally as described above in Brake Caliper Pad Adjustment and Clearance. Shimano® recommends pad clearance of 0.2–0.4mm on each side of the rotor.

The pads of the Shimano caliper are held in place with a pad fixing screw. Replace pads when pad material is less than 0.5mm thick, not including pad holder. To replace pads, remove wheel and then remove any clip at end of pad screw and remove screw. Push pads and pad-return spring out from caliper body (figure 11.45). Install new pads with new pad return spring into caliper body. Install and secure pad fixing screw and install clip if present. Install wheel and adjust new pads to rotor.

FIGURE: 11.45

Remove pad-fixing screw to remove pads

Tektro® Mechanical Disc Calipers

Tektro® mechanical calipers align laterally as described above in Brake Caliper Pad Adjustment and Clearance. Tektro® recommends a 0.3mm clearance from each pad to the rotor.

Tektro® brand pads are made with a wear indicator. A circular hole in the pad will appear as the pad thins and requires replacement. Pads are held in place with a pad fixing screw (figure 11.46). Remove wheel and remove pad-fixing screw. Push pads and pad return spring from caliper. Some models will use a magnet in the piston and have no return spring. To remove these pads, use tab on pad and lift pad away from stud on piston. Pull pad out.

FIGURE: 11.46

Pad fixing screw in the Tektro® brake

Hayes Mechanical Disc Calipers

Hayes® recommends a pad to rotor clearance of about 0.4mm – 0.5mm. To replace pads, remove wheel. Use tab on pad plate and pull outer pad first toward center and pull outward from caliper body. Pads are not symmetrical. Match replacement pad to old pad from caliper. Replace outer pad first, using tab to engage spring on to piston stud (figure 11.47). Install inner pad. Loosen pad adjusting screw(s), install wheel and set clearance to rotor. Some models use a magnetic pad holder without stud or clip system.

FIGURE: 11.47

Hayes® pad and pad stud on piston.

Avid® Mechanical Brake

Avid® disc caliper brakes use a ball-and-socket system for the caliper mounting bolts. This fixing system is similar to many brake pads on linear-pull caliper rim brakes (figure 11.48). The caliper body can move laterally as other brands but will also allow vertical rotation of the pad face to the rotor.

FIGURE: 11.48

Ball and socket system for pad and caliper alignment to rotor

Both the inner and outer pads of the Avid® brake can be adjusted for clearance with pad-adjusting knobs (figure 11.49). The moving outer pad flexes the rotor toward the fixed inner pad when the brake is operated. The dials use an indented "click" system with one complete revolution moving the pad approximately 1mm.

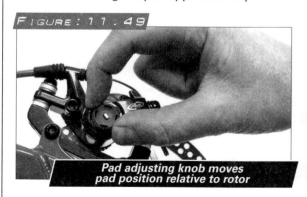

FIGURE: 11.49

Pad adjusting knob moves pad position relative to rotor

The Avid® caliper design is to have the inner pad-to-rotor gap about twice as large as the outer pad-to-rotor gap (figure 11.50). It can be difficult to measure and achieve this ratio, but the brake will still perform even if the ratio does not achieve this exact proportion.

FIGURE: 11.50

Gap from fixed pad to rotor should be larger than gap from moving pad to rotor

The procedure for Avid® mechanical caliper pad alignment:

a. If the caliper is attached to an adapter bracket, check that the bracket is fully secured to the frame or fork.
b. Loosen caliper-mounting bolts so the caliper is loose on bracket or post mounts.
c. Slacken cable with adjusting barrel or loosen brake wire pinch bolt if it is secured.
d. Check that both pad adjusting knob dials are turned fully counter-clockwise to move pads fully away from rotor. Turn the outer pad-adjusting knob approximately ½ turn clockwise.
e. Turn the inner pad-adjusting knob clockwise until inner pad fully secures and locks rotor. This aligns caliper body and pads to rotor face.
f. Snug each caliper-mounting bolt. Alternate turns to tighten one bolt and then the other until both are fully secure.
g. Draw slack from the brake wire and secure pinch bolt. Do not allow caliper arm to move upward when drawing slack from brake (figure 11.51).
h. Set pad clearance. Loosen outer pad-adjusting knob approximately ¼ turn counter-clockwise. Loosen inner pad-adjusting knob approximately ½ turn counter-clockwise. Inner pad (fixed pad) to rotor gap should appear larger than the outer pad to rotor gap.

i. Squeeze lever to test caliper brake. Adjust lever modulation setting by moving pads inward or outward from rotor by using both pad-adjusting knobs. To maintain the 2:1 ratio, turn the fixed pad-adjusting knob twice as many clicks as the moving pad-adjusting knob. For example, if a looser modulation is desired, turn the inner pad-adjusting knob counter-clockwise 4 clicks and the outer pad adjusting knob counter-clockwise only 2 clicks.

FIGURE: 11.51

Pull slack from cable, but do not move caliper arm

The caliper-actuating arm is designed to operate from a fully open position. Set cable tension at the adjusting barrel so actuating arm is fully opened or returned. Do not use the brake lever adjusting barrel or cable pinch bolt to account for pad wear. Caliper arm may bottom out on caliper body and prevent the pads from pressing on rotor.

As pads wear, use pad-adjusting knobs to move pads closer to rotor. Turn the fixed pad-adjusting knob clockwise twice as many clicks as the moving pad adjusting knob to maintain the 2:1 ratio of pad to rotor spacing. For example, if the inner (fixed) pad-adjusting knob is turned clockwise two clicks, turn the outer (moving) pad-adjusting knob clockwise one click.

Brake pads should be removed and replaced if the pad thickness, including the metal holder, is less than 3mm.

The procedure for Avid® mechanical caliper pad removal and replacement:

a. Remove the wheel.
b. Loosen each pad adjustment knob an equal amount.
c. Squeeze tabs at end of pad together and pull pads outward and away from caliper (figure 11.52). If pad return spring remains in caliper, push spring out from the top using hex wrench.
d. Note orientation of pad return spring and remove spring from pads.

e. Place new pads over pad return spring (figure 11.53). Spring should be sandwiched between new pads. Installation lever is set asymmetrically on pad. Align bridge of spring with caliper boss locators.

f. Gently squeeze return spring and pads. Engage pads into caliper body. Pad installation lever orients away from brace bolts. Push return spring and pads into place (figure 11.54). Pad locator will engage bosses in caliper boss.

g. Install wheel.

h. Align pads as described above.

FIGURE: 11.52

Push lever to center of caliper body and lift to remove

FIGURE: 11.53

Place spring between brake pads

FIGURE: 11.54

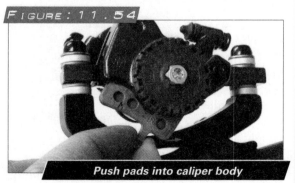

Push pads into caliper body

CHAPTER 12

Caliper Rim Brake System

A good brake system is more than an emergency stopping system. Properly adjusted brakes give the user subtle control and modulation in bike handling and speed control. Many small details affect the control of the bike, including the placement of the levers, how the cable system is installed, and the alignment of the brake pads.

The caliper rim brake system includes the brake lever, cables, caliper, and wheel rim. Rim calipers are attached to the frame and fork near the wheel rim. The calipers are fitted with brake cables and housing which attach to levers at the handlebars. Force is applied to the rim by the pads, which converts the speed and energy of the bicycle into heat to slow the bike.

Disc brake systems use a rotor attached to the hub. These brakes are discussed in Chapter 11 Caliper Disc Brake Systems.

This chapter will review cantilever, linear pull, dual pivot, and side pull rim brakes. For service of U-brake systems, see Repair Help at www.parktool.com

Brake Levers

The hand brake lever is fitted to the handlebar with a clamp. The lever increases the muscular force of the hand, which pulls the cable and transfers force to the pads. There are two basic types of hand brake levers: the upright bar brake lever and drop bar brake lever.

Upright Bar Brake Levers

Brake levers clamped to the handlebars should be positioned so they are easy and comfortable to reach. Upright bar (flat bar) brake levers should be rotated so they are in-line with the rider's arm. A common standard is to set the lever at 45 degrees from the horizontal plane (figure 12.1). This avoids bending the wrist to apply the brakes. Brake levers may be rotated on the bar by loosening the clamp-fixing bolt.

Figure: 12.1

Rotate levers for comfortable reach from saddle

Upright bar levers commonly have a setscrew on the lever body that allows the lever to be set closer to the grip. The lever reach can then be set according to the rider's hand size and riding style. Tighten the setscrews to bring the levers toward the grip to accommodate smaller hands or shorter fingers.

Upright bar levers typically allow for easy installation of the cable end into the cable anchor of the lever. Pull the lever and inspect for the cable anchor. Inspect also for slots in the adjusting barrel. Align the slots and then attach the cable to the anchor. Engage the brake cable between the slots in the barrel adjuster (figure 12.2).

Figure: 12.2

Use slots to easily engage cable end

Brake levers are designed to pull a certain amount of brake cable as the lever is squeezed. The distance from the cable head pivot to the lever pivot determines the amount of brake cable pulled. Linear pull or "long travel" brake levers will have a greater distance between cable end and lever pivot of approximately 30mm or more. Cantilever caliper levers will have a relatively shorter distance of less than 30mm. The brake lever should be compatible with the type of brake caliper used. Although the linear pull brake levers pull more cable, they pull with less force compared to the cantilever levers.

Some levers will adjust for either cantilever/ side pull travel or the greater pull of the linear pull brake. Mechanical pulley systems, such as the Travel Agent®, are available that attach to the linear pull caliper. These pulleys allow the use of cantilever or road caliper compatible levers with linear pull brakes.

Drop-Bar Brake Levers

Drop-bar brake levers may be moved up or down the curve of the drop bar for easier reach. Moving the lever down on the bar curve makes the levers easier to reach while riding in the drops. Moving the lever up on the bar makes them easier to reach when riding on the top of the bars. The handlebar tape must be removed to move the levers up or down.

These levers use a strap that pulls the body tight to the handlebar. The bolt or nut to tighten the strap may be inside the lever body or hidden under the rubber hood covers. It may be necessary to pull the cover up in order to insert the hex wrench when tightening the strap (figure 12.3).

F IGURE : 1 2 . 3

Adjust lever height for comfort and secure strap

The drop-bar lever should be tight to the handlebar. The user effectively uses the lever body as a "bar extension" when riding on the tops of the levers. If the levers were to move during use, it could result in a crash.

Brake cable ends are attached to the cable anchor in the lever. Pull the brake lever fully down and inspect inside. The anchor will have a socket fitting for the cable. The common aero-style lever will have a hole in the lever body for the cable end (figure 12.4). Feed the cut end of the cable into the socket first, and route it out the back of the lever body. Pull the cable and check that the end is fully seated into the anchor. The brake housing will fit into the back of the lever body.

F IGURE : 1 2 . 4

Insert brake cable from front of lever

Cable System

The cable system is made of the brake cable and housing. It connects the brake lever to the caliper. The brake cable is made of multiple strands of wire and a fitting on one end that sits in the lever. Brake cables often come double-ended, and each end is fitted with a different head for different brake levers. One end is used, and the other end is cut off using a cable cutter. The brake cable fitting sits in the brake lever, and the cut end of the cable is bolted into the caliper arm. Upright bar levers use a round disc-shaped end about 7mm (9/32") in diameter. Drop-bar levers use a "mushroom" or "tear-drop" shaped end (figure 12.5). Brake cables have a minimum diameter of 1.5mm (1/16"), which is larger than derailleur cables.

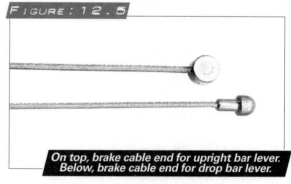

F IGURE : 1 2 . 5

**On top, brake cable end for upright bar lever.
Below, brake cable end for drop bar lever.**

Housing allows the cable to bend around corners on the way to the brake caliper. Wound-type brake housing is made of a plastic liner tube around which support wire is wound like a coil. It is then covered by plastic to help prevent rust (figure 12.6). Wound housing differs from the compressionless housing used on derailleur systems. The support wires of compressionless housing do not hold up to the higher stresses of braking.

ParkTool

FIGURE : 12.6

Common brake housing, with cut away to show inner support wire coil

"Braided" or "woven" housing is acceptable for either brake or indexing shift housing (figure 12.7). The outer support wires are woven in a mesh around the liner. This housing is especially effective on systems that seem to have excessive amounts of flex from coiled housing. This is felt as "sponginess" in the lever pull.

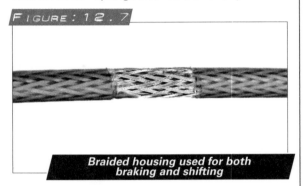

FIGURE : 12.7

Braided housing used for both braking and shifting

Another type is called "articulated housing." Small tubular segments are strung together over a plastic liner (figure 12.8). Articulated housing may be used for both brake housing and indexing shift housing.

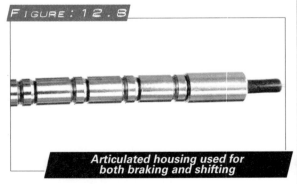

FIGURE : 12.8

Articulated housing used for both braking and shifting

Replace housing if it is twisted, rusty, split, or too short. It is a good idea to replace the housing even if it is simply old, as there is a plastic tube inside the wound housing which becomes dirty and worn with use.

Cable Lubrication

To prevent rust and to ensure smooth operation, apply a light lubricant to the brake cable where it passes through the housing. If the frame housing stops have a split, the housing and brake cable can be released from the stops for easier lubrication.

Release the brake caliper quick-release to relax the cable tension. Pull the housing back and out of the stop. Slide the housing back to expose the cable. Wipe the cable clean with a rag and lubricate. Re-install housing into the stops and close the caliper quick-release.

If removing the housing from the stops is not possible, rotate the bike so lubrication can be dripped down the brake cable into the housing. Some housing systems use a liner to cover the entire length of cable from lever to caliper, e.g. Gore-Tex® and Delta® systems. Do not lubricate the cable of these systems.

Cable Housing Length

When replacing housing, consider the housing length. Generally, housing should be as short as possible yet still entering straight into the housing stops (figure 12.9). If the housing is too long, it will pass an imaginary line created by the housing stop (figure 12.10). If it is too short, it will create kinks or severe bends. If it is likely the stem and bars are to be raised in the future, leave the housing somewhat longer than the ideal length.

FIGURE : 12.9

Housing enters stop in a straight line, indicating a good length

FIGURE : 12.10

Housing passes housing stop, indicating housing is too long

If the old housing was an acceptable length, cut new housing to the same length. If in doubt, cut housing longer and insert into stops, then inspect and cut shorter as required. For wound housing, cut with diagonal pliers (preferred) or with cable cutters. Bend brake housing where you wish to cut to open the wound coil (figure 12.11).

FIGURE: 12.11

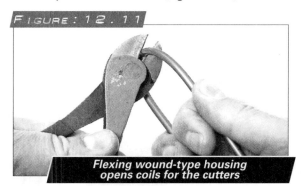

Flexing wound-type housing opens coils for the cutters

Wound housing is made of a single coiled wire. Any cutting tool tends to leave a sharp end or burr. The burr should be filed or ground smooth so the housing is flat (figure 12.12).

FIGURE: 12.12

File brake coil smooth to eliminate burr from cutting

Woven or braided housing is cut with cable cutters similarly as with index shift housing. Articulated housing is shortened similar to shortening a beaded string. Pieces are removed and the inner plastic liner cut with scissors.

Housing end caps should be used whenever they fit. The end cap will only improve the fit into a cable stop, but, if an end cap will not fit into a brake cable stop, the cap is not necessary. End caps are available in different designs (figure 12.13). The end diameters vary to better mate with frame fittings, and some may have extensions for protective liners.

FIGURE: 12.13

Various styles of housing end caps

After a brake cable is installed and the brake adjusted, the excess cable should be cut using a cable cutter, such as the Park Tool CN-10. The cutting jaws surround the cut and shear the wires. Leave approximately 3-4cm (1.5 to 2 inches) wire length past pinch bolt. After cutting the brake cable, use a cable end cap to prevent the end from fraying (figure 12.14).

FIGURE: 12.14

Use a cable end cap to prevent fraying

The brake cable is fixed to the rim caliper arm by a plate and bolt. The brake cable is pulled with great force by the hand lever, and the cable must not slip in the pinch bolt (figure 12.15). The brake cable will flatten with proper torque.

FIGURE: 12.15

Pinch bolt and brake cable

If the brake cable is frayed or sliced anywhere between the lever and the cable pinch bolt at the derailleur, it should be replaced. Even the failure of a single strand of wire will eventually lead to a cable break (figure 12.16).

ParkTool

FIGURE: 12.16

Inspect and replace cables with broken wire

Caliper Brakes

Note: When rim calipers are discussed in this chapter, "right" and "left" will be from the mechanic's point of view, not the rider's point of view. In other words, the left caliper arm of the front brake is the left one seen when standing in front the bike. The left caliper arm of the rear brake is the one on the left side of the bike while standing behind the bike.

The design of the brake caliper will determine how the brake pads are adjusted. Most caliper arms swing the pad on an arc as it approaches the rim. Certain caliper types swing the pad downward as it moves toward the rim. Other types move the pad upward as it moves toward the rim. Before adjusting pads, begin by determining the basic type of caliper used. Move the caliper arm and watch how the pads move toward rim. Arm movement will determine pad alignment (figure 12.17).

FIGURE: 12.17

This pad will move downward as the caliper swings to the rim

Brake Pads

Brake pads will wear with use and will require replacement. Some pads are made with a "wear line," which indicates the need for replacement. Age will also harden pad material and make it less effective. It is not uncommon for small amounts of aluminum from the rim-braking surface to become embedded in the pad. Inspect the brake

pad and remove pieces of grit and foreign material as necessary using a pick or small screwdriver.

Pads that are aligned too low on a rim will develop a lip on the low edge. This lip makes correct alignment impossible (figure 12.18). Replacement pads should be compatible with the type of caliper. There are many after-market pads available from all-around use to pads for wet conditions or specific rim compounds. Choose a pad set that meets your needs as a rider. A relatively soft pad, for example, will generally give high performance but will wear quickly.

FIGURE: 12.18

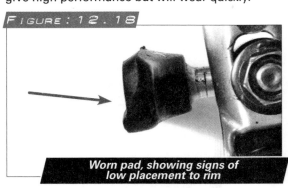

Worn pad, showing signs of low placement to rim

The brake pads may be replaced as an entire unit with pad material and pad holder and fastener all together. Some pad systems use a "cartridge pad" that allows for the pad material to be changed. The pad holder and fastener are re-used. To replace cartridge pads, inspect for and remove any screw or clip retaining the pad. Pull on the pad backwards, away from the rim rotation direction (figure 12.19). Install new pad by pushing it into holder and reinstall retaining screw or clip.

FIGURE: 12.19

Pull cartridge pad toward back to remove it from pad holder

It is common for some cantilever and linear pull caliper brake pads to have the mounting stud placed off-center, so one end of the pad is longer (figure 12.20). Look for the manufacture's marking for direction of rim rotation and marking for "front" and "back."

Off center brake pad mounting stud

Rim caliper pad adjustments depend upon the wheel being centered in the frame. A misaligned wheel will affect both pad centering and pad placement on the rim, and it is important that the wheel be centered before beginning pad adjustments (figure 12.21).

A misaligned wheel off to mechanic's left

A wheel can be misaligned from simply being placed in the frame incorrectly. Loosen quick-release or axle nuts and pull wheel fully into dropouts. It is also possible the wheel rim is not properly centered over the hub. As a test, flip the wheel around left-to-right and inspect again. If the centering is good, wheel centering will look the same either way. A wheel may be purposely "misdished" to correct for minor frame or fork misalignment. It is also possible the frame or fork was made with the left and right dropouts at slightly different heights. An effective solution is simply to hold the wheel centered when installing it, and then close the skewer tightly (or tighten axle nuts) to hold the wheel in place. Some frames have enough material that may allow filing to effectively raise one dropout. Consult a professional mechanic.

Brake pads are mounted to the caliper arms and are adjustable in several directions. There are four basic aspects to pad alignment: vertical height alignment, tangent alignment, vertical face alignment, and pad toe. Not every brand or model of brake caliper has every adjustment,

and sometimes it is necessary to compromise when setting pads.

Vertical Height Alignment

This is the setting up and down on the rim-braking surface, which is the flat section of rim. View caliper face-on and move the arms while watching the pads move to the rim. If the pad moves on an arc moving down, it should be set near the upper edge of the rim-braking surface (figure 12.22). If the pad travels upward toward the rim, it should be set near the lower edge of the rim-braking surface. As the brake pad wears, it gets thinner, and tends to move further upward or downward along its arc. Do not set pads so high that they strike the tire at any time, or so low that they are below the braking surface.

Pad on left is set at top of rim braking surface, while pad on right is at bottom of rim-braking surface

Tangent Alignment

This is the setting of the pad tilt. Viewed from the side, the front and back of the pad should be parallel to the rim. One side should not be higher or lower than the other side (figure 12.23). Use care when tightening the pad fixing bolt and hold the brake pad to keep it from rotating.

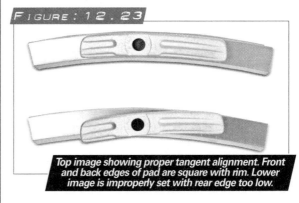

Top image showing proper tangent alignment. Front and back edges of pad are square with rim. Lower image is improperly set with rear edge too low.

3-way wrench for pad adj

to be used if brakes squeel

Vertical Face Alignment

This is the setting of the pad's face surface relative to the rim's vertical surface. The vertical face of the pad should be set parallel to the face of the braking surface as it strikes the rim (figure 12.24). Most cantilever and linear pull calipers have an adjustment for vertical alignment. Many side pull and dual pivot caliper pads do not allow for vertical alignment. These pads will simply wear in with use, or they can be sanded or filed to shape.

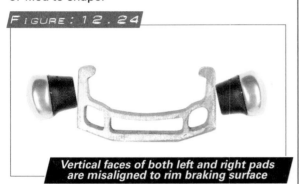

F I G U R E : 1 2 . 2 4

Vertical faces of both left and right pads are misaligned to rim braking surface

Pad Toeing

This is the setting of the pad angle as it touches the rim. Toeing refers to setting the pad so its front edge strikes first, with a slight gap of 0.25mm to 1mm at the back or trailing edge (figure 12.25). Toe helps to reduce squeal during braking. Caliper arms have play in the pivots. Additionally, the mechanism flexes with the wheel when the brake is applied. This creates a "slip and stick" phenomenon as the pads jerk backward, then forward again. The effect is much like that of a bow on a violin string. The result is "harmonic resonance" or squealing. With systems that are more rigid, there is less flex, and there tends to be less squealing. The stiffer the brake, the less it will tend to squeal even without pad toe. Generally, less toe angle is better than more. Too much angle will exacerbate brake caliper flex without providing power to the pads.

Some brake pad systems allow toe adjustment in the pad-fixing bolt. Side-pull and dual pull caliper arms can sometimes be bent slightly for pad toe. If the caliper arm is relatively thick or difficult to bend, however, toe may be cut into the pad with a file. It is simplest to first ride the bike and see if toe is required.

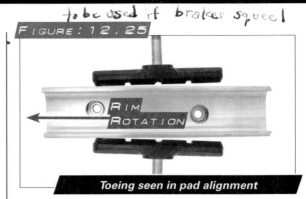

F I G U R E : 1 2 . 2 5

RIM ROTATION

Toeing seen in pad alignment

Cantilever Caliper Adjustment

Cantilever calipers may be found on mountain bikes, cyclo-cross bikes and touring bikes. Cantilever and linear pull caliper arms attach to separate frame or fork pivots on either side of the wheel rim. Attached to the frame or fork is a stud called the "braze-on." This stud is 16mm long and 8mm in diameter, with an internal thread for a 6mm bolt. Grease the surface of the braze-on before installing the calipers. Use a mild thread-locker inside the fitting and install the bolt to a relatively low torque. The cantilever should pivot freely when the bolt is secure. Over tightening may damage the fitting and cause the caliper to stick.

There may be several spring hole options in the braze-on as well as in the caliper (figure 12.26). Mount left and right caliper springs into mirror image holes. Spring hole options allow changes in spring tension. Generally, select the middle option and move both sides symmetrically if changing tension.

F I G U R E : 1 2 . 2 6

Braze-on for brake spring mounting

The cantilever caliper pads move downward on an arc as they travel to the rim (figure 12.27). Because of the downward arc, pads should be set high vertically on the rim but without interfering with the tire. Pad height will lower as pad face wears and the caliper arms get closer to the rim.

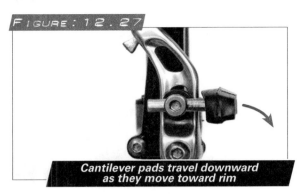

FIGURE: 12.27

Cantilever pads travel downward as they move toward rim

Cantilever calipers may have either a "threaded stud" or a "smooth stud" brake pad. Smooth stud brake pads are secured by pressure from a "pad-fixing bolt." Typically, a system of curved washers allows the brake post to rotate for setting toe (figure 12.28).

FIGURE: 12.28

Smooth stud pad with curved washer system

There are two basic systems for connecting the left and right calipers: the straddle wire carrier and the "link unit." The straddle wire carrier is centered over the wheel and uses a pinch bolt to secure the cable coming from the brake lever (figure 12.29). Place this type of carrier as low as practical for the best mechanical advantage to the brake pads. The bottom of the carrier should be approximately even with the lowest part of the rear seat stay bridge or front fork crown.

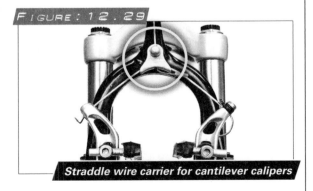

FIGURE: 12.29

Straddle wire carrier for cantilever calipers

The link unit uses housing and a head that is a fixed distance above the tire (figure 12.30). The height of the link unit determines the arm position. A longer link unit will allow more clearance above the tire.

FIGURE: 12.30

Straddle wire link unit

The procedure for cantilever caliper pad and caliper adjustment:

a. Mount bike in repair stand.
b. For link units, attach cable to brake lever and to caliper arm. For straddle wire carriers, attach cable to brake lever, then attach cable to carrier, and position the carrier above the tire. Fully secure carrier pinch bolt.
c. Turn brake lever barrel adjuster fully clockwise into lever body but then unthread two or three complete turns. This allows adjustment after setting pad placement.
d. Loosen brake pad fixing nuts on both sides of cantilever and lubricate threads, curved washers, and washer-to-arm contact points.
e. Point pads down, away from rim, and gently snug nut. This allows proper alignment of caliper arms before adjusting pads.
f. Position caliper arms parallel to one another (figure 12.31). Adjust cable at cable pinch bolt. Use the Park Tool BT-2 Cable Stretcher to help adjust brake cable.
g. View centering of caliper arms to rim. Most models use a centering setscrew on the caliper arm. Turning the setscrew changes spring tension in that arm. For example, to move both arms right, turn right side setscrew clockwise. To move both arms left, turn counter-clockwise. Squeeze lever to work calipers and check centering again. Caliper arms should be centered to rim. Do not center pads to rim; view only arms relative to rim.

Park Tool

h. Attach a rubber band around backside of pad. This is used in pad alignment only and is later removed (figure 12.32). The rubber band creates a shim to give "toe" to the brake pad. Some pads may have a built in toe-feature at the back end of the pad. Do not use a rubber band on these pads. Simply align the built-in toe feature flush to the rim.

i. Adjust pad alignment to rim. Push one pad until it is contacting rim. Use care not to move caliper arm. Align pad correctly for four positions.
Height: with pad close to top edge of braking surface.
Tangent: with front and back edge even to rim.
Vertical face: with pad face and rim parallel.
Toe: with slight gap at trailing edge of pad. The rubber band acts as a shim to hold the back of the pad out slightly.

j. Hold mounting bolt with hex wrench and tighten mounting nut. Pad should contact rim after adjustment.

k. Remove rubber band from rear and view toe. There should be a slight gap at back of pad. Double-check pad alignment by viewing from top, bottom, front, and side.

l. Loosen other pad and repeat steps h-k. Both pads should be contacting rim when pad adjustment is completed.

m. Squeeze lever multiple times to seat brake cable and test brake cable pinch bolt. Cable should not slip.

n. Set clearance at lever for rider preference. If brake feels tight, turn barrel adjuster clockwise to loosen brake cable tension. If brake feels loose, turn barrel adjuster counter-clockwise to tighten brake cable tension.

o. If barrel adjuster is all the way engaged at lever and brake lever is still too tight, loosen brake cable pinch bolt and allow slack to feed through pinch plate. Tighten pinch bolt and test again. Adjust at brake lever.

p. View pad centering to rim. If not adequately centered, use centering setscrew on arm (figure 12.33).

q. Inspect that the pads are not rubbing the tire. Readjust if necessary. Use care not to move brake pad stud in or out from caliper arm as this changes centering. Move pads only up/down.

FIGURE: 12.31
Adjust brake cable at pinch bolt until arms are close to parallel

FIGURE: 12.32
Adjust one pad at a time, using a rubber band to create toe

FIGURE: 12.33
Use spring tension to center pads to rim

Some brands and models of cantilever calipers have no centering setscrew or other system of pad-to-rim centering. In this case, move pad stud laterally as necessary in pad fixing bolt. Another option on some brands utilizes an adjustable spring tension nut on each caliper at the mounting bolt. Spring tension can be changed on either arm.

The cantilever may have a threaded stud brake pad. The arms cannot be moved until both are parallel. The threaded stud uses a ball and socket system.

The process for threaded stud brake pad cantilevers:

a. Mount bike in a repair stand.

b. Use straddle wire to bring pads to rim and secure pinch bolt. Pads should be touching rim-braking surface.

c. Align both pads correctly for four positions.

   Height: with pad close to top edge of braking surface.

   Tangent: with front and back edge even to rim.

   Vertical face: with pad face and rim parallel.

   Toe: with slight gap at trailing edge of pad.

d. Turn adjusting barrel into lever to clear pads from rim. Squeeze lever and set lever clearance as desired.

Linear Pull Caliper Adjustment

Linear pull brakes are similar to cantilever brakes. The arms pivot on frame or fork mounted studs at one end and are pulled by the cable at the other end. There is no extra straddle wire as with cantilevers. The primary cable from the brake lever passes through a metal cable-housing stop called the "noodle." The noodle is fitted to one arm, and the cable attaches to the second arm. Pulling the lever pulls the arms together and forces the pads into the rim-braking surface.

"Linear Pull" brakes and Shimano V-brakes® are common on many mountain bikes and hybrid bikes (figure 12.34). The caliper arm shares the same frame mounting system with cantilevers.

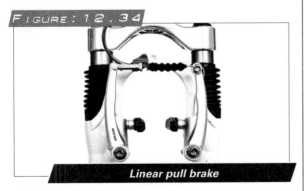

Linear pull brake

Linear pull calipers move the pads on an arc moving downward toward the rim. Pads should be set high vertically on the rim but without interfering with the tire. Pad height will lower as pad face wears.

Linear pull brake pads often use a washer system to set caliper arm position to the rim. Push both arms together until pads are touching rim and view caliper arms. Arms should be close to parallel with one another. If arms are forming a wide "V," swap the wide spacers inside the caliper for the narrower spacers outside the caliper. If the arms tilt inward when the pads are striking the rim, swap the narrow spacers inside the calipers for the wider spacers outside the calipers (figure 12.35).

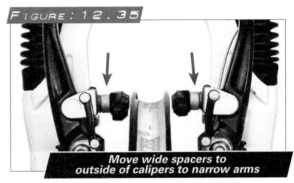

Move wide spacers to outside of calipers to narrow arms

Some models of the Shimano® XTR, XT, and LX brakes use a moving parallelogram for the pad-to-rim motion. These are called V-brakes® and differ in pad placement from other linear pull models. A linkage system allows the pads to move straight toward the rim, not on an arc. The pad is mounted to a moving plate attached to the caliper arm with a linkage system (figure 12.36). Set pad height to strike in the middle of rim braking surface for these caliper brakes.

Linkage system of Shimano® V-brake system

Linear pull calipers, like cantilevers, are attached to the frame or fork at the braze-on. Grease the outer surface of the braze-on before installing the calipers. Use a mild thread-locker inside the fitting and install the bolt to a relatively low torque. The cantilever should pivot freely. Over tightening may damage the fitting and cause the caliper to stick.

Most models of linear pull calipers use a threaded stud brake pad. A threaded bolt is fixed into the pad. The bolt is sandwiched to the caliper arm by a series of convex and concave washers. This "ball and socket" system allows the bolt and pad to move in the caliper arm for toe and vertical face alignment (figure 12.37). To change pad angle, loosen the bolt and move pad to desired position. Hold pad while securing nut/bolt.

FIGURE: 12.37

Ball and socket system of threaded brake pad

The procedure for linear pull caliper adjustment:

a. Attach brake cable to brake lever and through housing. Feed cable through the "noodle" and through the rubber boot, if available. Finally, feed brake cable through pinch mechanism and secure.

b. Push both arms together until pads are touching rim and inspect caliper arms. Arms should be close to parallel with one another. Move washers as necessary to position arms as described above.

c. Adjust one pad position to the rim at a time. Loosen pad nut/bolt and lubricate curved washers and thread. Install rubber band shim at back edge of pad (figure 12.38).

d. Push caliper arm to rim and view pad alignment. If practical, unhook spring from arm to make alignment easier. Align pad correctly for four positions.
Height: with pad close to top edge of braking surface.
Tangent: with front and back edge even to rim.
Vertical face: with pad face and rim parallel.
Toe: with slight gap at trailing edge of pad. The rubber band acts as a shim to hold the back of the pad out slightly.

e. Tighten pad nut and remove rubber band. Inspect pad alignment again.

f. Repeat pad adjustment on other side of caliper.

g. Squeeze lever hard several times and set pad clearance at lever for rider preference. If brake feels tight, turn barrel adjuster clockwise to loosen brake cable tension. If brake feels loose, turn barrel adjuster counter-clockwise to tighten brake cable tension. If barrel adjuster is all the way engaged at lever and brake lever is still too tight, loosen brake cable pinch bolt and allow slack to feed through pinch plate. Tighten pinch bolt and test again. Adjust at brake lever.

h. Inspect pad centering to rim. Use setscrew on sides of caliper to center pads to rim. Tighten setscrew on arm with pad that is closest to rim (figure 12.39).

i. Inspect that pads are not rubbing tire. Readjust if necessary.

If the linear pull caliper uses the smooth stud brake pads, the procedure is similar to cantilever calipers. Use the cable to set arms close to parallel and adjust pads. Use the barrel adjuster to back pads off rim for clearance.

FIGURE: 12.38

RIM ROTATION

Using a shim to create toe

FIGURE: 12.39

Use screw to change spring tension when centering pads to rim

Dual Pivot Caliper Adjustment

TOOLS & SUPPLIES:

- *Box or open end wrenches (Park Tool CBW-1 and CBW-4)*
- *Hex wrenches (Park Tool–various models)*
- *Fourth Hand (Park Tool BT-2)*

Dual pivot calipers are popular on many road bikes. They appear visually very similar to side pull brakes (figure 12.40). However, the left side and right side dual pivot brake caliper arms move on separate pivots, and the two arms arc in different directions. As seen from the mechanics point of view, the left pad swings downward toward the rim while the right pad swings upward. As with other calipers, the swing of the arm determines pad height.

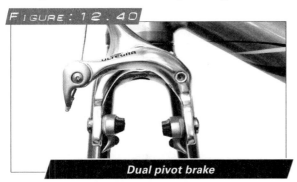

FIGURE: 12.40

Dual pivot brake

Dual pivot and side pull brake calipers secure in mounting holes in the frame and fork. These calipers secure to the frame with a single nut centered above the wheel (figure 12.41). The front brake-mounting bolt has longer threads, while the rear brake bolt has shorter threads. When mounting a dual or side pull caliper, hold caliper centered to wheel and tighten bolt.

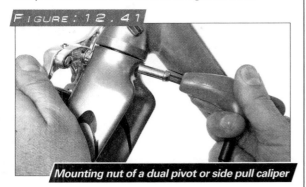

FIGURE: 12.41

Mounting nut of a dual pivot or side pull caliper

Some dual pivot brakes allow for only height and tangent alignment adjustments to rim. Toeing or vertical face alignments are possible with pads using a ball and socket system only. Dual pull caliper arms can sometimes be bent slightly for pad toe. If the caliper arm is relatively thick or seems difficult to bend, however, then toe may be cut into the pad with a file. It is simplest to first ride the bike and see if toe is required.

The procedure for dual pivot caliper and pad adjustment:

a. Feed brake cable through brake lever and through housing.
b. Attach brake cable to pinch bolt and secure.
c. Loosen and lubricate threads of pad bolt/nut.
d. Squeeze both pads to rim and adjust pads for height and tangent. Right pad should be set to lower edge of braking surface. Left should be set to upper edge of braking surface. Vertical face alignment to rim and toe alignment are not typically adjustable on dual pivot calipers. If desired, toe may be set by slightly bending arm. Grasp arm with small adjustable wrench and bend arm as needed. Use rag on arm to protect finish if surface scarring is a concern.
e. Tighten pad-fixing bolts.
f. Squeeze lever to test pad clearance.
g. Use barrel adjuster to adjust pad clearance. Set clearance for approximately 3-4mm (⅛") per side from pad to rim. Draw slack from system using brake cable pinch bolt if barrel adjuster is set out to its limit.
h. View pad centering to rim. If left pad appears closer to rim, tighten setscrew. If right pad appears closer, loosen setscrew (figure 12.42).

FIGURE: 12.42

Center pads to rim with setscrew in brake bridge

Park Tool

Side Pull Caliper Adjustment

Road-type bikes may also use a side pull brake (figure 12.43). Side pull calipers at first glance look like dual pivot calipers. Each arm, however, shares a single pivot bolt in the middle of the brake. The bolt for mounting the brake and for the arm pivot is centered over the rim. Both pads swing downward on an arc toward the rim and should be set high on the braking surface.

FIGURE: 12.43

Side pull caliper

The side pull caliper arm pivot can be adjusted if there is play (knocking) between the arms or if the caliper arms bind from being too tight. There are two basic types of pivot bolt systems: the double nut system and the safety pivot system.

TECH NOTE:

See www.parktool.com for detailed information on sidepull and dual arm pivot adjustments.

The procedure for side pull caliper adjustment:

a. Feed brake cable through lever and through housing.

b. Loosen each pad-fixing nut and lubricate threads.

c. Push one arm to rim and set pad alignment. Adjust pad to strike upper edge of braking surface. Pad front and back edges should be level. Most side pull pads adjust only for height and tangent. Vertical face alignment is not typically adjustable. Tighten pad-fixing bolt.

d. Repeat adjustment with other pad and tighten pad-fixing bolt.

e. Attach brake cable to pinch mechanism. Squeeze pads to rim and draw slack from cable. Secure brake cable pinch bolt.

f. Squeeze lever hard several times to test brake cable pinch bolt.

g. Check lever clearance to handlebar. Squeeze lever gently until pads contact rim. Gap to handlebar should be no less than one inch (25mm) at this point. Use adjusting barrel to change lever clearance to rider preference.

h. Check brake pad centering to rim.

i. If pads are not centered to rim, hold caliper arms with one hand while loosening rear nut. Move caliper so pads are centered to rim and tighten rear nut. Some models are fitted with a wrench flat in the center bolt. Use one wrench on the stud and another wrench on the mounting nut and move wrenches the same direction and the same amount (figure 12.44). One pad may contact the rim before the other when squeezed to the rim. This is not an issue with side pull calipers. It is only important that the pads are centered to the rim when they are fully open.

j. Set toe if necessary. Test ride bike and apply brakes. If brakes do not squeal, toe is not necessary. If desired, toe may be set by slightly bending arm. Grasp arm with small adjustable wrench and bend arm as needed. Use rag to protect arm if surface scarring is a concern.

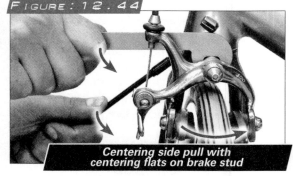

FIGURE: 12.44

Centering side pull with centering flats on brake stud

CHAPTER 13

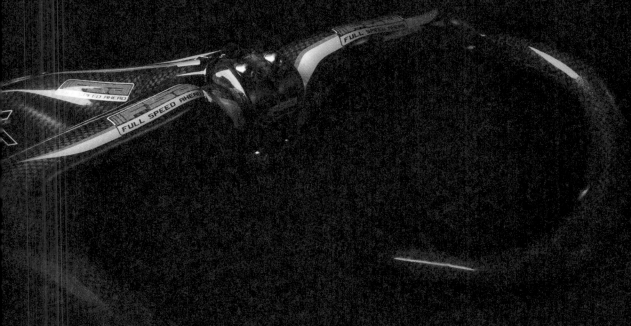

Handlebars, stems, Saddles & Seatposts

H andlebars support the rider's hands and are part of the steering system. The handlebars are one of the three contact points for the cyclist with the saddle and pedals. All of these components should be fitted and adjusted to the rider's body and riding style to maximize comfort and performance. Different models, sizes, and styles of these components may be changed for individual positioning needs.

Upright Bars

Upright style bars are commonly used on mountain bikes, hybrid bikes, BMX bikes, and cruisers. These bars typically have a slight bend to each side. Generally, these bars should be aligned to point straight back with the bar bend level to the ground (figure 13.1). If the bars are rotated, it will affect the reach for the brake and shift levers as well.

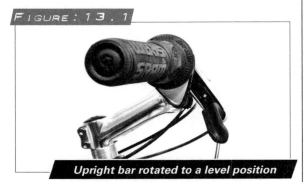

FIGURE: 13.1

Upright bar rotated to a level position

The upright bar typically uses a 22.2mm outside diameter at the ends for securing brake levers, shift levers, and bar-end extensions. The stem tightens on the handlebar center. The traditional size of 25.4mm is not directly interchangeable with the larger 31.8mm standard. Appropriate shims may be used to reduce the larger stem for the smaller 25.4mm bar.

Upright bars are available in different designs and can vary in width bend and/or rise (figure 13.2). The bar width is measured, end to end. The bars may bend or sweep back toward the rider. The amount of bend is measured in degrees from the bar center to the grip. The bar may also rise up from the bar center, and bars may vary from no rise to several centimeters.

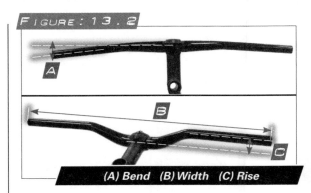

FIGURE: 13.2

(A) Bend   (B) Width   (C) Rise

Bar-ends, mounted either internally or externally to the ends of the handlebars, give the rider other hand position options (figure 13.3). Bar-ends may take nearly the entire body weight of the rider during use and should be tight and very secure on the bar. However external bar-ends may crush the ends of thin handlebars. If the inside diameter of the bar is greater than 19mm, a plug is required to provide internal support to prevent damage. Consult a professional mechanic or the manufacturer if in doubt.

FIGURE: 13.3

Bar-ends must be secure so they do not move under load

Bar grips vary in shape, color, compounds, size, and length, but all are designed to fit the 22.2mm bar diameter. Grips should not slip or move during the ride. Grips tend to expand and loosen, however, on the bar in time.

When installing new grips make sure the levers are positioned to allow the grips to slide fully onto the bar. It can help to lubricate the inside of the grip with non-oily liquids, such as rubbing alcohol, hair spray, window cleaner, or a fluid which will quickly evaporate. Do not use oil of any type. This prevents the grip from holding fast to the bar.

If the old grips are worn out and are being replaced, they may be cut off the bar. It is also possible to remove and re-use the grips if they are in adequate condition. Use a long, flat-tipped screwdriver worked gently under the inside edge of the grip. Drip or spray liquid such as window cleaner, hair spray, or rubbing alcohol in the gap (figure 13.4). Work the solvent around the grip to loosen the bond and slide the grip off the bar.

If the grip had a sealed end, it is also possible to remove it with compressed air. Use a blow tip and place inside end of grip. Wiggle the grip while pulling as blown air loosens grip from bar. It is necessary to have someone plug the exposed bar end to remove the second grip.

FIGURE: 13.4

Move levers inward, then lift grip to inject liquid spray

If the grips are slipping, it may be possible to improve the bond to the bar with glue. Contact cements and tubular tire cements are good choices. Use a thin layer inside the grip rather than the bar. Wire tying may also help. Stainless wire is secured and pulled tight at the end of grip. Cut wire end and then bend it back so sharp end does not cut into rider's hand.

Drop Style Handlebars (Road bars)

Drop style bars curve downward and form hooks for the hands. Bars will vary in width, reach of the drop, and shape of the bar. Select a bar for comfort. There are currently bar center diameter standards in 25.4mm, 25.8mm, 26.0mm, 26.4mm, 31.7mm, or 31.8mm. They can be considered interchangeable with the proper stem and/or shim. When in doubt, measure the diameter with a caliper.

The stem should match the standard of the bar center. For example, using a stem made for a 26.0 bar center with a 25.4 bar will mean the bar will not properly secure in the stem. This would be a very dangerous situation for the user. The bar would slip and move when used.

A difference of 0.1mm between stem and bar, however, is acceptable.

Drop bars are made with different designs and shapes. The bar width is measured at the ends. The common designation is to measure from center to center. Bar drop is measured center-to-center from the bar top downward to the lower section. Bar reach is measured from bar center, where it clamps in a stem, forward to the center of the bar at the curve (figure 13.5).

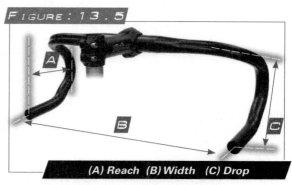

FIGURE: 13.5

(A) Reach (B) Width (C) Drop

Drop style bars can be rotated at the stem for comfort. There are rotational limits (figure 13.6). Too far up or down can sacrifice performance and safety. Drop bars experience a significant amount of stress at the stem clamp, and it is important that the drop bar be fully secure. Refer to Appendix C and with manufacturer's specifications for torque values.

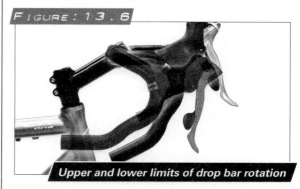

FIGURE: 13.6

Upper and lower limits of drop bar rotation

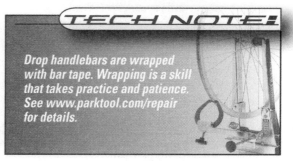

TECH NOTE!

Drop handlebars are wrapped with bar tape. Wrapping is a skill that takes practice and patience. See www.parktool.com/repair for details.

Several types of "aero" bar attachments are available, and each system offers different positions (figure 13.7). It is important the bars be fully secure before riding. Loose bars cause riders to lose control. Check manufacturer's specifications for torque and compatibility concerns.

FIGURE: 13.7

"Aero" clip-on handlebars

Stems

Stems connect the handlebars to the steering column or "steerer tube." Bikes with threaded steering columns use "quill stems" while bikes with threadless headsets use threadless stems.

A stem binds the bars using either a faceplate, or a one-piece pinch clamp. All binder bolts in the stem should be lubricated and secured tight. Do not, however, get grease or oil in the area where the bar meets the stem or column. The stem/bar interface may creak if not properly secured.

The removable faceplate of the stem presses against the bar center when the stem binder bolts are tightened. It is important that each bolt be turned the same amount, and the top and bottom gaps between the face-plate and the stem body are the same. If the gap size is different, the head of the bolt will be stressed as it rotates during tightening (figure 13.8).

FIGURE: 13.8

Uneven faceplate gaps may result in handlebar security failure

Quill Stems

The "quill" refers to the vertical post of the quill stem that inserts into the inside of the threaded steering column. A bolt draws up a wedge or cone to jam the stem tight in the column. The stem binder bolt, bolt head, wedge, and outside of the quill should be greased before installing and tightening (figure 13.9).

Quill stems measure length from the center of the stem binder to the center of the bar clamp. Stem angle is measured from the quill to a line representing the length. Quill stems will also a range of possible insertion height options (figure 13.9).

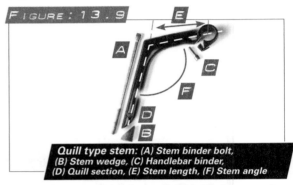

FIGURE: 13.9

Quill type stem: (A) Stem binder bolt, (B) Stem wedge, (C) Handlebar binder, (D) Quill section, (E) Stem length, (F) Stem angle

It is important that the stem's quill diameter is a correct match for the inside diameter of the steering column. The quill should be slightly smaller than the inside of the column. There are several different steering column sizes found on bikes. Quill stems of 22.2mm are used in the 1" (25.4mm) steering column. Quill stems of 25.4mm are used with the 1⅛" (28.6mm) column, and a 28.6mm quill are used in the 1¼" (31.8mm) column.

To change stem height on a quill stem, loosen the stem binder bolt at the top of the quill. Do not loosen the headset locknut to move the stem. Attempt to move the stem by twisting after loosening the binder bolt. If it will not move, strike the top of the stem binder bolt with a hammer or mallet to free the wedge. The stem must not be raised too high. Inspect the stem for a "max height" line and do not raise the stem past this mark (figure 13.10). Changes to stem height may also require adding longer housing and wire.

Stem is too high,
"max height" must not be visible

Align the stem with the front wheel. Alternatively, the handlebars provide a straight edge to help align the stem. Align the bars parallel to the front hub. It is useful to place a straight edge on the fork blades. Compare this line to the handlebar near the stem. If the two lines appear parallel, the stem is straight (figure 13.11 and Figure 13.12).

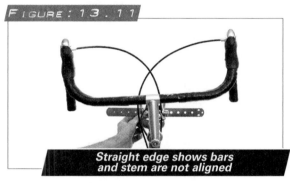

Straight edge shows bars
and stem are not aligned

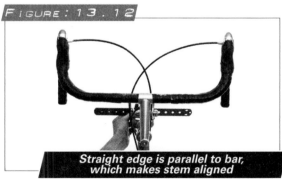

Straight edge is parallel to bar,
which makes stem aligned

Threadless Stems

Threadless stems clamp around the outside of the steering column. The stem also acts to lock the threadless headset bearing adjustment. Look for the adjusting cap at the top of the steering column. Do not confuse this cap for part of the stem. The threadless stem should be mounted only to a threadless steering column.

Threadless stem standards are determined by the outside diameter of the steering column. There several standards in use, the 25.4mm stem for 1" steering columns, the 28.6mm stem for 1⅛" columns, the 31.8mm stems for 1¼" columns, and 38.1mm stems for 1½" columns. A relatively larger stem may be shimmed down to a smaller steering column.

Threadless stems measure length from the center of the bar clamp to the center of the steering column. Stem angle is measured from the steering column to a line through the stem center. Threadless stems have a stem stack height, which is the length of stem along the steering column. (figure 13.13)

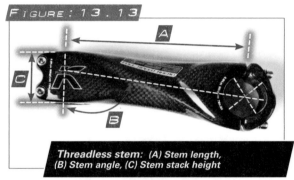

Threadless stem: (A) Stem length,
(B) Stem angle, (C) Stem stack height

Threadless stems generally offer limited height adjustment. To lower threadless stems, remove any extra spacers that are below the stem and stack them above the stem. It is important to keep at least one spacer between the stem and headset. This helps reduce stress on the steering column. After lowering the stem, if there is an excessive amount of steering column above the stem, the column may be cut and shortened. See Headsets, Unthreaded Steering Columns.

To raise a threadless stem, look for any spacers above the stem. Move these to below the stem, leaving enough of a gap for the top cap to allow for headset adjustment. If there are no spacers above the stem, install a different stem with a steeper upward angle. Changes to stem height may also require adding longer housing and wire.

Simply adding spacers below the current stem may compromise the stem-to-steering column engagement and make the bike unsafe. The steering column must have good engagement inside the threadless stem. The steering column should be slightly recessed below the stem top (figure 13.14). For most top caps, a 3mm gap between top of stem and column is adequate.

ParkTool

FIGURE: 13.14

Threadless steering column recessed below threadless stem

Threadless stem extensions are available (figure 13.15). These mount on the steering column and extend a post upward where the threadless stem clamps. It is important the extension have full engagement on the steering column. Consult manufacturer for height limits.

FIGURE: 13.15

Threadless column extender

Align stem to be in line with the front wheel. If this proves difficult, use a straight edge to extend the line of the fork blades. See the process with quill stems described above (figure 13.16). Fully secure stem binder bolts.

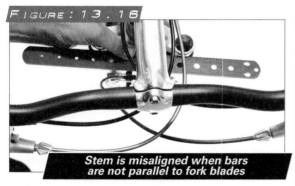

FIGURE: 13.16

Stem is misaligned when bars are not parallel to fork blades

It is critical for safety on carbon fiber columns to not over-tighten bolts as this may crack the carbon material (figure 13.17). Consult manufacturer for acceptable torque limits.

FIGURE: 13.17

Cracked steering column from stem binder bolts

Saddles

Bicycle saddles have rails mounted beneath the seat mold. The rails are secured to the seat post by saddle rail binder clamps (figure 13.18). Lubricate saddle rail binder bolts of post before tightening.

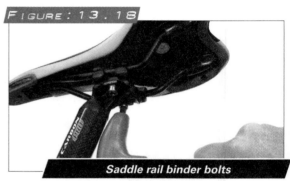

FIGURE: 13.18

Saddle rail binder bolts

To change the saddle, begin by noting the position of the current saddle. Place a straight edge on the saddle and measure the saddle tilt or angle using an angle finder. Note the distance of the saddle on the rails. Unbolt the old saddle from the seat post cradle. Lubricate saddle rail binder bolts with a light lubricant. Install the new saddle on the post clamp and secure binder bolts. Using an angle finder, measure saddle angle and position on the rails as compared to the previous saddle. Change position as necessary. The clamps can be adjusted so the saddle may point either up or down. Generally, begin with the saddle level, and then make changes in small increments upward or downward as necessary (figure 13.19).

Hard use and crashing may bend the saddle rails. Riding with bent rails may lead to breakage of the rail. Replace saddles with bent rails, rails that come out of the mold, or with cracked molds.

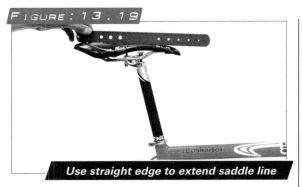
Use straight edge to extend saddle line

Seat Post

The seat post connects the saddle to the frame. Seat posts are available in different lengths. Posts may also vary in "offset" or "setback." This is the distance from center of the post to the center of bracket that holds the seat post. More offset allows the rider to sit farther back relative to cranks.

Bike frames typically have a compression slot cut into the top of the seat tube. A seat post binder bolt pinches the seat post tight. Lubricate bolt before tightening. The seat post binder bolt does not require a great deal of tension to hold the post from slipping downward. Generally, only tighten the binder until the saddle will not rotate when pressed with one hand. If it will not rotate with one hand, it is unlikely to slip downward (figure 13.20).

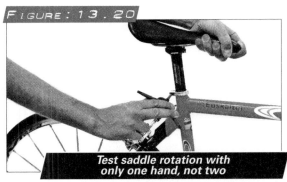
Test saddle rotation with only one hand, not two

There are many different sized seat tubes, and different seat post diameters are available to match. The seat post size may range from 22.2mm to 32.4mm. The post diameter should be approximately 0.1mm smaller than the inside frame diameter. Generally, if the frame is steel, titanium or aluminum, it is necessary to grease or anti-seize inside the seat tube to prevent rust and corrosion from seizing the post. If the seat post or frame are made of carbon, grease and oil are not recommended. Most manufacturers of carbon frames recommend installing a dry post dry without any treatment.

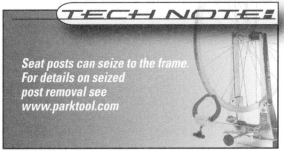
TECH NOTE!
Seat posts can seize to the frame. For details on seized post removal see www.parktool.com

Seat posts are usually marked with a "maximum extension" or "minimum insertion" line (figure 13.21). Do not raise the post above this line, or the post may break. Generally, always keep the end of the post inserted below the frame lug or weldment. Seat posts often sway and can bend permanently from impact and heavy use. A bent post is not repairable and should be replaced immediately.

There are some frame designs that use an "integrated seat post." An extended seat tube acts to hold the seat rail clamp. The seat tube is cut down to fit the rider with a saw guide such as the Park Tool SG-7. Other designs limit the seat post insertion, and the aero post must be trimmed to size for the rider (figure 13.22).

Post is too high; insert post so "max line" is not seen

Aero seat post is cut to size with the SG-7 saw guide

Park Tool

CHAPTER 14

Headsets

Two-wheeled vehicles, such as bicycles and motorcycles, make small self-corrections in steering while traveling forward. The headset is the bearing system that connects the bicycle fork to the main frame and allows the front wheel to steer smoothly while riding. If the headset is pitted or worn, the rider cannot make these corrections smoothly and handling suffers. Badly worn headsets tend to "lock up" when the front wheel is pointing straight. Pick up the front of the bike and gently swing the handlebars back and forth from center. Pitting in the cups will cause the headset to stick as it passes through the center position. A pitted headset should be replaced.

The upper and lower bearing races in a headset rest on the support surfaces or edges of the head tube. If the support surfaces are not machined parallel, the bearings will bind as the fork is rotated. This can lead to premature bearing wear and poor adjustment. The head tube can become deformed by welding or by inadequate manufacturing techniques. If necessary, the head tube can be machined (faced) so the surfaces are parallel by using the head tube reaming and facing tool (figure 14.1). The base of the fork steering column should also be cut square to the fork. If it is not properly machined, the fork crown race will not sit square to the steering column and will add to the binding effect. The fork can be machined with a crown race cutter. Facing the head tube and fork crown is best left to professional mechanics. Generally, the headset can be installed and then simply adjusted. If it adjusts well, with no binding, then the machining is adequate.

FIGURE: 14.1

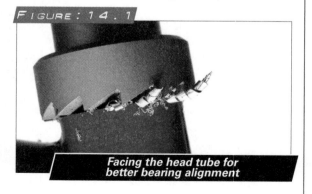

Facing the head tube for better bearing alignment

Headset Types

The two basic types are threaded and threadless. The threaded headsets use a threaded bearing race and locknut that secure onto a threaded steering column (figure 14.2). A quill stem insets down inside the steering column.

FIGURE: 14.2

Bike with conventional threaded headset

The threadless headset is used on steering columns with no threading (figure 14.3). The adjustment is done using a non-threaded adjusting race that slides onto the steering column. It is pushed onto the bearing by pressure from an adjusting cap at the top of the column. Pinch bolts on the stem lock the adjustable race and secure the stem.

FIGURE: 14.3

Bike with conventional threadless headset

The threaded and threadless headsets described above will be referred to as "conventional." These have been the traditional headset designs. They use cups pressed into the head tube. The bearing races may be caged ball bearings, loose ball bearings, or cartridge bearings. With the conventional design, the bearings sit outside (above and below) the head tube faces.

Threadless headsets have several variations. The "low-profile," "internal," and/or "zero stack" threadless systems use a relatively large diameter head tube, approximately 50mm outside diameter (figure 14.4). These are simply different names for the same headset system. Shallow headset cups are pressed into the lower and upper parts of the head tube. The bearings may be either caged balls or cartridge bearings. The bearings do not sit above and below the head tube faces. The bearings sit almost level with the head tube faces in this case.

FIGURE: 14.4

Bike with low-profile threadless headset

Integrated headsets are another variation of the threadless headset category (figure 14.5). Integrated headsets use cartridge bearings that are a slip fit into the frame. The frame is made with a headtube profile that accepts cartridge bearings dropped into place without pressed-in separate cups. The low-profile headset is not considered an integrated design because the bearings sit inside cups that are pressed into the frame. When a new low-profile headset is purchased, new cups as well as bearings are included. For integrated headsets, only the cartridge bearings and top cap parts are included.

FIGURE: 14.5

Bike with integrated threadless headset

There are several non-interchangeable industry standards for headset designs. It is important to know which standard the bike uses to find the correct replacement parts.

Headset Service

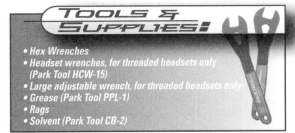

TOOLS & SUPPLIES:
- Hex Wrenches
- Headset wrenches, for threaded headsets only (Park Tool HCW-15)
- Large adjustable wrench, for threaded headsets only
- Grease (Park Tool PPL-1)
- Rags
- Solvent (Park Tool CB-2)

The front wheel throws dirt and water directly up at the lower headset bearing. An overhaul can extend the life of the headset by removing any foreign matter. If the headset feels gritty when turning, it should be overhauled. If the headset seems to stop as it rotates, then the races are dented. The headset should be replaced instead. Like any overhaul, taking notes regarding parts orientation during disassembly will help during reassembly.

The handlebars are in the way when servicing the headset. It is best to disconnect the cables from the brake calipers and derailleurs and completely remove the bars. This will prevent damage to housing and inner wires. Additionally, it is best to remove or disconnect handlebar-mounted computers to avoid damage to the wire.

Any pressed race may be left in the head tube and on the fork unless the headset is being replaced. Clean all bearings and races with a solvent. Use care on suspension forks not to get solvent into lower sliding legs.

Threadless Headset Service

The threadless headset service discussed here will include low-profile and integrated headsets. If the headset uses a cartridge bearing rather then caged ball bearings, simply replace the cartridge bearing as a unit. It is possible to use a seal pick and remove the seals of some cartridge bearings and to clean and re-grease the bearings. New grease will not smooth a pitted or rough bearing surface.

Park Tool

The procedure for threadless headset disassembly and assembly:

   a. Loosen stem bolts and remove stem from steering column. Remove any washers/spacers from the steering column.

   b. Pull fork from bike. It may be necessary to use a mallet and tap the top of the steering column, driving fork downward (figure 14.6). Once the fork is driven down a little, lift it back up and remove center cone from adjusting race.

   c. Remove fork from frame and note orientation of cage bearing retainers or cartridge bearings as they sit in headset (figure 14.7).

   d. Clean and inspect parts. View races for pitting and damage while looking for gouging and small, evenly spaced pits (figure 14.8). Use a ballpoint pen to trace the bearing path. Roughness and wear will be felt as the small ball of the pen passes over pitted areas. Again, any worn parts should be replaced.

   e. If the ball bearings have a shiny silver color and appear smooth, they can be re-used. If the ball bearings appear discolored, they should be replaced. The ball bearings are generally the last part of the system to wear out.

FIGURE: 14.6

If necessary, drive fork downward to remove fork

FIGURE: 14.7

Note orientation of retainer. Open side of retainer faces cone-shaped race

FIGURE: 14.8

Pitted headset cup

If the headset is using caged ball retainers, check the orientation of the retainers in relation to the races before installing. Retainers have only one correct orientation. The open side of the ball retainer should face the cone-shaped race, not the cup-shaped race (figure 14.9). Cups installed in the frame or made as part of the frame do not move. Point the bearing's open side towards the race that moves. If in doubt, place bearing into headset, use mating race, press downward on bearings with your hand, and rotate race side to side. If the bearing orientation is wrong, the race will have a rubbing feeling. If the orientation is correct, race rotates on balls and will feel smoother.

FIGURE: 14.9

Open side of bearing cage should face cone-shaped race

The procedure for threadless headset assembly:

   a. Grease bearing retainers and bearing race cups. For cartridge bearing headsets, drop cartridge in place.

   b. Install bearing retainers into upper and lower cup shaped races.

   c. Install fork steering column through head tube.

   d. Install race-centering cone onto column. Press centering cone into adjusting race to help hold fork.

   e. Install spacers and accessories as appropriate.

f. Install stem, tighten top cap bolt, and snug stem bolts. Check for adequate clearance from top of column to top of stem (figure 14.10). The recommended clearance is 2-3mm for aluminum and steel columns. Add spacers as necessary. Spacers may be placed either below or above the stem.

FIGURE: 14.10

Steel and aluminum columns must be recessed below top of stem

Note the height of the steering column relative to the stem. Steel and aluminum columns can be approximately 2-3mm (⅛") below the level of the stem. The stem needs to press down on the spacers in order to adjust the bearings. If the top cap presses on the steering column rather than the stem, there will be no load put on the adjusting race and bearings. It will be impossible to remove play. The column can be cut shorter, or alternatively, spacers can be added either above or below the stem to achieve a gap (figure 14.11).

FIGURE: 14.11

Spacers added to increase clearance between top cap and column

It is best for carbon fiber columns to protrude past the stem rather than be recessed. This permits the column to be fully secured by the stem and reduces the chance of cracking at the top of the column (figure 14.12). A spacer must then be used on top of the stem as described above to allow bearing adjustment.

FIGURE: 14.12

Recessed carbon column cracked at top by stem binder pressure

It is possible to replace retainer ball bearings with loose ball bearings of the same diameter. Loose balls, especially in the lower race, can move about which helps prevent the pitting that commonly ruins headsets. Installation and assembly with loose bearings is more difficult. It is important that the bearings stay aligned in the cup as the headset is assembled.

To use loose ball bearings, grease cups to hold bearings. Place balls into cup shaped races. Leave a gap equal to two to three ball bearings (figure 14.13). Do not attempt to fully fill cup with ball bearings. If possible, rotate bicycle upside down in the stand to assist assembly before installing fork. After assembly with loose ball bearings, rotate fork to check smooth rotation. Any popping or sudden change in feeling indicates a bearing out of place.

FIGURE: 14.13

Loose ball bearings in the headset cup with gap so balls can move freely

Threadless Headset Adjustment

Threadless headsets, including low-profile and integrated, all operate on the same principle. The bearing races must press against the bearings. The bolt in the top cap puts pressure on the stem. The stem presses on washers below the stem. The washers press on the bearing races. The races press against the bearings (figure 14.14). The stem is secured by the top cap bolt to maintain this pressure on the bearings.

The cap and bolt at the top of the threadless systems are used for bearing adjustment only. These caps do not secure the stem onto the steering column. The stem uses binder bolt(s) to secure the stem from moving once the adjustment is made.

If not already inspected in assembly, remove the top cap to inspect the star nut or plug inside the steering column. The cap bolt threads into this fitting and pulls on the fork against the headset bearing surfaces, which acts to tighten the adjustment.

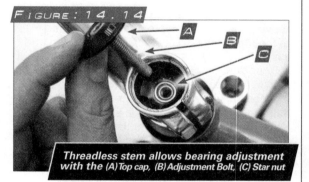

FIGURE: 14.14

Threadless stem allows bearing adjustment with the (A) Top cap, (B) Adjustment Bolt, (C) Star nut

The procedure for threadless headset adjustment:

a. Remove top cap bolt to inspect steering column length relative to cap. Lubricate bolt and re-install cap and bolt gently. Do not tighten cap bolt.

b. Loosen stem bolt(s) that secure stem to the steering column. Lubricate these bolts if they are dry.

c. Wiggle the stem side to side to ensure it is loose. If the stem is jammed or rusted frozen to the steering column, no adjustment can be made.

d. Align stem straight to wheel and gently secure the top bolt. Stop when resistance is felt (figure 14.15).

e. Tighten stem bolt(s) and check for play by pulling back and forth on fork. Turn the handlebar in different directions while checking for play. There may be play at this early setting. Grab the upper portion of suspension forks because the legs may have play.

f. To adjust bearings, loosen stem bolt(s).

g. Turn adjusting bolt in center cap ⅛ turn clockwise.

h. Secure stem bolts, check for play again.

i. Repeat adjustments as above until play disappears. Remember to loosen stem bolts before turning adjusting bolt in cap.

j. Check alignment of stem and tighten stem binder bolts fully.

FIGURE: 14.15

Make bearing adjustment at top cap only when stem bolts are loose

Another test for play is to place the bike on the ground and grab the front brake tightly. Press downward on the handlebars and rock the bike forward and back. A knocking sensation may indicate a loose headset. In effect this does the same thing as grabbing and pulling on the fork. However, play in the brake caliper arms may cause a knocking. Front suspension forks may also have play in the legs, which can also cause a knocking.

If a bearing adjustment cannot be found to be acceptable, there may be other problems in the headset. Bearing surfaces may be worn out; the ball bearing retainers may be upside down; or a seal may be improperly aligned. If play always seems present no matter the adjustment, the steering column may be too long and may be pressing into the top cap. Add spacers as necessary. Another source of play can be a loose press fit in either in the head tube or on the fork crown race.

Threaded Headset Service

The threaded race of a headset requires a narrow headset wrench. Use either the Park Tool HW-2 Headset Locknut Wrench, or a large adjustable wrench on the top locknut when possible. These wrenches allow more purchase of the top nut.

The procedure for threaded headset disassembly:

a. Loosen stem binder bolt. Attempt to move the stem by twisting. If stem will not move, strike the top of the stem binder bolt with a hammer or mallet to free the wedge (figure 14.16). Attempt to twist stem again.

b. Pull stem and handlebars from fork.

c. Install wheel into fork to act as a lever. Stand in front of bike and hold the wheel between your knees while working with the locknut and race.

d. Hold lower threaded race with thin headset wrench. Loosen and remove top locknut with second wrench, preferably large adjustable wrench or Park Tool HW-2 Headset Locknut Wrench.

e. Remove wheel.

f. Remove any spacers or brackets from under the locknut.

g. Unthread and remove the threaded race. Note orientation of upper and lower bearing retainers.

h. Pull fork from bike.

i. Clean and inspect parts. View races for pitting and damage, looking for gouging and small evenly spaced pits. See pit example page 188, Figure 14.8. Use a ballpoint pen to trace the bearing path. Roughness and wear will be felt as the small ball of the pen passes over bad areas. Wear in the races will not become smooth with new grease. Worn parts should be replaced. If the ball bearings have a shiny silver color and appear smooth, they can be reused. If the ball bearings appear discolored, they should be replaced. The ball bearings are generally the last part of the system to wear out.

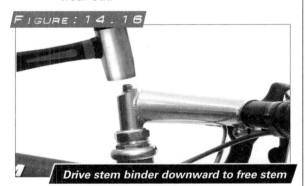
Drive stem binder downward to free stem

Threaded headsets commonly use a spacer with a notch or "tooth" on the inside diameter. This notch is designed to sit inside a groove running vertically in the column. However, these types of spacers will often rotate, causing damage as the notch cuts into the threads. This is especially the case when the spacer is made of steel and is relatively thin. Wide, aluminum spacers do not tend to damage fork threads. Inspect the threads of the fork. If any damage is present, file out the notch or get a new spacer without a notch.

If the headset is using bearing retainers, check the orientation of the retainers in relation to the races before installing. Retainers have only one correct orientation. The open side of the ball retainer should face the cone shaped race,

not the cup shaped race (figure 14.17). Bearing cups inside the frame do not move. Bearings do. Place the open side of the bearings against the races that move. If in doubt, place bearing into headset. Use mating race and press downward on bearings with your hand and rotate race side to side. If bearing orientation is wrong, race will have a rubbing feeling. If orientation is correct, race rotates on balls and will feel smoother.

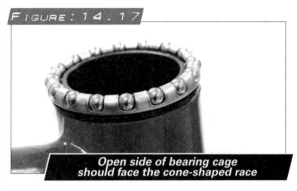
Open side of bearing cage should face the cone-shaped race

The procedure for threaded headsets assembly:

a. Grease bearing retainers and bearing race cups. Grease threads of steering column.

b. Install bearing retainers into upper and lower cup-shaped races.

c. Install fork steering column through head tube.

d. Thread on top race.

e. Install spacers and accessories as appropriate.

f. Thread on locknut. Inspect that steering column does not touch inner lip of locknut. Add spacers as necessary.

It is possible to replace retainer ball bearing with loose ball bearings of the same diameter. Loose balls, especially in the lower race, can move about which helps prevent the pitting that commonly ruins headsets. Assembly with loose bearings is more difficult. It is important that the bearings stay aligned in the cup as the headset is assembled.

To use loose ball bearings, grease cups to hold bearings. Place balls into cup-shaped races. Leave a gap the size of two to three ball bearings. See image example Figure 14.13, page 189. Do not attempt to fill cup completely with ball bearings. If possible, rotate bicycle upside down in the stand to assist assembly before installing fork. After assembly with loose ball bearings, rotate fork to check for smooth rotation. Any popping or sudden change in feeling indicates a bearing out of place.

Threaded Headset Adjustment

Threaded headsets are adjusted using a top locknut and threaded race. The stem has no effect on the bearing adjustment. The best bearing adjustment is as loose as possible but without bearing play or knocking. To achieve this, the following procedure will first create play in the adjustment. Proceed to incrementally tighten the race until play is gone.

The procedure for threaded headset adjustment:

a. Make sure headset locknut is loose. Use a headset wrench to hold threaded race. Use a large adjustable wrench or the Park Tool Headset Wrench HW-2 on the locknut.

b. By hand, turn threaded race clockwise until it contacts ball bearings. Turn race back counter-clockwise at least ¼ turn from this setting. Hold threaded race with headset wrench and tighten locknut. Tighten locknut fully (figure 14.18). This early setting is intended to have play.

c. Check for play by pulling back and forth on fork. A knocking sensation indicates play. Turn the handlebars in different directions while checking for play. There should be play at this early setting. If headset feels tight, loosen adjustment further until play is found. Grab the upper portion of suspension forks because the legs may have play.

d. Grab front wheel between knees and hold it in line with top tube. Front wheel will act as a lever to hold steering column. Threaded race will need to be adjusted slightly clockwise. Use a wrench to hold race and note orientation of wrench relative to front wheel.

e. Loosen locknut and rotate threaded race clockwise ¹⁄₃₂ of a turn relative to wheel.

f. Hold threaded race securely with wrench and tighten locknut fully. Check for play by rotating fork and moving fork forward and back at different positions.

g. If play is present, repeat steps "e" and "f" above until play disappears. Adjustment is finished when there is no play in any position, the fork rotates, and locknut is fully secure.

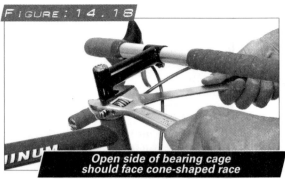

FIGURE: 14.18

Open side of bearing cage should face cone-shaped race

Another test for play is to place the bike on the ground and grab the front brake tightly. Press downward on the handlebars and rock the bike forward and back. A knocking sensation may indicate a loose headset. In effect this does the same thing as grabbing and pulling on the fork. Play in the brake caliper arms may also cause knocking. Front suspension forks may also have play in the stanchion and sliding legs, which can cause knocking.

If an acceptable bearing adjustment cannot be found, there may be other problems in the headset. Bearing surfaces may be worn out; the ball bearing retainers may be upside down; or a seal may be improperly aligned. Another source of play can be a loose press fit, either in the head tube or on the fork crown race. If the headset seems well-adjusted at one position but binds when rotated to another position, the head tube may require facing to improve bearing alignment. Consult a professional mechanic.

Headset Replacement & Installation

The headset may be replaced when worn or when upgrading to a better model. After installing the new headset, the procedure for assembly and adjustment is the same the same as the procedures above.

There are several standards for headsets found on bicycles. When selecting a new headset, it is important to get one that will fit the bike. This can be easier said than done. There are currently more than a dozen headset standards that do not interchange. Table 14.1 Headset Fit Standards reviews some of these standards. The table is not exhaustive, as some unusual and proprietary standards exist. There are also hybrid designs that mix standards. For example, a steering column can be 1⅛ inch at the top for the stem, but 1.5 inches at the fork crown. It will usually be necessary to remove the headset to know exactly what standard is being used. If in doubt, consult a professional mechanic for the correct standard for your bike.

TABLE: 14.1　　Headset Fit Standards

NAME OF STANDARD	STEERING COLUMN: THREADED OR THREADLESS	BEARING OR CUP FIT	STEERING COLUMN OUTSIDE DIAMETER	PRESSED RACE OR CARTRIDGE BEARING OUTSIDE DIAMETER
Conventional 1" Japanese Industrial Standard (JIS)	Threaded and Threadless 1"	Pressed races	1" (25.4mm)	30.0mm
Conventional 1" "European" Standard	Threaded & Threadless 1"	Pressed races	1" (25.4mm)	30.2mm
Integrated 1"	Threadless	Slip fit	1" (25.4mm)	30.2mm
Conventional 1 ⅛" Standard	Threadless & Threaded	Pressed races	1 ⅛" (28.6mm)	34.0mm
Conventional 1 ¼" Standard	Threadless & Threaded	Pressed races	1 ¼" (31.8mm)	37.0mm
One-point-five® (1.5 standard)	Threadless	Pressed races	1 ½" (38.1mm)	49.8mm
IS (Integrated Standard)	Threadless	Slip fit	1 ⅛" (28.6mm)	41mm
Campagnolo® Hiddenset Integrated Standard	Threadless	Slip fit	1 ⅛" (28.6mm)	42mm
Low-Profile (45-47mm head tube)	Threadless	Pressed races	1 ⅛" (28.6mm)	41.4mm
ED-36	Threadless	Slip fit	1 ⅛" (28.6mm)	41.5mm
Microtek®	Threadless	Pressed races	1 ⅛" (28.6mm)	42.0mm
Integrated 36° by 36° contact	Threadless	Slip fit	1 ⅛" (28.6mm)	44.0mm
Low Profile (50mm head tube)	Threadless	Pressed races	1 ⅛" (28.6mm)	44.0mm pressed cup (if used, cartridge bearing is 41mm)
Perdido®	Threadless	Pressed races	1 ⅛" (28.6mm)	44.5mm pressed races

Park Tool

It is sometimes possible to use a smaller steering column than the head tube was designed to use. Reducing rings are available and are pressed into the head tubes of the larger standards. Reducers are available to size the 1.5 standard head tube down to the 1⅛ inch standard, and to reduce the 1⅛ inch standard down to the 1-inch "European" standard. It is not possible to convert a bike upward. The head tube cannot accept a steering column larger than it was designed to accept.

The integrated headset systems use the frame to act as a holder for cartridge bearings (figure 14.19). Unlike conventional headsets, there are no pressed bearing races in the head tube. The integrated systems use cartridge bearings with an angular contact to fit inside the frame.

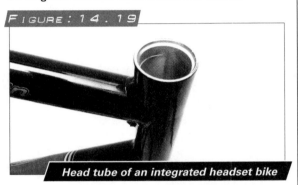

FIGURE: 14.19

Head tube of an integrated headset bike

There are several non-interchangeable standards of cartridge bearing diameter and contact angle. There are commonly two numbers listed on the cartridge bearings. The first number is the contact angle of the inner race, commonly 36-degrees. This refers to the fork race and compression ring. The second number is the contact angle of the outer race, which is the race surface contacting the frame. For example, a bearing marked 36-45 has a 36-degree contact angle for the inner race, and a 45-degree contact angle for the frame contact. To service an integrated headset, simply dismantle the headset. Cartridge bearings are lifted out by hand, and a new bearing is placed in the headset, again by hand (figure 14.20). The adjustment procedure is the same as for a conventional threadless headset.

FIGURE: 14.20

Removing the integrated headset bearing

Headset Stack Height

Headsets vary between brand and model in stack height. Stack height is the amount of steering column length the headset will occupy (figure 14.21). The steering column is always longer than the head tube. Headset stack height does not include the stem of threadless headsets, nor any sizing washers used to give extra rise to the stem.

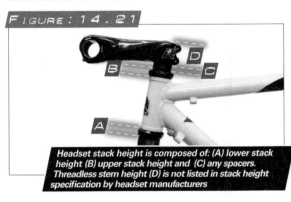

FIGURE: 14.21

Headset stack height is composed of: (A) lower stack height (B) upper stack height and (C) any spacers. Threadless stem height (D) is not listed in stack height specification by headset manufacturers

A new headset will have the stack height listed on the box or instructions. Generally, when replacing a headset, select one of equal or smaller stack height. Using a headset with more stack height may result in the column being too short for the bike or removing spacers from under the stem if possible.

Headset Removal

Begin headset replacement by removing the wheel, handlebars and fork. To remove pressed races, use a race removal tool such as the Park Tool RT-1 Race Tool or RT-2 for 1.5 inch headset cups. Install tool with smaller end first through the headset cup. Squeeze sides of prongs and pull tool fully into head tube. Do not press prongs with hand as prongs will close and pinch flesh. A clicking sound will be heard as tool prongs engage head tube cup. Use a steel hammer at the small end of the Park Tool RT-1 (or for 1.5 inch frames the RT-2) and drive cup from head tube (figure 14.22). Use care as cup approaches end of tube; the tool may fall to ground on the last blow of the hammer. Place RT-1 or RT-2 with small end first through remaining cup and repeat process to remove second race. A long punch can also be used to remove the head tube races. Alternate tapping left to right to "walk" out the race.

FIGURE: 14.22

Removing the pressed race with race remover RT-1

The fork crown race must be removed from the fork. Professionals will use the Park Tool CRP-1 Crown Race Puller (figure 14.23). An alternative is to use a punch or other tool that will engage race. In some cases this may scar the fork and crown race. Place the fork column downward on soft material such as wood to protect top of column. Using a hammer, tap race alternately first on one side, then the other side, driving the race off the crown seat (figure 14.24).

FIGURE: 14.23

Park Tool CRP-1 Crown Race Puller removing fork crown race

FIGURE: 14.24

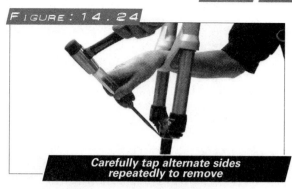

Carefully tap alternate sides repeatedly to remove

Pressed Headset Installation

Conventional and low-profile headset bearing races or cups require a press fit into the frame. The press fit (or interference fit) occurs when parts are held together by internal and external surfaces forced together. There must be a slight diameter difference between the two pressed surfaces. This tension is what keeps the cups tight in the frame. Generally, the difference in the press fit should be between 0.1mm and 0.2mm. A professional mechanic will be able to ream the head tube to improve the fit.

Use a caliper to measure the outside diameter of the cups. Next, measure the inside diameter of the head tube in two places: each 90 degrees from the other. Average the two readings (figure 14.25). The difference between the outside diameter and inside diameter is the amount of interference fit. See Table 14.2 Interference Fit Guidelines.

FIGURE: 14.25

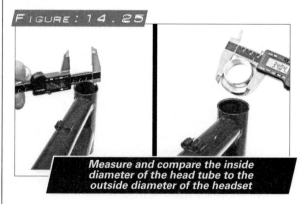

Measure and compare the inside diameter of the head tube to the outside diameter of the headset

Park Tool

TABLE: 14.2	Interference Fit Guidelines
DIFFERENCE BETWEEN RACE OUTSIDE DIAMETER AND HEAD TUBE INSIDE DIAMETER	**RESULT AND ACTION REQUIRED**
0.26mm or greater	Too great of press fit difference. Ream head tube inside diameter to improve fit.
0.1mm to 0.25mm	Acceptable tolerances for press fit.
0.01mm to 0.09mmm	Unacceptably small interference. Get a new race with larger diameter. It is also possible to use a retaining compound.
0mm or any negative number	No interference fit at all, headset is smaller than head tube. Use a different race if possible. Retaining compound may be tried if no other option is available.

Significant force is required to press headset races into the head tube. Additionally, the races should be pressed square to one another. It is best to use a bearing press (Park Tool HHP-2 or HHP-3 Bearing Press) for the head tube races. The HHP-2 Bearing Press comes with a pair of cup guides (#530-2) to help maintain cup alignment during pressing. The cup guides fit most 1-inch and 1⅛-inch conventional headset races.

The procedure for installing head tube races:

a. Determine the acceptability of the headset press fit as described above.

b. Adjust threaded press plate of HHP-2 until top is flush with end of hex shaft thread. For HHP-3, remove one handle and washers.

c. Remove HHP-2 sliding press plate and install cups onto guides.

d. Place upper headset cup on top of head tube. Hold guide onto top threaded press plate and lower assembly through upper headset cup.

e. Install second cup guide on sliding press plate and place lower cup onto guide (figure 14.26). If guides do not fit headset well, press one cup at a time using only the press plates. For HHP-3, press one cup at a time.

f. Engage HHP-2 sliding press plate onto hex shaft and push plate upward until headset cup meets head tube. Release lever. Sliding press plate lever must be engaged in one of seven hex shaft notches. Pull downward on lower press plate to test engagement.

g. HHP-2 and HHP-3 handle clockwise slowly and inspect alignment of cups as cups enter head tube. Press cups fully into head tube.

h. Inspect for full seating where cups meet frame. A gap between the frame and cup indicates incomplete pressing (figure 14.27).

i. Remove HHP-2 or HHP-3 from bike. For HHP-2, unthread handle one turn, press lever of sliding press plate, and remove tool from bike. If pressing one cup at a time, repeat process for second cup.

FIGURE: 14.26

Arrangement of cups and pressing guides for the HHP-2

FIGURE: 14.27

This cup is not fully seated into frame

It is sometimes possible to press a headset without the headset press. Substitute a large threaded rod, called all-thread, of ½ inch diameter with thick flat washers and two nuts fitting the rod. Press one cup at a time and use care when turning the nut with a large adjustable wrench.

Fork Crown Race Installation

The fork crown race is pressed to a crown race seat on the fork. Because the fork race is smaller than the crown race seat, it expands as it is pressed. Crown races are commonly made of bearing hard steel, which is very hard and brittle. It does not expand to the same extent as the head tube when the headset race is pressed. Measure the difference between the inside diameter of the fork crown race and the outside of the fork crown. The crown race seat should be larger than the race by only 0.1mm to 0.15mm. Greater differences then this between race and seat may stress and crack the bearing race. When the crown race seat is too large for the fork crown race, the crown race seat may be cut smaller. A professional mechanic will use a crown race seat cutter such as the Park Tool CRC-1. If the crown race seat is only slightly larger than the race (0.02 to 0.09mm) use a strong retaining compound. If the crown race seat is equal to or even smaller than the race, try to use a different race, and consult a professional mechanic.

The fork crown race must be pressed to the fork crown. Determine acceptability of press fit as described above. The Park Tool CRS-1 Crown Race Setter will drive on the race. Use the CRS-15 for 1.5 inch steering columns. Place race on fork crown and select most compatible Park Tool CRS aluminum ring. Place ring on tool and insert over fork. Use a steel hammer and strike top of tool until race fully seats (figure 14.28). The sound of the hammering will change as it seats. Inspect sides of race for full seating against fork.

Pressing the fork crown race

There are some models of headsets using cartridge bearings that use a lower race made with a split ring. These races press on and remove by hand. The race does not directly ride on the rotating bearings rather on inserts into the cartridge bearing race.

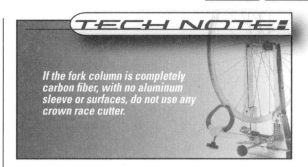

Star Nut & Compression Plug Installation

Threadless headsets are adjusted by pressure on the top bearing race. Pressure is applied when the bolt in the top cap is tightened. The bolt is threaded into either the "star nut" or a compression plug (figure 14.29).

Star nut on the left and compression plug on the right

Compression plugs are a threaded system installed into the steering column. A socket fitting is tightened to hold the plug secure. These plugs have an internal thread for the top cap. The plug diameter must be compatible with the diameter of the steering column. The compression plug is removable.

The star nut system is designed not to pull upward after installation. In other words, it is not meant to be removed. The star nut has flanges with an outer diameter slightly larger than the inside diameter of the fork column. This allows the flanges to bite into the fork walls and hold tight.

To install a star nut, use a tool such as the Park Tool TNS-1 or TNS-4 Threadless Nut Setter. The tool will drive the star nut about 15mm (⁹⁄₁₆") below the top of the steering column. This allows the adjusting bolt to thread fully into the nut for adjustment pre-load. Mount the nut with concave side toward tool thread. Hold TNS-1 over steering column. Use care to align TNS-1 with the column. Tap squarely on top of TNS-1 with steel hammer. Continue until TNS-1 is fully seated (figure 14.30).

FIGURE: 14.30

Seating the star nut

The TNS-4 uses a sleeved guiding system to drive the star nut into the column. Thread the star nut into the tool and slide the tool over the column (figure 14.31). Use a hammer to drive down the mandrel until the star nut is fully seated.

FIGURE: 14.31

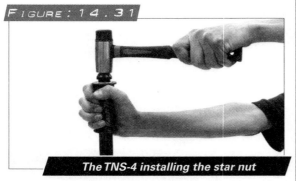

The TNS-4 installing the star nut

An alternate technique to the TNS tools is to create a driving system. For example use a short wooden dowel to drive in the star nut. It will require careful use of the hammer to tap the nut in straight. Another alternative is to thread the bolt into the nut, then tap the bolt to drive in the nut.

Fork Sizing and Cutting

The steering columns on new forks are typically longer than required, and the column is cut to fit the rider. Threadless columns must be long enough to fit the stem and any spacers. Threaded columns must be long enough to engage the locknut. Steering columns that are too long will prevent bearing adjustment.

Unthreaded Steering Columns

For threadless steering columns, the column length will limit the height of the stem and handlebars. When installing a new fork, consider where you would like the handlebars to be. It is possible to cut a threadless column relatively long and to use spacers under the stem to raise the bars. However, there are limits to how far

the stem can safely be raised above the headset. For steel and aluminum steering columns, do not exceed 40mm between the stem and headset. If more stem and bar height is required than this limit will allow, consider purchasing a new stem with more height or rise. It is also possible to cut a column purposely too long, and stack spacers above the stem to allow bearing adjustment.

Carbon fiber steering columns also have limits on the height of spacers between stem and frame. Generally, manufacturers recommend no more than 25mm additional stack height between stem and upper race. Contact the fork manufacturer for limits in regards to your fork.

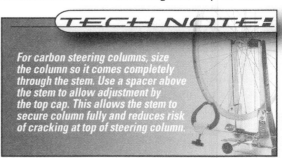

TECH NOTE!

For carbon steering columns, size the column so it comes completely through the stem. Use a spacer above the stem to allow adjustment by the top cap. This allows the stem to secure column fully and reduces risk of cracking at top of steering column.

The safest and most practical method to determine column length is to install the fork first without cutting. Mark the fork at the appropriate point and then remove it for cutting. When cutting unthreaded columns, use the ParkTool SG-6 or SG-7 Saw Guide. The SG-7 Saw Guide is for the 1.5 inch columns.

The procedure for cutting threadless steering columns:

a. Assemble steering column into the head tube with bearings and parts in place. Install stem and all desired spacers.
b. Press downward on stem to simulate an adjusted headset and snug stem bolts. Remove what play you can, but the adjustment need not be perfect.
c. Scribe or mark steering column at top of stem (figure 14.32).
d. Remove fork from bike. Measure an additional 3mm from mark toward fork crown, and mark column. This will be the cut line. This allows the top of the column to sit slightly below the top of the stem.
e. Place fork inside ParkTool SG-6 or SG-7 Saw Guide. Loosely secure handle. Move SG-6 Saw Guide opening over mark on column and secure handle. Place saw guide in vise. If no vise is available, hold column in repair stand jaws. For 1.5 inch forks, hold column in repair stand, not vise.

f. Cut through column using proper hacksaw techniques and a good blade (figure 14.33). Apply pressure forward in the direction of cutting teeth and release pressure drawing the blade backwards.

g. Loosen handle and push column further into saw guide.

h. Use a flat file to finish and bevel end of steel or aluminum columns. Hold file at approximately a 45-degree angle to bevel the end of the column. Use a round file or de-burring tool to remove the sharp inside edge of the column. Carbon forks can be beveled with fine sand paper.

i. Remove fork from saw guide and install on bike.

FIGURE: 14.32

Mark column for cutting

FIGURE: 14.33

Cut the fork square using the SG-6 Saw Guide

Steel columns tend to be relatively thin. A pipe cutter can substitute for the hacksaw technique described above. The cutting wheel will leave a burr at the end of the tubing, which must be filed off.

Alternatively, if no saw guide is available, it is possible to use a hacksaw and steel radiator hose clamps for a guide. Measure and mark the column. Mount and secure one clamp on each side of the mark while leaving a gap wide enough for the hacksaw blade. After cutting, finish the end flat and square with a file.

For carbon fiber steering columns, a fine 32 TPI blade is recommended. Cut using moderate pressure only, do not force the blade. Carbon dust is a potential health risk due to the small size of the dust particulates. Take normal precautions of wearing a dust mask and working in a well ventilated area. Additionally, to minimize dust from the carbon, keep the blade wet. Use a fine emery cloth to finish the end, again wetting the paper.

Threaded Steering Columns

The threaded steering columns require enough thread for the threaded race to press on the bearings. However, the column should not have too many threads. The threads should never extend past the depth of the quill stem. If the column cannot be shortened to permit the quill to extend past the threads, a new fork should be installed with less threading.

The procedure for cutting and sizing threaded steering columns:

a. Assemble the threaded fork in the bike with all spacers.

b. Measure how much steering column extends past the top spacer and write this number down.

c. Turn the locknut upside down and measure the amount of depth of locknut to "lip" at the end of the nut. This is the amount of available threading in the nut. The steering column should not contact this inner lip when the locknut is secured (figure 14.34). Deduct an additional millimeter from this number to allow a small gap between nut and column.

d. Deduct the available threaded height in the locknut from the amount of steering column extending past the spacers. For example, a steering column extends 27mm above the spacers. The threaded locknut measures 7mm down to the lip. Deduct one millimeter from the nut, making only 6mm of threading available. Cut 21mm off the column.

e. Use a saw guide such as the Park Tool SG-1 Saw Guide (1" column), or SG-2 (1⅛" column) to ensure that the cut is square to the fork. Thread fork into saw guide until it reaches desired cut length at the gap for the blade. Clamp the guide in a vise. If no vise is available, hold column in repair stand jaws. Use a hacksaw and cut fork.

f. The threads at the end of the fork will
    require extra finishing after the cut.
    Thread the fork farther into the guide to
    expose freshly cut threads. Hold a flat file
    at approximately a 45-degree angle to
    bevel the threads at the end of the fork
    (figure 14.35). Rotate the fork into the
    file as the file is pushed forward. Use a
    round file to finish the inside of the fork,
    removing any sharp edges or burrs.

FIGURE: 14.34

Cutaway of locknut on threaded column.
Locknut lip should not contact top of column.

If no Park Tool Saw Guide is available, it is
possible to use a steel threaded race as a saw
guide. Thread race on column and measure
exposed threads. Hold column in bike repair
clamp. Press race to clamp so it cannot move.
Cut the column using a hacksaw, holding the
blade against the face of the race. Finish the cut
with a file to bevel the end of the column.

It is common for threaded columns to be made
with a machined groove running along the axis
of the threads. Threaded headsets may come
with spacers with a notch or "tooth" on the
inside diameter. The fork groove is for this notch.
Shortening a fork may remove the groove. Do
not attempt to extend or create a new groove for
the notched washer. Simply file the notch away
or get a new spacer without the notch.

FIGURE: 14.35

Bevel end of fork thread

CHAPTER 15

Frame and Fork

The frame and front fork form the skeleton of the bike to connect the two wheels. The frame also supports the rider and the various components of the bike. The front fork allows the wheel to pivot, which permits steering. The front wheel is designed to be in line with the rear wheel. As we ride, it is the rider's balance that keeps the bike upright. Like motorcycles, bicycles have a "self-steering" feature that helps the vehicle maintain a straight line. The bicycle is steered by leaning in combination with turning the handlebars.

The frame has different parts or sections (figure 15.1). Bicycle designers will manipulate the length and angle of each section, tube, or tube junction to obtain certain ride and handling characteristics. As an example, headtube angles differing by just one degree may cause two different bicycles to handle differently. Bicycle design is a complex topic because there are many interacting variables, including the rider's body and performance expectations.

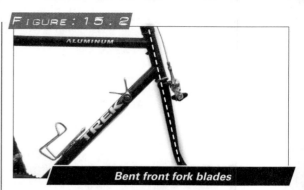
Bent front fork blades

A suspension fork will have moving parts that allow the wheel to move relative to the bike when riding over uneven terrain. For more discussion of suspension forks see Chapter 16, Suspension Systems.

Head tube
This is the frame tube that houses the fork's steering column. Headset bearings are seated here to allow rotation and steering. The head tube length will affect handlebar height. The inside diameter and design will determine the type of headset used.

Top tube
The top tube is the connection between the head tube and the seat tube. The top tube is vitally important to bike fit because the length will affect bar placement and rider comfort. This tube sees relatively low stress and is typically made lighter and thinner than other parts of the frame.

Down Tube
This tube is the connection between the headtube and bottom bracket. It also experiences stress from pedaling and handling of the bike. It may also be fitted with water bottle cage nuts or threads. The common fitting used is the "pemnut", which is fit into the tubing and then expanded to hold seat permanently (figure 15.3).

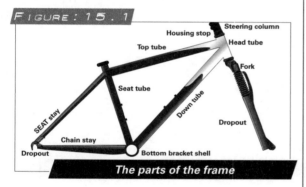
The parts of the frame

Fork
The fork is the connection between front wheel and main triangle of the frame. Fork dropouts hold the wheel at the end of the fork blades. Fork blades meet at the fork crown, which attaches to the steering column. The column passes through the head tube and is supported by the headset bearing system. Forks vary in length to fit specific sizes of wheels. The fork will also have a "rake" or offset that puts the contact patch of the tire beyond the head tube. This gives bicycles their "self steering" ability.

The stress of riding tends to flex fork legs, which transmits stress to the fork crown. This area of the bike experiences a lot of stress, even from casual riding. Fork failure is especially dangerous because the results are often a loss of control and a wheel coming off the bike (figure 15.2).

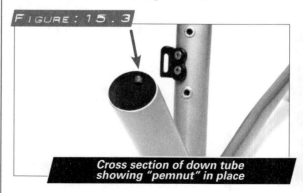
Cross section of down tube showing "pemnut" in place

Seat tube

The seat tube connects the bottom bracket to the saddle or seat post. Frames are generally sized according to the seat tube length. The seat tube may also be fitted with water bottle mounts. It may also have a fitting or brackets for the front derailleur.

Chain stay

These connect the rear dropouts to the bottom bracket and see a relatively high amount of stress from riding. The length of the stay is designed for the type and size of wheel used as well as bicycle performance.

Seat stay

This is the connection from the rear dropouts to the seat tube. These two tubes see less stress than the chain stays but still support the bike over the rear wheel. The rear brake caliper, either rim or disc, is commonly mounted to the seat stays.

Dropouts

Dropouts are the fittings at the end of the front fork and the rear stays that accept the hubs and wheels. Traditionally, the front dropouts accept a 9mm axle, while the rear dropouts accept a 10mm axle (figure 15.4). Through-axle dropouts on downhill and freeride bikes can use a 12mm axle in the rear and a 20mm axle or a 15mm axle in the front. There are also proprietary dropout designs made to fit unique hub/frame systems.

FIGURE: 15.4

Rear vertical dropouts

Bottom bracket shell

This is a short tube between the cranks that hold the bottom bracket bearings. It is connected to the down tube, the seat tube, and the chainstays. Traditionally, this has an internal threading for attaching the bearing cups (figure 15.5). The shell width may be 68, 70, 73, 85, or 100mm depending upon the design. There are also unthreaded designs that use pressed bearings.

FIGURE: 15.5

Threaded bottom bracket shell

Swing arm

A swing arm is the rear part of the frame of some full suspension bicycle designs. These function as moveable stays that react to impact on the rear wheel. The swing arm is attached to the main frame with bearings. A spring system keeps the swing arm extended and allows it to pivot. Bearing design in the swing arm is generally proprietary and bearing service varies with each model.

Frame Construction and Service

Frame material may be steel, aluminum, titanium, carbon fiber, magnesium, special plastics, or a combination of any of the above. Each type of material has different properties, which will affect the ride of the bike. All these materials flex under loads or stresses but to varying degrees. Additionally, each material will require different manufacturing processes and will have limits for repairability.

Like any mechanical part subjected to stress, the frame may fail. If the frame was poorly designed, improperly constructed, or simply subjected to excessive loads and abuse, cracks and bends can occur.

Regardless of the material, when a frame fails, it tends to fall apart at the tubing joints. This is the area where stress is concentrated. In some cases, a joint may be poorly made, or the design may simply be too weak for the use. Failure may also be the result of a crash. The tubing joints yield or weaken and begin cracking or failing. The repeated stress of riding creates a "stress cycle," loading and unloading of the part. This may in time cause cracks and eventually failure. A severe impact or crash may bend steel or aluminum. Repair by re-bending deformed tubing is typically impractical and will create a stress riser or weak spot in the area of the repair.

Bicycle frames are best inspected during cleaning. Most types of paint tend to be somewhat brittle and will crack if the material has moved under it (figure 15.6). This is often a sign of failure or future failure. Cracked paint may simply be paint coming off the surface or poor paint bonding. Inspect to confirm a failure or crack and consult a professional mechanic if in doubt.

FIGURE: 15.6

Bent metal on down tube from impact

Steel
Different types of welding typically join steel tubing. Tubes may be fit into a lug, and then brazed or welded with alloys of silver. Tubes can also be mitered and welded by sophisticated electrical welding know as "tig" or "mig" welding (figure 15.7). Steel frames are susceptible to rust or oxidation. Water inside the frame and lack of paint can worsen issues of rust, even to the point of frame failure. It is also recommended to use grease or an anti-seize on any frame threaded fitting or press fit, such as bottom bracket threads or headtubes. A good frame builder is able to repair some failures of steel frame. In welded steel frames, tubing can sometimes be replaced.

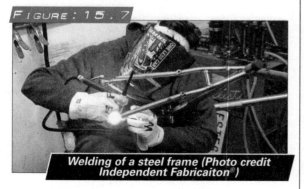

FIGURE: 15.7

Welding of a steel frame (Photo credit Independent Fabricaiton®)

Aluminum
Aluminum is a very common material for many uses and is easily worked and welded. Frames may also be bonded together with lugs. Aluminum is a relatively lightweight metal, but it can require more material to match the strength of steel. Aluminum does not rust, but it can corrode. This results in pitting on the surfaces. The consequence is components may seize in the aluminum such as a seat post or a bearing cup. As with steel, it is useful to grease or anti-seize. Local repair to aluminum frames is difficult because of the special skills needed and the need for heat treatment of the frame after welding.

Titanium
Titanium is a very strong material, but it can be difficult and expensive to work and shape. It is difficult to form it to the desired shape. Titanium is commonly welded for bicycle frames. There is very little issue with corrosion, but greasing the fittings is still recommended. Local repair of titanium is difficult due to the special skills and equipment involved.

Carbon
Carbon fiber is a fabric material held in place by epoxies, called the "matrix." The carbon cloth or fabric is laid into a mold and the matrix applied. This can create tubing, or entire sections of the frame. When carbon fiber tubing is jointed, it is often with a thermal-set epoxy (figure 15.8). Often the carbon fabric will be laid up with fittings or metal tubing to add strength or to allow installation of components. For example, carbon fiber is a poor material for threading, so metal inserts are installed for threaded parts such as the bottom bracket or water bottle fittings.

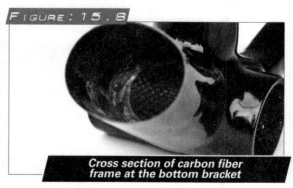

FIGURE: 15.8

Cross section of carbon fiber frame at the bottom bracket

Repair of damaged carbon fiber is difficult and often not practical. Not even by the manufacturer. Composite frames are susceptible to cracking or tearing from bonding failure (figure 15.9).

FIGURE: 15.9

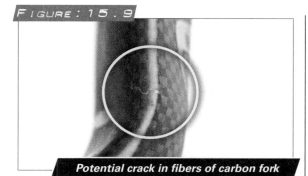

Potential crack in fibers of carbon fork

Park Tool

CHAPTER 16

Suspension

Bicycle suspension is a system of pivots, levers, and even sliders built into the bicycle that allow the rider to maintain a steady line or path on unsteady terrain. "Rigid" (non-suspension) bicycles have no pivots or linkage. If a rider uses any kind of suspension system, the wheels can track the terrain independently of him or her. Suspension on any vehicle allows the wheels to move up and down to accommodate bumps and dips in the trail or road. Suspension can help both rider comfort and performance. Suspension systems provide more "forgiveness" for the rider's errors as they choose the best line off-road.

For many years, spring systems were used for forks and even saddle rails. A stress or load flexes the spring, and then the spring returned all the energy as it moves back. Damped suspension systems then became common in off-road forks (figure 16.1). These were the telescoping forks that used a spring system to keep the entire fork extended where the lower legs slide on the upper legs. The speed of the return motion was controlled by an internal damping system.

FIGURE: 16.1

Suspension fork compressing from impact

The movements of a suspension system can be split up into two basic actions: compression and extension (also called rebound). The compression is the upward motion of the wheel(s) from the road or trail. The compression cycle occurs due to a load or impact. The spring system compresses, which momentarily stores energy.

The extension cycle controls the return motion wheels. Extension acts as the downward motion of the wheel(s) back to the terrain. When the force stored in the spring from compression is greater than the load put on it, the spring extends and returns all the energy it has stored. In other words, a tightened spring wants to relax. This relaxation is the extension cycle.

Suspension systems are built with "sag." The weight of the cyclist partially compresses the suspension system to create sag, often just by sitting on the bike. This is desirable because it allows for movement of the wheel over dips and depressions as well as bumps. The ride height of the bike also changes with the amount of sag.

Spring systems in shocks have a "spring rate" (deflection rate). This is the amount of force that is required to compress a spring a given amount. For example, if it takes 400 pounds of force to compress a spring one inch, the spring rate is 400 pounds per inch.

Many systems allow the rider to set the spring pressure. Whatever type of spring is used, it is generally better to use the lowest spring rate possible. Softer springs reduce the impact to the bike and suspension system. Softer springs also allow more of the suspension travel to be used. There are several spring systems in use on bicycles:

Helical compression springs:
Commonly called "coil" springs, these are typically made of steel and are common on car suspension systems. Coil springs are common on rear suspension systems (figure 16.2). Metal springs generally are not effected by changes in temperature. Coil springs have consistent compression rates.

FIGURE: 16.2

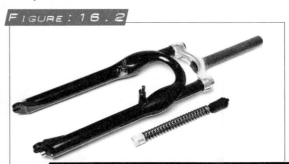

Helical compression spring from a shock fork

Elastomer and rubber springs:
Elastomer and rubber springs are similar to steel helical springs because they have fairly consistent or linear spring rate. The spring rate can vary with different types of polymer and other synthetic compounds. Unlike steel springs, elastomer spring rates tend to change with temperature. Colder temperatures stiffen polymers, and this will raise spring rates and make them stiffer. Elastomer springs can be found inside shock forks and on some suspension seat post systems (figure 16.3).

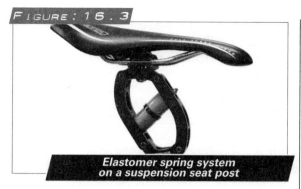
Elastomer spring system on a suspension seat post

Air (gas) Springs:

Air can also be used as a spring in suspension systems (figure 16.4). Gas, usually ambient air, is contained in a sealed cylinder with a piston to compress the gas. The gas pressure can be raised or lowered for changes in spring rate. Assuming the temperature remains constant, the spring rate of gas tends to be progressive. As the suspension system is compressed, the air is pushed into a smaller space, and the spring rate increases.

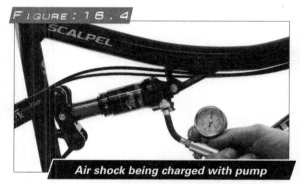
Air shock being charged with pump

Both air temperature and working temperature will affect the spring rate of shock gas. Colder temperatures cause the gas to contract, reduce the pressure of the gas, and lower the spring rate. Warmer temperatures will cause the gas to expand and raise the spring rate.

Shocks (Dampers)

A more precise term for "shock" is damper. An example of this type is the car suspension with coil or leaf springs and a separate damper unit. Generally, the cycling industry uses the word "shock" to mean both spring and damper. This two-part system of steel spring and damper is also seen on some bicycle suspension units (Figure 16.5).

Rear shock on full suspension bike

Damping systems are designed to help control motion. A common place to see damping is on automatic, self-closing doors. As you push the door open, a spring is worked (either expanding or contracting). When you let go, the spring forces the door back closed, but it closes slowly because there is a damper to slow its return.

Damping in suspension shocks can occur both on the compression cycle and on the extension cycle. With simple dampers, the amount of damping is the same for both compression and extension. Sophisticated shock systems will be adjustable for the different amounts of compression and extension damping (figure 16.6).

Internal damping system of a shock fork

Stiffer compression damping means the suspension linkage moves less, and there will be less compression of the springs. More energy is transmitted to the rider and makes a harsher ride. A lighter damping setting will allow the linkage to move relatively easily, but too light a setting can cause the system to bottom out on large or even moderate impacts-jolting the rider and the bike.

Suspension Linkages

The design of suspension linkage systems should permit the wheels to move only up and down in the vertical plane. If the wheel is allowed to move side-to-side while the suspension is working, the ride will be unpredictable and good handling will be sacrificed.

On rear suspension bikes, the rear wheel is connected to the rest of the bike with a moveable "swing arm" (figure 16.7). The swing arm is the back end of the bike. Typically the chain stays and seat stays act as a unit, and it's bolted to the main triangle by pivots. The placement and design of the pivots will affect the performance. The rear wheel should be allowed to swing independently of the main frame. As the rear wheel moves upward, some of the force that would throw the bike upward is now stored in the swing arm spring. The forces involved are the same with a rigid bike, but the effect on a suspension bike and rider is spread out over time. The impact to the ride is reduced, and the wheels stay closer to the trail.

Swing arm system of a full suspension bike

Service and Tuning

Play or lateral movement can develop in both front and rear systems. In telescopic front fork systems, bushings are used to allow the outer legs to travel over the upper tubing. With use and time, play may develop in the bushing, which reduces performance.

Some rear suspension linkage systems move on pivots. Some pivots use an adjustable bushing system. Play can be adjusted out by tightening a bolt or nut. Other systems use replaceable washers, but a few systems have no provision for removing wear or play.

Rear suspension bushings or sleeves may also be pressed into a fitting in the frame and suspension system (figure 16.8). These are usually brand specific diameters and widths, and this typically requires the use of brand specific tool and parts for servicing. Grab the rear wheel and main triangle frame and pull the rear wheel side to side. Note any play in the system. If play is felt, track the area where the play coming from to diagnose the problem. A professional mechanic should be consulted for bushing replacement.

Bearings inside linkage pivot

Tuning the suspension system is making modifications to change handling for the rider. Designers attempt to make the bike and its suspension system useable by a wide range of riders. The system may need adjustment, however, to suit the rider's particular expectations.

When tuning a system, attempt to change one variable at a time. Tuning is considered a skill acquired with experience and time. This type of work can be slow and tedious at first, but with experience you will learn what procedures work in each scenario and what doesn't. For example, a stiff rear swing arm would tend to tip the bike forward and compress the front fork. In a series of bumps, it might appear to the rider that the fork is too stiff, but there may just be too much preload from the transferring of weight from the stiff rear end.

There are various aspects that affect the handling of a bike. Some of the various aspects of the bike these will be very adjustable, others will be more or less fixed. Changes to handling may be affected by the following:

Spring Preload:

Preload is typically the easiest thing to change in a system. Most companies design ways to change spring preload, such as by increasing air pressure or by compressing or relaxing the steel/elastomer spring.

Fluid Viscosity:

Some damper designs allow for changing the suspension fluid to different viscosities. This will affect damping. A fluid with a higher viscosity rating (thicker) will move more slowly through porting in the shock system. This has a tendency to slow rebound. Fluid with a lower viscosity rating is lighter and moves more quickly through the holes in the ports. Consult a professional mechanic for fluid changes.

Valving:

If there is access to a hydraulic system valving, there may be changes that can be made to affect the flow of oil. Polishing ports, drilling new ports, or changing internal spring tensions are done by professional mechanics.

Linkage:

Some designs of full suspension systems have different positions for strut mounts and shock mounts. This changes the leverage of the wheel over the shock. By doing this, vehicles can be changed to better suit the racing situation.

Cyclist Posture:

The cyclist's posture and position on the bike also greatly influences weight distribution and hence the bike handling. Moving the saddle rails forward or back; raising or lowering the saddle; changing the stem's length, height or angle; or any combination of these also alters weight distribution and the vehicle's center of gravity.

Tire Contact:

An often-overlooked area of handling is in the tires. Tire width, casing, rubber tread design, and air pressure have a large influence on handling of any bike. A harder tire firms the suspension. A softer tire gives the bike more give on rough terrain. Many racers say the best suspension on any bike is between the wheel and the ground.

CHAPTER 17

On-Ride Repair

Mechanical problems can and do occur while riding on the trail or road. The best way to prevent these problems is to regularly clean, lubricate, and inspect the bike. Keeping your bike well maintained will prevent many of the mechanical problems described below, even when riding off-road.

Tool Choices

Be prepared with a few tools if problems arise. When selecting tools for the ride, consider the type of bike components being used by you and others in your group. Consider the weight of the tools and the amount of space available for carrying. Your budget and level of mechanical skill will also affect your choice of tools. See table 17.1.

There are numerous possibilities for tool options and pre-packaged tools kits. One versatile tool choice is the "multi-tool." These contain several tools, including hex wrenches, screwdrivers, spoke wrenches, tire levers, and others in one unit. This type of tool is compact and cost effective. You may assemble your own take-a-long kit of tools. The list below outlines recommended tools for a typical off-road or road ride.

TABLE: 17.1

ITEM DESCRIPTION	PARK TOOL NO.
Multi Tool	MTB-3, MTB-7, IB-3 (may include several functions of tools listed below)
Chain Tool	CT-5, MTB-3, IB-3
Tire Levers	TL-1 or TL-4
Patch kit	GP-2 or VP-1
Spoke Wrench	SW-7, SW-0, SW-1, SW-2
Screwdriver	MTB-3, MTB-7, IB-3
Tire Boot	TB-2
Inner Tubes	Matched to valve and size of existing tube
Hex wrench set	AWS-10, AWS-9, also on multi tools

Repair Procedures

Repairs made during the ride have some limitations. The right tools or parts are not always available. Some bikes can simply be flipped upside down to work on them, but be careful to not damage shift and brake levers or housing. Additionally, some hydraulic brake systems should not be turned upside down. If it is necessary to turn a hydraulic brake system upside down, allow it to sit upright several minutes after the repair, then test the brake to ensure no air has entered the brake line.

The following text outlines problems that may occur on the ride and gives suggestions for addressing them. If a repair seems questionable, walk the bike home or call for a lift. Do not ride an unsafe bike.

Flat Tire

Always carry a spare tube. On long or group rides, carry two tubes if possible. A patch kit and a tire lever are also essential. To clean the tube before patching, carry a foil sealed alcohol wipe. These are available in drug stores.

Cut or Ripped Tire

Use a tire boot such as the Park Tool TB-2. Replace the tire as soon as possible.

Broken Spoke

The only permanent repair for a broken spoke is to replace the spoke and re-true the wheel. If a single spoke is broken, the lateral true can be improved by loosening the two spokes immediately adjacent to the broken one. This will somewhat bring the wheel back into lateral true, but opening the rim brake caliper, if possible, may be necessary. It may be possible to continue the ride. If the wheel has 28 or fewer spokes, having one spoke missing or broken may make the wheel unsafe to use. Bent spokes, even severely bent ones, are less of a problem. If the wheel is still adequately true, continue the ride. True the wheel as necessary, and then replace the spokes after the ride.

Dented Rim

Rims can become dented from striking objects on the ground. First determine the extent of the dent. If the braking is not badly affected, it may be best to leave it alone and finish the ride. Have the rim repaired or replaced after the ride. With rim caliper brakes, severe dents will be felt during braking and may lock up the wheel unexpectedly. A badly dented rim can also affect the seating of the tire bead. In either of these cases, it is best to not ride the bike.

Broken Chains

A broken chain can usually be shortened as an emergency repair. If you have extra links, these may be added, but the chain will be compromised and should be replaced with a new chain as soon as possible. Note that outer plates must be joined to inner plates and remove links accordingly. If the chain was shortened, use care not to shift into the largest rear sprocket and largest front chainring combination. The most common cause for a broken link is improper installation. When installing a chain, inspect all pins and links to prevent on-the-ride chain problems. Inspect all rivets and links after repairing. If there was one bad link, there are likely to be more.

Chain Suck

Chain suck occurs when a chainring will not release the chain at the six o'clock position. The chain gets stuck on a tooth and continues upward with the chainring and eventually jams into the frame. If it is not too jammed, grasp the chain at the bottom, and pull down while turning the crank backwards. Scarring of the paint and frame is likely. If pulling the chain doesn't work, it may be possible to disconnect a link of chain, and unthread the chain from the frame and reinstall correctly. The last option is to remove the right crank, which requires a crank puller. Inspect the chain after pulling it free. The chain may have become twisted or damaged. Inspect the chainring teeth as well, which may be the cause of the problem. If a tooth is bent, avoid using that chainring if possible.

Twisted Chain

Chains can twist from being shifted into the spokes or from jamming against the frame during chain suck. It may be possible to twist the chain back using a pair of pliers, but it is difficult to do so by hand. Isolate the twisted section and use the rear cog to hold one end of the chain. Twist the chain back using pliers at the end of the twist. Replace the chain as soon as possible after the ride. chain may have become twisted or damaged. Inspect the chainring teeth as well, which may be the cause of the problem. If a tooth is bent, avoid using that chainring if possible.

Squeaky and Noisy Chain

A squeaky chain is caused by the lack of lubrication in the links. It is usually not necessary to carry chain lubricant on shorter rides if the chain has been lubricated as part of regular maintenance. If the ride is especially wet, the lubricant may wash away. In this case, almost anything that will penetrate the link will provide some temporary lubrication. Sunscreen oils or creams, bug repellent creams and cooking oils can provide some short-term relief from a noisy chain. Clean and lubricate the chain properly after the ride.

Rear Derailleur Shifting into the Spokes or Frame

This problem is typically the result of improper limit screw settings. The limits of the rear derailleur act as a stop to the derailleur body. If the derailleur or derailleur hanger is bent, the previous limit screw settings will no longer be appropriate. View the derailleur from the back and sight that the pulley wheels are parallel to the cogs. If the derailleur hanger or pulley cage appears to be pushed inward toward the spokes, something has been bent. It may be possible to pull the derailleur back. Insert a hex wrench in the mounting bolt and pull upward until the derailleur appears parallel with sprockets (figure 17.1).

FIGURE: 17.1

Bend hanger back until visually straight

Check shifting and reset H-limit screw and L-limit screw as necessary. Take the bike to a professional shop for proper hanger alignment after the ride, or see Derailleur Hanger Alignment & Repair, page 127, to do it yourself.

Derailleur not Indexing Properly

The common cause of derailleurs not indexing properly is poor derailleur cable tension adjustment. Apply the same skills and procedures as with routine derailleur adjustment. Have someone hold the bike by the saddle while you pedal and make adjustments to the barrel adjuster.

ParkTool

Broken Derailleur Body, Cage, or Hanger

If the rear derailleur body, pulley wheel cage, or derailleur hanger has broken, shifting is no longer possible. The bike may be converted to a single speed to get back home.

a. Remove the chain.
b. Remove the derailleur or other affected parts.
c. Choose a gear. For triple chainring bikes, use the middle ring and one of the middle rear sprockets. For two chainring bikes, use the smallest ring.
d. Run the chain from the chosen rear sprocket to the front chainring and determine the correct pin to remove in order to shorten the chain. It may be necessary to change rear sprocket choices to get better chain tension.
e. Cut the chain and connect the links. The chain should be tight enough to prevent it it from coming off the front sprocket (figure 17.2).
f. Pedal the bike and bounce the chain up and down to check tension.

FIGURE: 17.2

By-pass derailleur to create a make–shift one speed

Missing Derailleur Pulleys

Look for missing parts if possible on the trail or road behind you. If parts are not available, convert to a one-speed as described in Broken Derailleur Body, Cage, or Hanger.

Front Derailleur Cage Bent or Twisted

The front derailleur cage can get twisted if a chain jams during a shift, or if it is struck. Realign the cage if it has twisted. Outer cage should be approximately straight to chainrings. The derailleur may not properly shift after the realignment, so select the preferred chainring and use cable tension or limit screw to keep the derailleur on that chainring.

Crank Falling Off

If the crank has completely fallen off, the bolt may be missing. In this case, walk the bike back. It would be dangerous to attempt riding it with the arm simply shoved back in place. If you have the bolt, reinstall the arm. The torque for crank bolts is relatively high, around 300 inch-pounds. Tighten the bolt as much as you feel the tool will be able to withstand.

Pedals Falling Off

A loose pedal may be secured with a correct fitting wrench. The Park Tool MTB-3 Rescue Tool comes with a short pedal wrench. If no wrench is available, it is best to walk the bike. Riding with a loose pedal in the crank may cause the thread to pull out of the arm, resulting in a ruined crank arm or a catastrophic crash for the rider.

Bent Crank

If a bike has crashed with much force, the crank arm may bend. The pedal surface and your foot will then oscillate as the bike is ridden. If the crank clears the frame, it is best to finish the ride by riding lower gears and going slowly. Replace the arm. If the crank does not clear the fame, walk the bike or get a ride. Attempting to unbend a bent arm may lead to failure.

Bottom Bracket Loose or Falling Apart

Depending on the specific bottom bracket, there may be very little repair that is possible. It is impractical to carry bottom bracket tools on the ride. If the bottom bracket is so loose that the cranks strike the frame, do not ride the bike.

Broken Derailleur Cable

If a derailleur cable has become frayed between the lever and cable pinch bolt, it is more likely to fail. Avoid using the derailleur if possible. Broken gear cables usually mean a non-functioning derailleur.

If a front derailleur cable has broken, and a spare is not available, consider the route of the remainder of the ride, then choose the most comfortable chainring for completing the ride. Typically the middle chainring is best. Pull the cage up to the middle ring by hand and tighten the L-limit screw. For rear derailleurs, again consider the remainder of the ride. Choose one of the middle cogs and tighten the H-limit screw to hold the derailleur in that position. Broken cables will tend to get caught in moving parts. Remove the old cable and store until it can be properly disposed.

Broken Brake Cable

Do not attempt to patch or tie together broken brake cables. If the cable fails again, the consequences could be disastrous. Ride the remainder of the ride with caution, and replace the cable as soon as possible. If in doubt, walk the bike rather than ride it. Remove and store the broken brake cable until it can be properly disposed.

Twisted or Bent Handlebars or Stem

Handlebars may become misaligned from crashing. To realign, stand in front of the bike and grab wheel firmly between knees. Loosen stem binder bolt(s) and pull stem back into alignment until bars appear parallel with front hub or dropouts, Stem should be aligned with the wheel. Secure binder bolt(s). It may be necessary to readjust the headset if the binder bolt(s) of a threadless stem are loosened. It is possible to ride with a slight misalignment in the bars. If the crash has actually bent the bars or twisted the stem, it is best not to continue riding. A bent bar or stem may fail without warning. Replace it as soon as possible.

Bent Frame or Fork

Very severe crashes may bend either the frame or fork. Inspect the frame, especially behind the head tube. Look for paint cracks, and wrinkles in the metal, indicating bent frame tubing (figure 17.3). If the frame is bent, it should be considered unsafe. Do not ride this bike. Fork blades and fork crowns can also bend. View the bike from the side to see if the alignment looks odd or not parallel. Again, a bent fork makes the bike unsafe to ride.

FIGURE : 17 . 3

Bent frame at head tube

Bent Saddle or Seat Post

If the saddle has come loose on the post, it may simply be realigned and tightened. If the clamp is broken, it will be difficult to repair away from home. In this case, remove both entire seat post and the saddle. Simply removing the seat and leaving the post installed is inviting an accident to happen.

ParkTool

CHAPTER 18

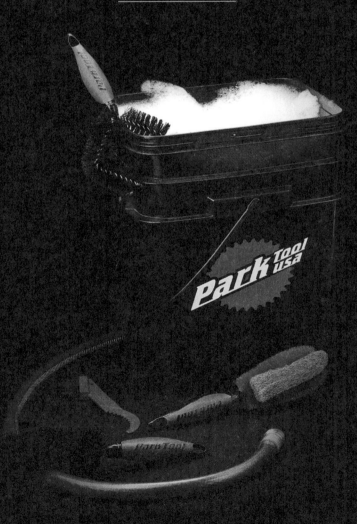

Bike Wash

Cleaning the bike adds to its life and performance by removing dirt, grime, salt, and grit. Washing also allows you to more closely inspect the frame and component parts. Keeping the bike clean also adds to one's feeling of peace-of-mind. Although cleaning helps the bike's performance, overzealous washing and rinsing can also wash out grease from bearings. Avoid using high-pressure car washes or blasting the bike with streams of water from the hose.

It is possible to clean the bike by wiping off the frame and parts using rags. This is a slower process and will also consume a lot of rags. Use a mild cleaning solvent such as a window cleaner or furniture polish to cut grime on the frame.

Cleaning with soap and water is very effective but messy, just like washing a car. Bike washing is common with race mechanics, who often clean several dirty bikes in succession. Washing is best done outdoors in a place where the water can drain. Wear appropriate clothing and rubber gloves. It is always best to use biodegradable cleaners whenever possible (figure 18.1). Avoid using diesel or kerosene as a cleaner.

For the most detailed cleaning, it is best to remove wheels from the bike. It is also a good idea to remove frame pumps, water bottles, and clip-on accessories.

FIGURE: 18.1

Useful equipment and supplies for bike washing

The procedures for washing the bike:

a. Begin by filling two buckets with warm water. Just as when washing dishes, warm or even hot water cleans better. Mix a biodegradable soap, such as for dishwashing, into one of the buckets. Use the other bucket for clean rinse water if a hose is not available.

b. Sponge the area to be clamped clean of dirt and grit. This will prevent marring the finish where it is clamped. Also clean the jaws of the clamp (figure 18.2).

c. Clamp the bike in the repair stand.

d. Apply the degreaser to the chain and allow it to soak in. Also apply degreaser to chainrings if they are very dirty.

e. Designate one stiff bristle brush and one of the smaller sponges as "drive train" only tools. These will become quite dirty and should not be used on other parts of the bike. Apply degreaser to brush and brush other components, such as the derailleurs and brakes, if they are very dirty. Brush chainrings and rear pulley wheels with the stiff bristle brush and degreaser (figure 18.3). Also scrub the rear sprockets with the stiff bristle brush. If necessary, use a flat-tipped screwdriver to scrape dirt from pulleys. Use care not to get degreaser into bearings such as the bottom bracket, hubs, or headset.

f. Use chain cleaner if available, following manufacturer's instructions (figure 18.4). If chain cleaner isn't available, use a stiff bristle brush. Shift the chain to the largest chainring and scrub outer side plates at chainring. Turn pedals to move the chain through chainring. Move to left side of bike and scrub left side chain plates. Next, scrub rollers from the top between the bottom of the rear cogs and the chainrings.

g. Clean the degreaser from the drive train before moving to the rest of the bike. Wrap the small drive train sponge around the chain and pedal the bike to flush the chain clean with soapy water. The sponge will become contaminated with oils and should not be used on the rest of the bike. Repeat until the water falling from the chain is relatively clean looking. Use the same sponge to wipe off the chainrings, derailleur, and rear pulley wheels. Drip soapy water over the rear cogs. To wipe between cogs, use a rag pulled taut.

h. Wipe down the frame with soapy water using the non-drive train sponges and brushes (figure 18.5). If the brakes are extremely dirty, use the drive train sponge to clean, then follow up with other sponges.

i. Wash hub center. If available, use a "bottle brush" (figure 18.6).

j. Wash rims and rim braking surfaces. Use care not to scrape or harm the tire sidewall (figure 18.7). For glued tubular tires, use damp rag to clean rim, but do not soak or scrub tires.

k. If no hose is available, use a discarded water bottle or plastic tub to rinse using the second bucket of clean water. Rinse from the top of the bike down. Spin the wheels and chain to help remove excess water.

l. If rinsing with a hose, use gentle spray. Do not blast the bike using a jet stream of water.

m. Remove the bike from the stand.

n. Bounce bike on the ground to shake off water. If no air compressor is available, use a rag to wipe the chain dry. If an air compressor is used, blow-dry the chain but use care not to blast air at the bearings as it may remove grease.

o. Lubricate chain and all accessible pivot points with light lubricant. Use care not to lubricate axle bearings or bottom bracket bearings with the liquid lubricant.

FIGURE: 18.4

Chain cleaners can thoroughly and quickly clean the chain

FIGURE: 18.5

Clean frame with soapy sponge

FIGURE: 18.2

Clean jaws before clamping

FIGURE: 18.6

Use bottle brush to clean hub

FIGURE: 18.3

Scrub chainrings with solvent on the brush

FIGURE: 18.7

Wash rims but do not scrub at tire sidewalls

Park Tool

APPENDIX A-D

The tool list below will stock a very complete "home mechanic shop." The list does not duplicate a professional shop. For example, there are no bottom bracket taps, head tube reaming tools and other tools a full service center at a retail bicycle shop would use. There are often several choices for a particular piece of equipment. It will be necessary to research these choices to make the best decision for your specific circumstances.

TOOL	PARK TOOL OPTIONS
Repair stand	PCS-10 Home Mechanic Repair Stand
	PCS-11 Super Lite Home Mechanic Repair Stand
	PCS-12 Bench Mount Home Mechanic Repair Stand
	PCS-9 Home Mechanic Repair Stand
	PRS-2 OS Deluxe Double Arm Repair Stand
	PRS-3 OS Deluxe Single Arm Repair Stand
	PRS-4 OS Deluxe Bench Mount Repair Stand
	PRS-4W Deluxe Wall Mount Repair Stand
	PRS-15 Professional Race Stand
	PRS-20 Team Race Stand
	PRS-21 Super Lite Team Race Stand
Floor pump	PFP-3 Home Mechanic Floor Pump
	PFP-4 Professional Mechanic Floor Pump
Spoke wrenches	SW-0 Professional Spoke Wrench (3.23mm nipples)
	SW-1 Professional Spoke Wrench (3.3mm nipples)
	SW-7 Triple Spoke Wrench (3.23mm. 3.3mm, and 3.45mm nipples)
	SW-13 Spoke Wrench for Mavic Spokes
	SW-14 Spoke Wrench for Shimano Wheels
	SW-15 Spoke Wrench for internal nipples
	SW-40 Four-sided Spoke Wrench 3.23 nipples
	SW-42 Four-sided Spoke Wrench 3.45 nipples
Truing stand	TS-2 Professional Wheel Truing Stand
	TS-8 Home Mechanic Wheel Truing Stand
Spoke tension meter	TM-1 Spoke Tension Meter

TOOL	PARK TOOL OPTIONS
Dishing tool	WAG-3 Portable Wheel Dishing Gauge
	WAG-4 Deluxe Wheel Dishing Gauge
Spoke ruler	SBC-1 Spoke, Bearing, and Cotter Gauge
Tire levers	TL-1 Tire Lever Set
	TL-4 Tire Lever Set (thin, flat type)
	TL-5 Heavy Duty Steel Tire Lever Set
Valve core remover	No Park Tool Option, see hardware/tool store
Inner tube patch kit	VP-1 Vulcanizing Patch Kit
	GP-2 Pre-Glued Super Patch Kit
Tire Boot	TB-2 Emergency Tire Boot
Bottom bracket tools	BBT-22 or BBT-32 Bottom Bracket Tool for 20-tooth internally splined Shimano® (and other) bottom brackets.
	BBT-5 Bottom Bracket Tool for 12-tooth internally splined Campagnolo® bottom brackets
	BBT-4 Bottom Bracket Tool for 6-notch Campagnolo® bottom brackets
	BBT-18 Bottom Bracket Tool for 8-notch Shimano®, Truvativ®, and Bontrager® bottom brackets
	BBT-9 Bottom Bracket Tool for 16-notch external bearing bottom brackets
	BBT-19 Socket-type Bottom Bracket Tool for 16-notch external bearing bottom brackets
Fixed cup spanner-36mm	HCW-4 36mm Box End Spanner / Pin Spanner
Lockring spanner	HCW-5 Double-Sided Lockring Spanner
Pin spanner	SPA-2 Pin Spanner
	SPA-6 Heavy Duty Adjustable Pin Spanner
Bearing cup press	HHP-2 or HHP-3 Bearing Cup Press
Fork crown race setting tool	CRS-1 Crown Race Setting System
Headset race remover	RT-1 Head Cup Remover for 1" and 1-1/8"
	RT-2 Head cup Remover for 1-1/4" and 1-1/2"
Fork saw guide	SG-6 Threadless Saw Guide for 1", 1-1/8", 1-1/4"
	SG-7 Oversized Saw Guide for 1.5" and aero

Park Tool

TOOL	PARK TOOL OPTIONS
Threadless star nut setter	TNS-1 Threadless Nut Setter for 1" and 1 1/8"
	TNS-4 Threadless Nut Setter with Guide for 1" and 1 1/8"
Headset wrenches	HCW-15 32mm and 36mm Headset Wrench
	HCW-7 30mm and 32mm Headset Wrench
	HW-2 32mm and 36mm Headset Locknut Wrench
Crank Puller	CCP-2 Crank Puller for square hole crank arms
	CCP-4 Crank Puller for splined hole crank arms
	CWP-6 Crank Puller for square and splined hole arms
Crank bolt wrench	HR-8 8mm Hex Tool with Handle
	HR-10 10mm Hex Tool with Handle
	PH-10 10mm P-handle Hex Wrench
	CCW-5 Crank Bolt Wrench, 8mm hex and 14mm socket
Chainring nut wrench	CNW-2 Chainring Nut Wrench
Chain tool	CT-3 Heavy Duty Screw Type Chain Tool
	CT-5 Mini Chain Brite Chain Tool
	CT-4 Professional Chain Tool
	CT-7 Chain Tool for 3/16" and 1/8" chain only
Chain wear indicator	CC-2 Chain Checker
	CC-3 Chain Wear Indicator
Pedal wrench	PW-3 15mm and 9/16" Pedal Wrench
	PW-4 Professional 15mm Pedal Wrench
	HCW-16 15mm Pedal Wrench/Chain Whip
	HR-6 6mm Hex Tool with Handle
	HR-8 8mm Hex Tool with Handle
Derailleur hanger alignment gauge	DAG-1 Derailleur Hanger Alignment Gauge

TOOL	PARK TOOL OPTIONS
Cone wrenches	SCW-13–19 13mm through 19mm Shop Cone Wrenches
	DCW-1 13mm/ 14mm Double Ended Cone Wrench
	DCW-2 15mm/ 16mm Double Ended Cone Wrench
	DCW-3 17mm/ 18mm Double Ended Cone Wrench
	DCW-4 13mm/ 15mm Double Ended Cone Wrench
Axle vise	AV-1 Axle Vise
	AV-4 Heavy Duty Axle and Pedal Vise
Freewheel removers	FR-1 Freewheel Remover for 12-tooth splined Shimano® freewheels
	FR-2 Freewheel Remover for 2-notch Suntour® freewheels
	FR-3 Freewheel Remover for 4-notch Suntour® freewheels
	FR-4 Freewheel Remover for 20-tooth splined freewheels
	FR-6 Freewheel Remover for 4-notch single speed freewheels (1.37 x 24 tpi)
	FR-7 Freewheel Remover for 12-tooth splined Falcon® freewheels
Cassette lockring tool	FR-5 Cassette Lockring Tool
	FR-5G Cassette Lockring Tool with Guide Pin
	BBT-5 Cassette Lockring Tool for Campagnolo®
Chain whip	SR-1 Chain Whip / Sprocket Remover
	SR-2 Heavy Duty Shop Chain Whip / Sprocket Remover
	HCW-16 Chain Whip/ 15mm Pedal Wrench
4th hand/cable stretcher	BT-2 4th Hand/ Cable Stretcher
Cable/housing cutter	CN-10 Cable and Housing Cutter
Hex wrench set	AWS-1 4, 5, and 6mm 3-way Hex Wrench Set
	AWS-3 2, 2.5, and 3mm 3-way Hex Wrench Set
	AWS-10 Fold Up Hex Wrench Set (1.5mm - 6mm)
	AWS-11 Fold Up Hex Wrench Set (3mm - 10mm)
	HXS-1 L-Shaped Hex Wrench Set (2mm - 10mm)
	HXS-2 L-Shaped Hex Wrench Set (2mm - 10mm) with Holder
	PH-1 P-Handled Hex Wrench Set (2mm - 10mm) with Holder

Park Tool™

TOOL	PARK TOOL OPTIONS
Star wrenches	TWS-2 Fold-Up Star Wrench Set (T7 – T40)
	PH-T25 P-Handled T25 Torx Wrench
Torque wrench	TW-1 Torque Wrench, 0 to 60 inch pounds
	TW-2 Torque Wrench, 0 to 600 inch pounds
Hex bits 4, 5, 6, 8mm	No Park Tool option, see hardware/tool store
Sockets 8, 9, 10, 14, 15, 17mm	No Park Tool option, see hardware/tool store
3/8 inch drive ratchet wrench	No Park Tool option, see hardware/tool store
Taps	TAP-6 9/16" x 20 tpi Pedal Tap Set
	TAP-8 5mm x 0.8 tap for water bottle and rack/fender bolts
	TAP-9 6mm x 1.0 tap for cantilever bosses and rack/fender bolts
	TAP-10 10mm x 1.0 tap for derailleur hanger
Tap handle	No Park Tool option, see hardware/tool store
Frame alignment gauge	FAG-2 Frame Alignment Gauge
Bench vise, 4 inch	No Park Tool option, see hardware/tool store
Air compressor	No Park Tool option, see hardware/tool store
Ball peen hammer, 12 oz.	HMR-2 Hammer
Rubber/plastic mallet	HMR-2 Hammer
Punches, various sizes	No Park Tool option, see hardware/tool store
Metric tape measure	RR-12 Tape Measure
Metric measuring caliper	No Park Tool Option, see hardware/tool store
Screwdriver, straight blade 5/32 inch tip	SD-3 Screwdriver
Screwdriver, straight blade 3/16 inch tip	SD-6 Screwdriver
Screwdriver, cross tip "Phillips" #0 or #1	SD-0 Screwdriver
Screwdriver, cross tip "Phillips" #2	SD-2 Screwdriver
Diagonal side cutter pliers	No Park Tool option, see hardware/tool store
Long nose pliers (needle nose)	No Park Tool option, see hardware/tool store

TOOL	PARK TOOL OPTIONS
File - round	No Park Tool option, see hardware/tool store
File-10-inch mill bastard	No Park Tool option, see hardware/tool store
Hacksaw	SAW-1 Hacksaw
Combination wrenches	MW-SET 7 to 15mm
8-inch adjustable wrench	No Park Tool option, see hardware/tool store
12-inch adjustable wrench	PAW-12 Adjustable Wrench
Flashlight	No Park Tool option, see hardware/tool store
Scissors	No Park Tool option, see hardware/tool store
Lubricant- liquid	CL-1 Synthetic Blend Chain Lube
Lubricant-grease	PPL-1 PolyLube 1000, 4 oz.
	PPL-2 PolyLube 1000, 16 oz.
Chain cleaner	CM-5 Cyclone Chain Scrubber
	CG-2 ChainGang Chain Cleaning System
Solvent	CB-2 Citrus ChainBrite Chain and Component Cleaning Fluid
Cleaning brushes	GSC-1 GearClean Brush
	BCB-4 Bike Cleaning Brush Set
Shop apron	SA-1 Shop Apron
	SA-3 Heavy Duty Shop Apron
Anti-Seize Thread Prep	ASC-1 Anti-Seize Compound
Bike polish	No Park Tool option, see hardware/tool store
Rags	No Park Tool option, see hardware/tool store

Adjustable cup. The left side bearing cup of an adjustable bottom bracket.

Adjusting race. A movable bearing surface typically mounted to a thread that is used to adjust bearing play and movement.

Allen® Wrench. See hex wrench.

Articulated housing. Brake and derailleur index housing made of small hollow metal segments strung together over a liner.

ATB. All terrain bike, or mountain bike.

Axle nut. A threaded nut that secures wheel to bike. Used with solid axle hubs.

Bead seat diameter. Rim diameter measured where the tire bead is seated.

Bolt circle diameter. Diameter of a circle transcribed by the chainring mounting bolts.

Bottom bracket. The bearings, cups, and spindle connecting both crankarms.

Bottom bracket shell. The bottom of the frame that holds the bottom bracket.

Bottom bracket spindle. The axle in the bottom bracket. It connects both crankarms.

Braided housing. A cable housing made of woven wire around an inner liner.

Brake bridge. The frame tubing connection between seatstays. Located above tire and used for mounting side pull and dual pivot brakecalipers on some bikes.

Brake cable. Wound, multiple strand wire that connects brake lever with brake caliper.

Brake cable carrier. Transverse connection between brake caliper arms. Found on cantilever brakes.

Brake cable pinch bolt/nut. Fastener that secures brake cable to caliper arm.

Brake caliper. The lever arms that move brake pads to rim or rotor to apply friction needed to slow and stop the bicycle.

Brake centering screw. The screw that changes spring tension between caliper arms, allowing pads to center over wheel rim.

Brake fluid. Either a mineral fluid or a D.O.T. brake fluid for hydraulic brake systems.

Brake lever. The mechanism pulled by hand to activate brake caliper and pads.

Brake pad. Synthetic rubber block fastened to caliper arm. Pad is forced against moving rim or disc causing friction, to slow rim rotation.

Brake pad fixing bolt/nut. Fastener system that holds brake pad to rim caliper arm.

Brake pad toe. An adjustment to the brake pad used to reduce brake squeal. Pad surface adjusted to strike braking surface at a slight angle. Usually with leading edge striking first or "toe in."

Brake quick release. Mechanism found on rim brake caliper to open brake arms allowing wide tires to pass brake pads. The mechanism is sometimes found on the brake lever.

Braking surface. Part of the rim or rotor disc that is rubbed by brake pads.

British Standard Cycle (BSC). A thread standard system used by the British and adopted by much of the world.

B-screw. Body-screw on rear derailleur that changes the placement of the derailleur body and upper pulley (G-pulley) to the rear sprockets.

Cable. Wound, multiple strand wire used for brake calipers and derailleurs.

Cable adjusting barrel. Hollow bolt that acts as housing stop. Adjusts in or out component to effectively change housing length and cable tension on brake and derailleur systems.

Cable pinch bolt. Bolt and washer system that flattens and holds secure the cut end of the cable. Found on derailleurs and brakes.

Caliper rim brake. A brake system that applies friction directly to the rim for slowing and stopping the bike.

Cantilever brake. Brake system found on mountain bikes and touring road bikes. Consists of two separate arms pivoting off studs fixed to the frame or fork.

Cassette. Sprocket and spacer assembly mounted to a freehub mechanism on the rear wheel.

Centerline. Mid plane of the bike running in line with wheels.

Chain. A connected series of flexible links used to transfer motion of front chainrings to rear sprockets.

Chain rivet. Small pin that connects two outer chain plates, usually considered a permanent part of chain.

Chainring. Sprocket attached to the crank.

Chainring bolt. Special bolts that secure chainring to crank.

Chainring nut. Thin-walled nut used with chainring bolt.

Chainring nut wrench. Wrench with two pegs used to hold chainring nut.

Chainstay. Frame tubes connecting the rear dropouts and the bottom bracket shell.

Cleats. Fitting mounted to a cycling shoe that attaches the shoe to the pedal.

Cogs. Sprockets attached to rear hub.

Compressionless housing. Outer plastic and metal sheath that covers derailleur inner cable, allowing it to pass around corners and between moving parts of the frame. Differs from other housing in that outer support wires run longitudinally with inner cable. Also called SIS™ housing by Shimano®.

Cone. A curved bearing race that rides against ball bearings.

Cone wrench. Thin wrench made to fit the narrow wrench fittings of a hub cone.

Crank (Crank arm). The lever arm between the pedal and the bottom bracket.

Crank bolt. Bolt that secures crank to bottom bracket spindle.

Crank puller. Tool used to remove cranks by pulling them from bottom bracket spindle.

Crankset. Rotating mechanism turned by feet, includes chainrings, cranks, arms, & chainring bolts/nuts.

Crown (fork crown). Horizontal portion of fork, located at top of fork blades.

Derailleur. Mechanism used to push chain from one cog or chainring to another.

Derailleur cable. The inner cable of the derailleur cable system. Sometimes called gear cable.

Derailleur capacity. The rated ability of a rear derailleur to take up chain slack from the gear combinations on the bike. Given as the sum of rear sprocket differences plus front chainring differences.

Derailleur hanger. The fitting on a bicycle frame that holds the rear derailleur. On some bikes this piece is replaceable.

Derailleur limit screw. Screw that stops derailleur travel. One screw stops inward travel, a second screw stops outward travel.

Disc brake. Caliper brake system using rotor bolted to hub as the braking surface. Brake caliper attaches to either fork end or frame adjacent to hub.

Dishing Tool. A gauge used to measure the centering of the wheel rim over the hub.

D.O.T. brake fluid. Hydraulic brake fluid approved by the US Department of Transportation. Does NOT interchange with mineral brake fluid.

Down tube. Frame tube connecting lower portion of the head tube to the bottom bracket shell.

Drop bars. Curved handlebars made with two bends, with the outermost section being lower than the top and offset 90-degrees. Most frequently used on road bikes.

Dropout. Part of frame and fork slotted to accept wheel axle.

Dual pivot brake. Road type brake with two arms pivoting off separate studs mounted to a center bracket. One arm swings on an arc moving up and the other arm swings on an arc moving down.

E-plate derailleur. A front derailleur design that permanently mounts the derailleur to a plate held by the bottom bracket.

E-plate derailleur. A front derailleur design that permanently mounts the derailleur to a plate held by the bottom bracket.

ETRTO. European Tire and Rim Technical Organization, an organization developing industry standards around tires and tubes.

Fixed cup. The right side cup of an adjustable bottom bracket.

Flat bars. A handlebar style where the handlebars bend very slightly from the center. Also called up right bars.

Foot-pound. A measurement of torque used mainly in the United States.

Fork. Mechanism used to hold the front wheel.

Fork blades. Tubes connecting fork dropouts to fork crown.

Frame. Supporting structure for the components and wheels of a bike.

Frame housing stops. Fittings on the frame that hold either brake or derailleur cable housing ends.

Freehub. Ratcheting body bolted internally to hub of rear wheel. Holds cassette cogs. Mechanism does not remove when cogs are removed.

Freewheel. Ratcheting mechanism on the rear wheel fitted with one or more cogs. Cogs and ratcheting body unthread from hub as a unit.

Front derailleur. Mechanism located above front chainrings that pushes the chain from one chainring to another.

Gear cable. See derailleur cable.

Guide pulley. (G-pulley) Uppermost pulley on rear derailleur. Guides chain onto rear cogs.

Gripshift®. Twist shifter manufactured by the SRAM® Corporation.

Handlebars. Connector between stem and cyclist's hands.

Head tube. Tube connecting down tube and top tube, contains headset and steering column of fork.

Headset. Bearing assembly connecting the head tube and fork. Allows fork to rotate.

Hex wrench. Metal wrench of six sides (hex-shaped) made to fit inside bolts or other mechanical fittings. Also known as Allen® Wrench.

High normal derailleur. See top normal derailleur.

Housing. The outer plastic and metal sheath that covers brake or derailleur cable , allowing cable to pass around corners and between moving parts of the frame.

Housing end cap (ferrule). Small metal or plastic cap that fits over end of housing.

Hub. The center of the wheel, contains bearings and an axle.

Hub brake. Braking system located at the center of the wheel inside the hub.

Hydraulic brake. A brake system that uses fluid to transmit power from the rider's hand to the brake caliper.

Hydraulic-mechanical brake. A brake system that combines hydraulic and mechanical systems.

Inch-pound. A measurement of torque used mostly in the United States.

Indexing. Shifting system that uses "clicks" or dwell to indicate each sprocket location.

Inner tube. Rubber bladder inside tire that holds air.

Innermost. Closest point relative to the centerline of the bike.

Interference fit. A method of assembly where one part is slightly larger than its intended fitting. Parts are held together by the force of assembly.

Internal headset. A headset type that uses a pressed head tube cup that allows bearings to sit inside head tube. Also called Zero-stack or low-profile headset.

International Standards Organization. A group dedicated to setting standards for all industries involved in international trade, such as the bicycling industry.

ISIS Drive®. International Splined Interface System. A crank and bottom bracket spindle interface standard using 10 splines.

ISO. See International Standards Organization

Integrated headset. A headset design where the frame acts as a holder for the bearings. Bearings are held inside head tube. Service or installation does not involve pressing cups.

Kilogram force. A force equal to a kilogram weight or a one-kilogram mass times the acceleration of gravity. Approximately equal to 2.2 pounds force.

Limit screw. Screws on front and rear derailleurs to stop the extreme range of derailleur motion.

Linear pull brakes. A caliper brake with two long arms holding pads. System uses housing stop in one arm, no straddle cable.

Locknut. Nut used to lock a cone, threaded race, or other threaded item to keep it from moving or unthreading.

Low normal derailluer. A rear derailleur design where with no cable tension the derailleur returns to the innermost (largest) sprocket position. Sometimes referred to as "low normal." Also called Rapid Rise®.

Low profile headset. A headset that uses a pressed head tube cup that allows bearings to sit inside headtube. Also called Zero-stack or internal headset.

Master link. Linkage system used to join the ends of a chain.

Maximum extension line. A line on a seat post or quill stem indicating the maximum amount the item should be raised above the frame or fork steering column. Also called the "minimum insertion line."

Maximum tooth size. The largest rear spocket size a rear derailleur will be able to shift.

Mechanical disc brake. A disc brake that uses a cable system and has no hydraulic fittings.

Mineral Fluid. A type of fluid, based on mineral oil, used in some models of hydraulic brakes. Does not interchange with DOT brake fluid.

Minimum insertion line. See minimum extension line.

Mountain bike. Bicycle design intended for rugged, off road use. Also called "ATB", or all terrain bike.

MTB. See mountain bike.

Nipple. See spoke nipple.

Octalink®. Registered trademark of Shimano® Inc. for a crank and spindle interface standard using 8 splines. Octalink® includes the non-interchangeable V1 and V2 systems.

One-key release. Crank system that allows removal of the crank without a crank puller.

One-piece crank. Crank that uses a single piece of metal for the arms and spindle. Also called "Ashtabula" crank.

Outermost. Farthest position laterally from centerline of bike.

Pawl. Articulating tooth on a ratcheting system. Used commonly in freehubs and freewheels.

Pipe Billet spindle. A splined bottom bracket spindle from Shimano® Inc. Cranks and spindles do not interchange with square spindles or square holed cranks.

Presta valve. Narrow valve system found on inner tubes.

Pulley wheel. Small wheel on the rear derailleur that wraps the chain.

Quick release skewer. Metal shaft and lever with cam, fitted into hollow axle. Allows easy and quick removal of wheel.

Quill Stem. A type of stem that inserts and secures inside a threaded steering column.

Rapid Rise®. See low normal derailluer.

Rear derailleur. Shifting mechanism attached to the frame that moves chain from one sprocket to another.

Rear sprockets. The toothed cogs or gears on the rear wheel.

Repair stand. Fixture designed to hold bike while doing repairs.

Retaining compound. Liquid adhesive designed to expand and harden in press fit situations.

Rim. Metal or composite hoop suspended around hub by spokes.

Rim strip. Protective strip covering holes between rim and inner tube.

Rotor. Round disc plate mounted to hub for disc brake caliper.

Saddle. Support for posterior of bicyclist.

Schrader valve. Inner tube valve commonly seen on many bicycle and car tires.

Seat post. Connection between saddle and frame.

Seat tube. Frame tube connecting top tube and bottom bracket. Seat post inserts into top of tube.

Seatstay. Frame tube connecting rear dropout and upper portion of seat tube.

Setscrew. Small screw used primarily for adjustments. Found commonly on brake levers and caliper brakes.

Self-vulcanizing fluid. Special fluid used on an inner tube to adhere patch.

Shift lever. Control mechanism designed to pull cable and control derailleur.

Sidepull brake. Caliper brake using one pivot for both arms and mounted to brake bridge above center of wheel.

Slip fit. Method of assembly where one part slides without force into its fitting.

Spanner. Wrench.

Spindle. Axle for the bottom bracket.

Spider. Arms that hold the chainrings to the crank.

Splined spindle. A tubular shaped bottom bracket axle with ends having machined notches and recesses. The splines mate to splines in the crank.

Spoke. Long thin bolt, connecting hub to rim. Threaded on one end with a hook or fitting on other end.

Spoke nipple. Nut located at threaded end of spoke.

Sprocket. Toothed gear or wheel used to connect with the chain.

Square spindle. A spindle design where the spindle ends are a square shaped stud. Fits into a square hole in the crank.

Star nut (Star fangled nut). A nut designed to press into the inside of the fork steering column. Nut provides method for headset bearing adjustment.

Steering column. Tubing that connects fork crown to stem.

Stem. Connector between fork and handlebars.

Tensiometer. Tool used to determine the amount of tension of spokes.

Tension. Tensile force, pulling along the axis line of an object.

Tension meter. See tensiometer.

Thread locker. A special adhesive designed to expand and harden in the threads of a fastener.

Thread pitch. Distance from one thread crest to the next thread crest.

Threadless stem. Stem that fastens to the outside of an unthreaded steering column.

Tire. Rubber and fabric casing which encloses the inner tube and contacts ground.

Tire bead. Wire or fabric molded into the tire edge. Holds tire down onto rim when tire is under pressure.

Tire lever. Lever with smooth, rounded edge used to remove tire bead from rim.

Tire Sealant. A liquid placed in the tire or inner tube. The purpose is to block minor leaks.

Top normal derailleur. A rear derailleur design where with no cable tension the derailleur returns to the outermost (smallest) sprocket position. Also called high normal.

Top tube. Frame tube connecting head tube to seat tube.

Torque. Force applied around an axis.

True. Refers to wheel rim spinning laterally straight and round.

Tubeless tire. Tire and rim system that maintains air pressure without an inner tube. Similar to automotive and motorcycle tubeless tire systems.

Twist grip. Shift lever fitted as part of handgrip that actuates by rotation.

Valve core. Mechanism in inner tube for inflating and deflating tube.

V-brakes®. Registered trademark of Shimano® Inc. for a type of linear pull brake. Pads move on parallelgram attached to caliper arms.

Wheel. A composite of the rim, hub and spokes. May also include tire and tube.

Zero stack headset. A headset type that uses a pressed headtube cup that allows bearings to sit inside headtube. Also called low profile or internal headset.

Zip tie. Thin plastic straps used to secure most anything.

Specifications in the table below are in Newton meter (Nm). Inch-pound (in lbs) are given in paranthases. Some component companies do not specify torque for certain components or parts. Contact the manufacturer for the most up to date specifications.

HEADSET, HANDLEBAR, SEAT & SEAT POST AREA	
Threaded headset locknut	Chris King® Gripnut type 14.6-17 Nm (130-150 in lbs)
	Tange-Seiki® 24.5 Nm (217 in lbs)
Stem binder bolt- quill type	Control Tech® 16.3-19 Nm (144-168 in lbs)
	Shimano® 19.6-29.4 Nm (174-260 in lbs)
Threadless stem steering column binder bolts	Control Tech 13.6-16.2 Nm (120-144 in lbs)
	Deda® 8 Nm (71 in lbs)
	FSA® carbon 8.8 Nm (78 in lbs)
	Syncros® cotter bolt type 10.1 Nm (90 in lbs)
	Thomson® 5.4 Nm (48 in lbs)
	Time® Monolink 5 Nm (45 in lbs)
	Race Face 6.2 Nm (55 in lbs)
Handlebar binder One bolt or two bolt models	Shimano® 19.6-29.4 Nm (174-260 in lbs)
	Control Tech® 13.6-16.3 Nm (120-144 in lbs)
Handlebar binders- 4 bolts face plate models	Control Tech® 13.6-16.3 Nm (120-144 in lbs)
	Deda® magnesium 8 Nm (71 in lbs)
	Thomson® 5.4 Nm (48 in lbs)
	FSA® OS-115 carbon 8.8 Nm (78 in lbs)
	Time® Monolink 6 Nm (53 in lbs)
	Race Face 6.2 Nm (55 in lbs)
MTB handle bar end extensions	Cane Creek® 7.9 Nm (70 in lbs)
	Control Tech® 16.3 Nm (144 in lbs)
Seat rail binder	Control Tech®, 2 bolt type 16.3 Nm (144 in lbs)
	Control Tech®, single bolt 33.9 Nm (300 in lbs)
	Shimano® 20-30 Nm (174-260 in lbs)
	Syncros® each bolt 5 Nm (45 in lbs)
	Time® Monolink-5 Nm (44 in lbs)
	Travativ® (M8 bolt: 195-212. M6 bolt: 53-63)
	Campagnolo® 22 Nm (194 in lbs)
Seat post binder Note: Seat posts require only minimal tightening to not slip downward. Avoid over tightening	Campagnolo® 4-6.8 Nm (36-60 in lbs)

Park Tool™

PEDAL, CRANKSET & BOTTOM BRACKET AREA	
Pedal into crank	Campagnolo® 40 Nm (354 in lbs)
	Ritchey® 34.7 Nm (307 in lbs)
	Shimano® 35 Nm minimum (304 in lbs)
	Truvativ® 31.2-33.9 Nm (276-300 in lbs)
Shimano® Octalink XTR crankarm bolts (M15 thread)	Shimano® 40.3-49 Nm (357-435 in lbs)
Shimano® Hollowtech II bottom bracket bearing cup	34.5-49.1 Nm (305-435 in lbs)
Shimano® Hollowtech II crank bolt pinch screws	9.9-14.9 Nm (88-132 in lbs)
Shimano® Hollowtech II Left-hand fixing cap	4-6
FSA® MegaExo crank adjusting cap	3.6-6
FSA® MegaExo crank fixing screws	87-100
PEDAL, CRANKSET & BOTTOM BRACKET AREA	
Crank bolt (including splinetype cranks and square-spindle cranks)	Shimano® 305-391
	Campagnolo® 32-38 Nm (282-336 in lbs)
	Campagnolo® Ultra-torque 42 Nm (371 in lbs)
	FSA® (M8 bolt) 304-347
	FSA® (M14 steel) 434-521
	Race Face® 480
	Syncros® 27 Nm (240 in lbs)
	Truvativ® ISIS drive (384-420 in lbs)
	Truvativ® square spindle (336-372 in lbs)
	White Ind® 27-34 Nm (240-300 in lbs)
Crank bolt one-key release cap	Shimano® 44-60
	Truvativ® 107-124
Chainring cassette to crankarm (lockring)	Shimano® 443-620
Chainring bolt–Steel	Shimano® 70-95
	Campagnolo® 8 Nm (71 in lbs)
	Race Face® 100
	Truvativ® 107-124

PEDAL, CRANKSET & BOTTOM BRACKET AREA

Chainring bolt–Aluminum	Shimano® 44-88
	Truvativ® 72-80
Bottom bracket–Cartridge	Shimano® 435-608
	Campagnolo® (three piece type) 70 Nm (612 in lbs)
	Campagnolo® Ultra-Torque cups 35 Nm (310 in lbs)
	FSA® 39.2-49 Nm (347-434 in lbs)
	Race Face® 47.5 Nm (420 in lbs)
	Truvativ® 300-360
	White Ind.® 27 Nm (240 in lbs)

DERAILLEUR & SHIFT LEVER AREA

Drop bar dual control brake lever/shift lever clamp bolt	Shimano® STI 6-8 Nm (52-69 in lbs)
	Campagnolo 10 Nm (89 in lbs)
	Campagnolo®
Shift lever - upright / flat bar type	Shimano® 5-7.4 Nm (44-69 lbs)
Shift lever - twist grip	Shimano® Revo 53-70
	SRAM® 17
Front Derailleur clamp bolt	Campagnolo® 7 Nm (62 in lbs)
	Mavic® 26-35
	Shimano® 5-7 Nm (44-60 in lbs)
	SRAM® 44-60
Front derailleur cable pinch	Campagnolo® 5 Nm (44 in lbs)
	Mavic® 44-62
	Shimano® 5-7 Nm (44-60 in lbs)
	SRAM® 40
Rear derailleur mounting bolt	Campagnolo® 15 Nm (133 in lbs)
	Shimano® 8-10 Nm (70-86 in lbs)
	SRAM® 70-85

DERAILLEUR & SHIFT LEVER AREA	
Rear derailleur cable pinch bolt	Shimano® 5-7Nm (44-60 in lbs)
	Campagnolo® 6 Nm (53 in lbs)
	SRAM® 35-45
Rear derailleur pulley wheel (idler wheel) bolt	Shimano® 2.9 -3.9 Nm (27-34 in lbs)
	SRAM
	Campagnolo

WHEEL, HUB, REAR COG AREA	
Spoke Tension Torque is typically not used in wheels. Spokes tension is measured by deflection. Contact rim manufacturer for specific tension recommendations.	
Quick release at wheel. Measured torque not typically used. Common industry practice is resistance at lever half way through swing from open to fully closed.	
Wheel axle nuts to frame	Shimano® 260-390
	SRAM® 266-350
Cassette sprocket lockring	Shimano® 260-434
	Campagnolo® 50 Nm (442 in lbs)
Hub cone locking nut	Bontrager® 17 Nm (150 in lbs)
	Chris King® 12.2 Nm (100 in lbs)
	Shimano® 9.8- 24.5 Nm (87-217 in lbs)
Freehub body	Bontrager® 45 Nm (400 in lbs)
	Shimano® 35-50 Nm (305-434 in lbs)
	Shimano FH-M975/970 using 14mm hex 45-50 Nm (392-434 in lbs)

DISC BRAKE SYSTEMS	
Disc rotor to hub-lockring models	Shimano® 40 Nm (350 in lbs)
Disc rotor to hub (M5 bolts, six per rotor)	Shimano® 2-4 Nm (18-35 in lbs)
	Hayes® 5.6 Nm (50 in lbs)
	Avid® 55
	Magura® 3.8 Nm (34 in lbs)
Caliper mount	Avid® 80-90
	Magura® 5.7 Nm (51 in lbs)
	Shimano® 6-8 Nm (53-69 in lbs)
Hydraulic hose fittings	Hayes® 6.2 Nm (55 in lbs)

BRAKE CALIPER & LEVER AREA

Upright bar brake levers	Shimano® 6-8 Nm (53-69 in lbs)
	SRAM
	Avid
	Campagnolo® 10 Nm (89 in lbs)
Brake caliper mount to frame, side/dual/center pull	Cane Creek® 7.7-8.1 Nm (68-72 in lbs)
	Shimano® 7.84-9.8 Nm (70-86 in lbs)
Linear pull or cantilever caliper mount to frame	Avid® 43-61
	Control Tech® 11.3-13.6 Nm (100-120 in lbs)
	Shimano® 8-10 Nm (69-87 in lbs)
	SRAM® 45-60
Brake pad- threaded stud	Avid® 52-69
	Campagnolo® 8 Nm (71 in lbs)
	Cane Creek® 6.3-6.7 Nm (56-60 in lbs)
	Mavic® 7-9 Nm (62-80 in lbs)
	Shimano® 5-7 Nm (43-61 in lbs)
	SRAM® 5.7-7.9 Nm (50-70 in lbs)
Brake pad- smooth stud	Shimano® 7.9-8.8 Nm (70-78 in lbs)
Brake cable pinch bolt- linear pull or cantilever	Control Tech® 40-60
	Shimano® 53-69
	SRAM® 50-70
Brake cable pinch bolt sidepull/dual pivot	Campagnolo® 5 Nm (44 in lbs)
	Cane Creek® 68-72
	Mavic® 62-80
	Shimano® 6-8 Nm (52-69 in lbs)
Sidepull/dual pivot brake pad bolt	Cane Creek® 6.3-6.7 Nm (56-60 in lbs)
	Shimano® 6-8 Nm (52-69 in lbs)
Cantilever straddle wire carrier pinch bolt (M5 thread)	Control Tech® 40-60
	Shimano® 3.9-4.9 Nm (35-43 in lbs)

ParkTool

BRAKE CALIPER & LEVER AREA	
Brake caliper wire pinch linear pull/cantilever (M6 thread)	Avid® 52-69
	Shimano® 50-75
Brake lever-MTB type	Avid® 40-60 (clamping built into body)
	Avid® strap type 28-36
	Cane Creek® 53-80
	Shimano® 53-69
	SRAM® 30
	Brake lever-drop bar
	Campagnolo® 88
	Mavic® 62-80
	Shimano® 53-69

The chart below is a quick conversion between inch-pounds, foot-pounds, and Newton-meters. For exact figures, use the formulas below.

INCH POUND IN-LB	APPROX. FOOT POUND FT-LB	APPROX. NEWTON-METER NM	INCH POUND IN-LB	APPROX. FOOT POUND FT-LB	APPROX. NEWTON-METER NM
10	0.8	1.1	260	21.7	29.4
20	1.7	2.3	270	22.5	30.5
30	2.5	3.4	280	23.3	31.6
40	3	3 4.5	290	24.2	32.8
50	4.2	5.6	300	25.0	33.9
60	5.0	6.8	310	25.8	35.0
70	5.8	7.9	320	26.7	36.2
80	6.7	9.0	330	27.2	37.3
90	7.5	10.2	340	28.3	38.4
100	8.3	11.3	350	29.2	39.5
110	9.2	12.4	360	30.0	40.7
120	10	13.6	370	30.8	41.8
130	10.8	14.7	380	31.7	42.9
140	11.7	15.8	390	32.5	44.0
150	12.5	16.9	400	33.3	45.2
160	13.3	18.1	410	34.2	46.3
170	14.2	19.2	420	35.0	47.5
180	15.0	20.3	430	35.8	48.6
190	15.8	21.5	440	36.7	49.7
200	16.7	22.6	450	37.5	50.8
200	17.5	23.7	460	38.3	52.0
220	18.3	24.9	470	39.2	53.1
230	19.2	26.0	480	40	54.2
240	20.0	27.1	490	40.8	55.4
250	20.8	28.2	500	41.7	56.5

The following formulas will convert other torque designations into inch-pounds (in-lb).

$$in\text{-}lb = ft\text{-}lb \times 12$$
$$in\text{-}lb = Nm \times 8.851$$
$$in\text{-}lb = kgf\text{-}cm \times 0.87$$

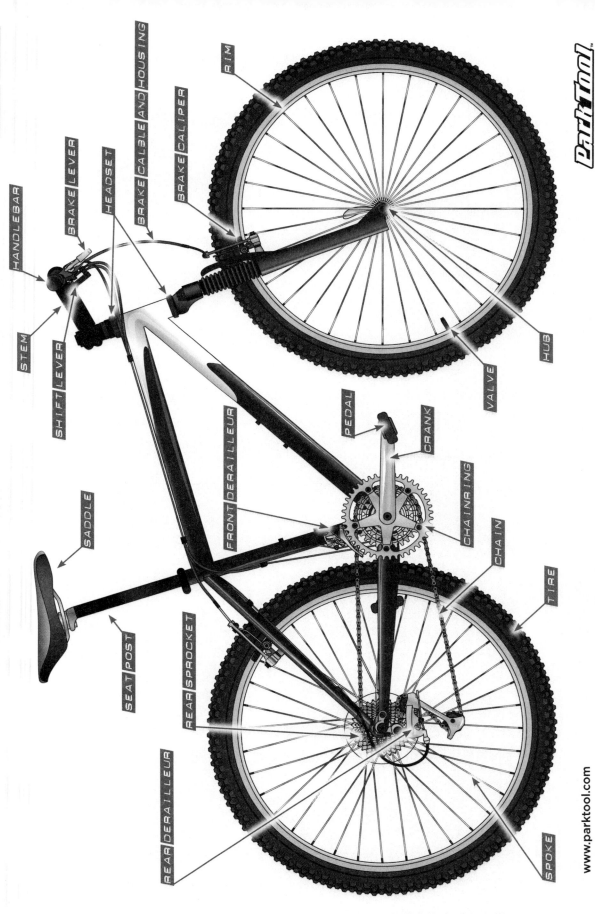

HANDLEBAR

BRAKE LEVER

HEADSET

BRAKE CABLE AND HOUSING

BRAKE CALIPER

RIM

STEM

SHIFT LEVER

SADDLE

FRONT DERAILLEUR

PEDAL

CRANK

CHAINRING

CHAIN

HUB

VALVE

SEAT POST

REAR SPROCKET

REAR DERAILLEUR

TIRE

SPOKE

ParkTool™